Your life is a reflection of your inner state, and by changing your moods, you can change your life. In this timeless classic, renowned New Thought author Elsie Lincoln Benedict teaches you how to direct your energies towards achieving your deepest desires, by cultivating a mindset that attracts success, health, and happiness.

Whether you seek financial abundance, personal growth, or unshakable confidence, these fourteen lessons, published for the first time in a single volume, provide the keys to unlocking your full potential. Let Benedict's wisdom inspire you to take control of your destiny and live the life you've always dreamed of.

HOW TO GET ANYTHING YOU WANT

ELSIE LINCOLN
BENEDICT
School of Opportunity

Originally Copyrighted
1923

by

ELSIE LINCOLN BENEDICT

and

RALPH PAINE BENEDICT

HOW TO GET ANYTHING YOU WANT

ELSIE LINCOLN
BENEDICT
School of Opportunity

SECRETS OF SUCCESS

Copyright © 2025 by Prime Mover Publishing
Published by Prime Mover Publishing
Licensed by Secrets of Success, LLC

All rights reserved.

The original *How To Get Anything You Want* by Elsie Lincoln Benedict is in the public domain. All original additions, including illustrations and written content, are copyright © 2025 by Prime Mover Publishing and may not be reproduced in any form without written permission from the publisher or author, except as permitted by U.S. copyright law.

Publishing Manager: Jenny Sage
Production Editor: Paul Neuviale
Edits by Maria Bengston, Toni Rexroat, Erika Steeves, and Julie Willson
Cover Art by Julie Dransfield-Myers
Replicated Layout by John Perrin and Julie Dransfield-Myers

The author(s) of this book do not dispense business or medical advice. They only offer information of a general nature to help you in your quest for business and personal success. This book is not designed to be a definitive guide or to take the place of advice from qualified professionals, and there is no guarantee that the methods suggested in this book will be successful, owing to the risk that is involved in business of almost any kind. Thus, neither the publisher nor the author(s) assume liability for any losses that may be sustained by relying solely on the methods described in this book, and any such liability is hereby expressly disclaimed.

The views and opinions expressed in this book are those of the author(s) and do not necessarily reflect the official policy or position of the publisher. The publisher disclaims any responsibility or liability for any statements or opinions expressed in this book.

ISBN 978-1-966993-02-5 (PB), 978-1-966993-01-8 (HC)

SECRETS OF SUCCESS

www.SecretsOfSuccess.com

To You

This is a lesson-lecture, as delivered by Elsie Lincoln Benedict to her one hundred thousand class students in the various cities of the United States.

It has been printed at the request of these students, who desired it in permanent form, and is made into this small volume for carrying with you as inspiration in your daily life.

When you have read it, read it again and again, until it becomes a part of you. Then pass it on to those you love, that it may help them as it has helped the many thousands who have already remade their lives by it.

CONTENTS

LESSON I — 1
How Your Predominant Moods Make Your Life

LESSON II — 25
How to Remake Our Moods for Mastery

LESSON III — 48
How to Know What You Want Most

LESSON IV — 71
How to Set the Next Gage for What You Want

LESSON V — 92
How to Prepare for What You Want

LESSON VI — 114
How to Find the Open Doors to What You Want

LESSON VII — 136
How to Make Your Desires Materialize

LESSON VIII — 158
Your Secret, Subconscious Self

LESSON IX — 181
Your Emotions

LESSON X — 204
Mental Miracles

LESSON XI — 227
Love, Courtship and Marriage

LESSON XII — 252
Success and Your Supreme Wish

LESSON XIII — 275
Healing Ourselves and Helping Others

LESSON XIV — 296
How to Let Your Subconscious Help You in Your Work

LESSON I

How Your Predominant Moods Make Your Life

A MAN on a country road stopped another and said, "If I keep walking this direction, how far will I have to go to reach Chicago?"

"If you keep going in the direction you are headed now it will be about twenty-five thousand miles," the other answered, "but if you will turn around and go in the opposite direction it is about a mile and a half." If you, dear friend, have been wondering why you did not reach the place in life or acquire the things you desired, perhaps you have been expending your energies in exactly the opposite direction from what you should.

If you have been getting some of the things you wanted but failed at others you have been headed right on some and wrong on others.

Now there are certain things inside every one of us that keep turning us, like a weather vane, in certain directions, and those things are our predominant moods.

You cannot entertain a certain mood and not act upon it sooner or later, any more than a man walking straight toward a thing could fail to reach it ultimately. The moods that PREDOMINATE deep, deep inside our hearts are living, vital forces, and they create actualities in our lives which exactly correspond to their own nature.

What happens down through the years, in the by and large of a man's life, fits these predominant moods of his just as if they were coats made to order.

For that is what the outer conditions of our lives really are—garments made by ourselves when we least suspected it, in exact accordance with the pattern we carried in our subconscious minds.

Since this is an unchanging law, operating in every one of us in precisely the same way, whether we recognize it or not, and for ourselves every hour, one of the most important things for any human being to know is how the law works.

My first word to you, therefore, is this: Take hold of my hand and we will go over the ground together. I will explain every step of the way as we come to it and make it so clear you will plant your feet solidly on each one till we reach the top.

From there you can see the whole road yourself from the heights. After that you will be able to travel it independently to whatever you desire and will, I hope, help many others to find it too.

In taking you over this "Road to Your Desires" I have but one request to make: that is, that you will give your entire attention to each step as we come to it and NOT keep looking ahead, wondering what lies farther along; for if you do you are sure to stumble.

Moreover, you will miss the best part of each lesson unless you give your whole mind to it.

I saw something once that perfectly illustrated this. It was early morning, following a deep snow in a mountain village. A man and his two little sons came out of the house across from the window where I was sitting, and started up the street.

Nobody had been out and there were no paths broken. But the father of course knew where the sidewalks were and took the lead to break a path, telling the boys to use the steps he had made for them. He was very careful to take short ones so they could follow easily, just as I shall do in this course of study.

One of the boys did as directed, planting his little boots straight down into father's steps, and kept up with him. But the other boy, though older and supposedly more sensible, kept leaning out on either side, looking ahead to see what was coming next instead of watching where he was going.

He kept wobbling and falling until he was far behind.

In this course of lessons I will break the trail for you to the land of your dearest, deepest desires, for I have traveled it myself and know where the road lies.

Through following this trail I have left Poverty, Ill Health, Unhappiness and Failure far behind me.

By following the rules laid down in this course, just as I shall ask YOU to follow them, I have reached the mountainsides where the things I longed for abide, and you can do the same.

I know this, because I have pointed out this road to more than one hundred thousand men and women, and every one who made even slight efforts to follow it has reported progress that is beautiful to see.

The very first thing for you to know as we start out on this journey is that our lives are not just a series of accidental happenings, as we have supposed, but are the OUTER CIRCUMSTANCES built directly or indirectly, innocently, usually unknowingly but nevertheless inevitably, by groups of INNER FEELINGS.

These INNER FEELINGS constitute our moods. The "feeling" (not the thought) you have about any given thing or person is your predominant attitude toward that person or thing.

This is especially true of those feelings you cannot explain—that don't seem to be based in reason or fact or anything you can lay your hand on, but which just ARE. These prepare the soil in the garden of your subconscious.

Each and every seed brings forth something sooner or later, and that something is always of the nature of the seed.

A tomato seed cannot bring forth an American Beauty rose. But if you plant rose seeds year in and year out, no matter how poor the soil, you are going to harvest roses sometime.

The acts of every person spring from the secret seeds which he has planted or allowed to be planted in his subconscious mind.

A man's acts bring the results you see in his life, but the act, in every case, was rooted in a thought or feeling which he could have controlled had he known how.

To show you how to select, plant, cultivate and nurture only those things you want to grow out into the daylight of your life is the aim of this course.

You will get a better idea of just how these moods build the realities of your life if you will think of yourself as owning a very powerful cannon. This is your own subconscious mind. Now this cannon is different from any you ever saw in real life, in that it is constructed on the boomerang principle. Every shot fired from this queer piece of artillery comes back to you, AND IT DOESN'T COME BACK ALONE. It returns to your feet LADEN WITH RESULTS, REALITIES, ACTUAL OCCURRENCES.

Whether these actualities are helpful or harmful, destructive or constructive, what you desire or what you despise, depends entirely on THE DIRECTION IN WHICH YOU KEEP YOUR CANNON POINTED MOST OF THE TIME. This direction or LEANING of your powerful subconscious points to good or evil, health or disease, every hour of your life, according to your PREDOMINANT MOODS. The separate thoughts you encourage constitute the ammunition.

The subconscious and conscious minds differ in that the subconscious points your cannon in the exact direction of your predominant FEELINGS while the conscious mind deals in THOUGHTS that fill it until ultimately it explodes.

Sometimes it goes off when we least expect it, especially when we say and do things that shock ourselves and others—things that are at variance with all our previous external acts. But these explosions are in accordance with SECRET THOUGHTS which we stuffed or jammed (repressed) down into the subconscious.

The world is full of good and evil. All the things we want and all those we hope to avoid are in it. Those we want lie in the exactly opposite direction from those we want to avoid, and all the gradations lie between.

> "I hold it true that thoughts are things
> Endowed with being, breath and wings,
> And that we send them forth to fill
> The world with good results—or ill.
>
> "That which we call our secret thought
> Speeds to the earth's remotest spot,
> And leaves its blessings or its woes
> Like tracks behind it as it goes.
>
> "It is God's law. Remember it
> In your still chamber as you sit
> With thoughts you would not dare have known,
> And yet make comrades when alone.
>
> "For after you have quite forgot,
> Or all outgrown some vanished thought,
> Back to your life to make its home,
> A dove or raven it will come.
>
> "Thoughts follow the law of the universe,
> Each thing creates its kind;
> And they speed o'er the track to bring you back
> Whatever went out from your mind."

The force that turns your subconscious cannon toward the desirable or undesirable is the INNER FEELING you maintain concerning what You want. If you build up a constructive mood your inner forces are turned TOWARD what you desire. If you keep up this mood nothing on earth can prevent your eventually getting that thing or something better along the same line.

But if your mood about the thing you want is one of ANXIETY LEST YOU WON'T GET IT your great inner forces are turned in the opposite direction, and the fruits brought back from that land will be the ashes of what you desired, the Dead Sea fruit that always grows in the Land of Fear.

Bear in mind that it is not what you SAY, DO or PRETEND which turns this powerful cannon on its axis and points it toward that Land of Desire or the Land of Despair; it is what you FEEL. The subconscious is a storehouse of living forces, each and every one of which works its way up out of the darkness of that basement into the light of day by creating the events, occurrences and so-called "accidents" of our everyday lives.

It builds your Health or Disease, your Happiness or Unhappiness, your Wealth or Poverty, your Success or Failure.

It builds with the thought-bricks you have piled away down there. It has no materials save those YOU have stored in it.

To see how you have thus been unknowingly and innocently building what you dreaded instead of what you desired, and exactly HOW to furnish your Inner Self with just the materials required for building what you want, is not only simple but interesting and fascinating.

The world of thought and feeling is a hidden world, but that hidden world is the producer of all things in the external world around us, and especially of our own success or failure.

Someone has said, "God made the world, but he doesn't make your world." We make our own, and we make it by our predominant moods.

> "We build our future thought by thought,
> For good or evil, and know it not;
> Yet so the universe was wrought.
> Thought is another name for Fate;
> Choose now thy destiny, do not wait,
> Knowing love brings love and hate brings hate."

There are no accidents. Everything that happens in our individual world, just as every occurrence in the material universe, is brought about by the operation of law.

The person who is constantly meeting unhappiness, poverty, disease and failure in his life is creating these things for himself. He may be ever so well-meaning. Personal hells too are often "paved with good intentions."

We make or unmake ourselves. In the great subconscious armory we forge the weapons that destroy us or the tools by which we build palaces of peace, power and prosperity.

No one outside yourself can ruin your life. No one but yourself can make your life successful or happy. Whatever comes to you HABITUALLY comes because of your HABITUAL attitudes. Whatever keeps bobbing up in your life CONSTANTLY is the ripened fruit of the feelings entertained more or less constantly in the subconscious over a long period.

You hold the key to every situation. You have within yourself that regenerative and transforming power by which you may make of yourself what you will, the agency by which you can get anything in this world you really want.

You are the master of your own life, the maker of your own destiny. No man ever sunk so low that he lost this complete mastery. But when he allows himself to become weak or fearful he is what the Good Book calls the "foolish master misgoverning his household." To become the wise master of your own future you must do three things:

First, you must recognize that this responsibility IS your own, and face it, instead of seeking, as most people do, to fasten it upon someone else or something else.

Second, you must read the lessons in this course carefully and conscientiously.

Third, you must not be content simply with knowing that the laws laid down herein are immutable. You must LIVE in accordance with them, put them to work in your life, begin at once to apply them in your everyday experience.

From the hour you do so you will note changes coming into your life. At first they may be so small you will be inclined to believe they are accidental. But as they continue to happen and increase in importance you will recognize them for what they are—the fruits of your new moods—and thereafter more and more beautiful things will happen to you as you consciously and expertly apply these scientific principles.

If it is difficult for you to see, at first glance, that your environment, your life as a whole, and the sum total of your experiences are the MASSED RESULTS of your own moods, do not resist this great truth or try to deny it. Simply leave it alone for a while.

Put it aside and forget it while I direct you on a little sightseeing tour amongst your friends.

Anyone that comes into your mind will do as a starting point. You can extend the investigation as far as the list of your friends or acquaintances reach. Every one, without exception, will illustrate this law.

There is the friend, for instance, who is always having something nice happen to her. She isn't the best looking or the most brilliant woman among your acquaintances, by a long way, and she has several drawbacks you know you do not have. Yet just one lovely experience after another comes to that woman!

"Right out of a clear sky," her friends say. And so it seems to the innocent bystander, or, to be exact, the ignorant bystander.

"Why SHE should have all the good things without half trying for them, while the rest of us who are much better looking and much better educated miss so many of them, is a mystery," they say.

Look a little closer, in the light this great law of moods sheds upon the situation, and the "mystery" will be solved.

You will note that this woman has been in the habit of keeping an uplifted, optimistic attitude toward her future and toward people, pretty much without regard to the actual events of her life. Sometimes perhaps she even seemed to you slightly inane, especially if you happen to be one of those over-serious people who take hold of everything with a "life-and-death" grip.

I knew a woman who used to be one of those dead-serious, "take-it--hard" kind, and I knew her well, for she lived in my skin. That YOU can stop trying to run the universe and also cure yourself of thinking it is going straight to the bow-wows every time one of your little plans goes awry, I know for a certainty, because I taught that woman how to do it, and I have taught thousands of others.

Over yonder is a man who has made and lost several fortunes. Study his real nature and you will see that every time he loses one he jumps up as though nothing had happened and goes after another, often making a bigger one than ever. He capitalizes what failure taught him (using it constructively) instead of letting it down him.

Such is the history of practically every big money-maker in the world.

Big fortunes are never made by bare facts and acts but by the main attitudes down inside the person. The money any man makes is the tangible result, the external symbol of internal, subconscious moods.

There is the woman who is always ill. One ailment after another descends upon her.

One week it is a bad cold, the next a sick headache, the next indigestion, and so on. You never see her that she is not just getting over or just "taking down" with something.

If you have been believing this woman is the victim of fate or "bad luck," or that germs just naturally choose her organism out of the entire population as their pet playground, take another glance—and look with your eyes open.

You will see a woman who, no matter what else she does or fails to do, is forever EXPECTING illness, thinking illness, talking illness, preparing to go more than halfway to meet it.

Such a one actually often says, in response to your invitation, "Yes, I'll come—if I'm well."

She has allowed herself to become the slave rather than the mistress of her habit-mind.

Your subconscious is like a garden. You can cultivate it intelligently or you can allow it to run wild. In either case it will bring forth in exact accordance with the seeds your habit-self has been dropping into the soil.

A sensible gardener takes care of his plot of ground, keeps the weeds out and carefully plants, waters, cultivates and nurtures the things he wants, AND NO OTHERS.

Thus and thus only can you ever produce in your life the things you desire. Certain rules govern the planting, growing and reaping of different kinds of fruits, and so it is in your own life. The specific rules for growing Health, Wealth, Peace and Achievement, and the general rules for growing anything else you want, make up the easy, simple yet wonderfully helpful lessons in this course.

Every thought-seed sown or permitted to take root in the mind produces its own harvest.

First that seed produces a tiny sprout that can be easily snipped off if attacked as soon as it appears above the surface. But if watered with further leanings, impulses and thoughts along the same line, it grows and grows. Sooner or later it will BLOSSOM INTO AN ACT, then other acts of a like nature will appear till it is covered with flowers—beautiful ones if the original seed was beautiful, or poisonous ones if the thought was destructive.

The act-flowers which have sprung from thought-seeds produce the fruit we daily see in the form of environment. Unless we take matters into our own hands and prevent it, the seeds of that fruit will fall back again into the soil many times multiplied, and bring forth a new and larger crop.

No matter what you have been planting in your life-garden and no matter how bitter its fruit, remember YOU own the garden and you are its only gardener.

You can uproot, much more easily than you suppose, the bad plants that have been growing there, plant new ones of ANY KIND YOU REALLY

WANT, and reap their lovely harvests more fully and more quickly than you have ever dreamed possible.

Nothing is impossible to the great, inner subconsciousness of man. "Miracles" are performed every day in the realm of disease, of business, of bad habits, in the intimate realms of human character and in the outward world of achievement.

The only thing necessary is to LEARN HOW, and then DO IT.

Few people change themselves or their lives, because they maintain the attitude that it is impossible to change. They keep pointing their cannons in the wrong direction and then lose hope because they accomplish wrong results.

Only learn this law of moods and apply it. You will soon see why you have hitherto failed to realize your ambitions.

No man arrives at the jail or the poorhouse unexpectedly. His friends may be surprised, but HE knows he has been traveling toward that place for a long while, and that the road was paved by his habitual feelings and moods.

A famous nerve specialist once said to me, "There ARE no such things as 'sudden breakdowns.' The victim of nervous prostration or any unexpected giving way has been preparing for and bringing about that very thing for a long while before-hand."

No sudden external force, no influence OUTSIDE himself induces a man to commit a crime save when that external circumstance, that sudden temptation, accords with thoughts and feelings long encouraged by his inner self.

One's "sudden" acts of goodness or evil merely reveal the accumulated power of tendencies that have been slowly gathering inwardly. The "pure in heart" can not indulge in degraded acts nor can he who does indulge in base thoughts make a practice of uplifting deeds.

The feelings each person fosters in his inmost heart write themselves out in his life so plainly that "he who runs may read." How many times you have been aware of this with regard to another. In fact, there is not one among your associates or acquaintances whose experiences do not tally with the mental outlooks that have characterized him for years.

That his inner attitudes have matched these outer manifestations, regardless of all his pretenses to the contrary, has been apparent not only to you but to others.

Recall any person whose friends are shocked to hear that he is a victim of a secret vice. Though he may have taken every precaution to conceal it, though every incident connected with it has been guarded against discovery, though not one overt act has betrayed him, yet you had been realizing for a long while that "there was something." What we are does get over. And the feelings we habitually entertain make us what we are. What we really ARE determines how far and how fast we shall go in the world.

There is no escaping the penalty or the profit of our innermost feelings.

> "Then let thy secret thoughts be fair;
> They have a vital part and share
> In making worlds and molding fate,
> God's system is so intricate."

Equally do our secret virtues betray themselves. Though we speak no word, though no opportunities come for expressing to any living person the ideals which dominate us, even strangers see in our faces a radiance that speaks for us.

And some day, perhaps after we have ceased to look for it or when we least expect it, the reward will come. That reward will be greater and finer the longer we have waited for it, for the Big Bank of Life pays with compound interest.

Our fleeting, transient thoughts, whims and fancies may be balked at every turn, but our deepest desires are food and fuel unto themselves.

The "divinity that shapes our ends" lies within ourselves and shapes them in exact accordance with our inmost attitudes. The "rough hewing" we do by means of pretense and sham only hacks the surface.

A woman I used to know is a good illustration of the fact that our PREDOMINANT MOOD, and not our superficial acts, brings the results.

"Good people, deserving people stay poor," she would say, "and wicked people become rich and ride in limousines. Look at me. I'm virtuous and hardworking. I pay my bills and do my duty. But I'm not rich and never will be. I have barely enough to get along with. It's entirely unfair!"

Needless to say, she never became rich. Also, needless to say, she continued to have "barely enough to get along with." Life paid her in her own coin, paid her just as she paid others—exactly what was earned but never a penny over.

That habit of never giving one iota more in kind words, love or money than was in the letter of the law built her life. Not her hard work and "virtue," but that inmost attitude, manufactured her experiences.

The thing it constructed for her was as perfect a materialization of that attitude as a house is of its blue prints.

True it is that rich people often have vices, just as this woman her virtues. But the person who makes money cultivates a mood ABOUT money the exact opposite of hers.

I shall tell you more about this in a later lesson devoted exclusively to the attainment of prosperity. But for the purposes of this illustration it is only necessary for you to bring to mind any money-maker whom you know intimately. Regardless of his virtues or vices, note this: his mental attitude CONCERNING MONEY is one that says, "I'm going to make money."

On the strength of this inner certainty he invests money, LETS GO, gives it a chance to grow. A man's habit of banking his money, putting it in a safety-deposit box or hiding it instead of investing it is always stated by the SECRET CONVICTION that he is destined to have so little he dare not risk any.

Such an attitude also keeps him pinching and scrimping. It leads him the life of a pauper even after he has saved something. His money is useless to him, for since he dare not spend any of it he is figuratively and literally poverty-stricken.

He thinks if he could only look ahead and know how many more years he has to live, he would begin to get some benefit of it. But the same mood paralyzes him. It makes him poor and keeps him poor to the last moment of his life.

This man is a wonderful example of the truth that it is not the bare facts but the inner feelings that create our lives. The facts in this case are that HE HAS MONEY IN THE BANK. But he lives and dies poor just the same—because of what went on inside his subconscious mind.

Order, not chaos, rules the universe; law, not accident, lies back of every general condition we have with us. Of all the laws operating in human life none is more vital than this.

Only so far as we acquaint ourselves with it and adapt ourselves to it shall we ever be healthy, happy or successful.

When we study it one of the first things we discover is that neither external things, events nor other people make our lives what they are. Each of us spins his own environment as a spider its web.

Our immediate surroundings come directly or indirectly, but nevertheless inevitably, from inside ourselves.

The moment we cease looking outside of, away from, beyond or behind ourselves for the cause of our undesirable financial, physical, intellectual or material condition we have taken a long step toward the conditions we desire.

The moment we begin to "inquire within" for the cause of our external conditions we begin to progress. As we look honestly for their roots in the soil of past thoughts and feelings, long-held resentments, fears, hates or jealousies, we discover the exact cause of our troubles.

From the hour when we begin to reverse these attitudes—to feel courage instead of fear, love instead of hate, forgiveness instead of resentment—the conditions around us begin to reverse themselves and soon comes a decided change for the better.

Start today to improve your own moods. Within a week you will note that several joys of real importance have come to you—joys that have been passing you by, joys you have longed for but kept at a distance through your wrong attitudes of mind and heart.

If you adhere to the right attitudes for three months your friends will begin to exclaim over the beautiful change in you. If you lengthen it to six months the world will be an entirely different and wonderful place. If you keep it up for a year—not without a single falling from grace, of course, but by getting right up every time you fall down—life will be glorious.

In five years your entire nature, your health, popularity, bank account—everything in your personal world—will be made over. The increase, improvement and expansion of everything in it will be beyond belief.

A long-continued attitude of mind, whether it be strong or weak, lovely or evil, invariably creates conditions in conformity with it. In doing so it develops from stage to stage, like a disease, showing the symptoms as it goes along which are accompaniments of that stage, and passing to others in an orderly and inevitable progress.

What you say and do today regarding any particular thing are symptoms showing what stage you have reached in the development of the inner mood regarding that thing.

The man who has put evil out of his mind, who forgives and forgets, shows by unmistakable signs that no destructive feeling rankles in his heart. But he who only pretends to have conquered these feelings while secretly nurturing them betrays himself whether he speaks or keeps silent.

Speaking of silence, have you noted that there are many sorts of it? There is the silence that is truly "golden," the one that is leaden, and many other kinds. But there is no silence that does not talk. What it tells is the MOOD of the person in question.

Many people think to disguise their real feelings by saying nothing with their tongues. They do not realize that man is a creature of law, and that every cause brings an effect. One of the greatest of these is that every disturbance taking place within anything in the universe is revealed ultimately by changes that have taken place upon its outer surface.

Not only does the general state of a man's mind reveal itself to those who know him, but it stamps itself into his character and thus raises or lowers him to that extent. It either weakens or strengthens him, it hurts or helps him, it stimulates or depresses him for the battle of life.

We all face emergencies when they arise, not in accordance with the circumstances of the emergencies themselves, but with the vigor or flabbiness born of our PREVIOUSLY INDULGED MOODS.

The weakest man can train himself to face life and conquer it. Regardless of what your past experiences have been, remember you are not bound by them. They were the outgrowth of the moods which preceded them.

To make the future what you wish it to be, to reverse the conditions, you have but to reverse your moods. Just as a thermometer registers changes in the temperature, so do the conditions in your life tell the true story of what was previously your inner "temperature."

So certain is it that these outer conditions change to match inner ones that no man can hope to remain in any high place in the world unless he keep his thoughts and feelings also on a high plane.

He may occupy a great office or position of distinction. To retain it he must not relax but hold on the high resolves, the ideals and lofty standards on which he dwelt mentally to get there. If he allows himself to sink mentally or spiritually for any appreciable period he will begin to fall from his pinnacle, at first almost imperceptibly, then obviously and at last completely.

In a recent article in the Saturday Evening Post entitled "Why Men Break," an anonymous author who is well acquainted with many of the most distinguished men of America referred to the working out of this great law.

He told how men of abstemious habits, of plain living and high thinking, deserted all these after being sent to Washington, D. C., for instance, and how in less than a year the disintegration was shockingly apparent to their friends.

Because we are living organisms, possessed of unbelievable power, and because we are never static but always building our tomorrows, we can make any change for the better we truly desire, and we can make it so complete that all who know us will be amazed at the change.

Every accomplishment, whether in the business, social or personal world, is the product of HABITUAL TRENDS OF THOUGHT, REITERATED FEELINGS—in other words, of PREDOMINANT MOODS.

The ignorant, the thoughtless and especially the indolent are always talking of "luck" and chance. They see only the effect, not the cause. They see a boyhood friend drive by in a handsome car and say, "What a lucky dog!"

They compare their own financial condition with his and say, "But I am so unlucky! Why is it that chance never favors me?"

Instead they should know there is no such thing as chance in this orderly universe; that the force which keeps millions of earths, suns and constellations swinging through illimitable space for unfathomable periods of time without ever an accident does not leave human life to chance.

Such a man should be devoting his energies to THE STUDY OF THE LAWS BACK OF HIS FRIEND'S RICHES. Then he could make his own to order.

I have in mind a well-known actress, a woman who attained fame so early in life that many think she did not earn it. They call her "fortunate," say she was "born under a lucky star," and so on.

But if you will read her life story you will find that one big idea saturated her mind from the time she was a tiny child.

Instead of meeting what we call "good luck" she had all kinds of "bad luck"—grinding poverty, heartrending discouragements, innumerable disappointments. Her father was dead and she helped support her mother, a brother and a sister, all of whom she loved so dearly it almost broke her heart to see them in need.

But she kept that one Big Idea in front of her mind's eye every hour. She cultivated and clung to the determination that she WOULD WIN.

When things got so dark she couldn't see even one day ahead and she could make no progress at all she hung on to her ideal with all the strength she had.

She refused to yield, she refused to give way to the external facts. She turned her eyes inward and looked and looked and looked, harder than ever, at her Great Desire.

Did it come true? The fame of Mary Pickford is the answer.

And while we are on this subject is the best time to speak of another misconception that thousands of people have. They console themselves for their own failures by saying that honor must be bartered if one is to rise to great financial or professional achievements.

Quite the contrary is true. And the career of this Marvelous Mary proves this also. She has built not alone a famous name but a beautiful character and retained in the face of world homage a sweet, sincere simplicity.

In every human life there are casual, isolated events, experiences and happenings. These may be likened to the scraps that fill in the chinks. These casual events may or may not be altogether of your own making, though THEIR EFFECT UPON YOU, which is the important thing, is absolutely of your own making. Then there are the KINDS of things that happen to us OVER AND OVER AGAIN. These fall into certain classifications, they consist of certain SORTS of things. These you will find are ALWAYS AND INVARIABLY created by certain long-continued, HABITUAL feelings.

They match, conform to and exactly FIT these habitual attitudes, as a glove fits the hand.

Now these secret feelings are the things which each of us must watch. For instead of being inconsequential, as we have often supposed, they are the real builders of our lives.

To guard them carefully from the light of day is not enough. We must meet and master them or they will master us.

We must fearlessly inventory our stock of "feelings," especially those which are most intense and those which have prevailed in our hearts over long periods. For we shall make no headway in life until we do. Even then we shall make none unless we APPLY what we have learned to improve our habitual moods.

We shall not find the right path by closing our eyes to the facts. Such a course will certainly lead us to further trouble, exactly as it would a chauffeur who drove with his eyes shut. Constant bumps, jars, wobblings and ultimate disaster would certainly come to him.

This lesson is designed with one end in view—to prepare you to open your eyes to one of the most far-reaching principles in human life; to gently, kindly point out to you the proof, so evident in the lives of others, that "as a man thinketh in his heart so is he."

For as a man thinketh in his heart so does he ACT; as he acts so does he BUILD HABITS; and habits, in the final analysis, literally create our lives and all the important things in them.

You will note that this famous phrase is, "As a man thinketh IN HIS HEART." Because the thinking that really makes or unmakes our lives is not done in our heads by our cool, logical reason, but by the Subconscious.

Now the Subconscious does not really think. It FEELS. And feeling is a matter more of the heart than the head.

As I have already pointed out, it is not what you say or do or pretend or even think now and then that creates a big general condition of good or evil in your life. It is what you "FEEL IN YOUR BONES," as the saying goes.

This saying did not arise by accident. If so it would have become extinct long ago. It became popular and is used frequently because it exactly expresses what we mean by a deep mood—a feeling that isn't on the surface, that seems to lie in the very marrow of our bones.

You hear a man say, "There, I told you that awful thing was going to happen to me! I felt it in my bones." Feeling it in his bones he brought it to pass, just as we all tend to do.

A mother of my acquaintance told me once, "I don't want my son to marry that girl, yet I just feel in my bones he is going to."

"Is he especially attentive to her?" I asked.

"No, not yet, but I am so afraid he is going to be. I'm doing and saying everything in my power to prevent it. I've forbidden him to see her and I cut her whenever I meet her now. I am so afraid, though!"

You do not need to be told that the boy did marry the girl. Not because he really wanted to nor because she specially desired it, but because of the opposition and fear that drove them together. They were divorced within a year, to their mutual satisfaction.

Many people imagine that they have this "feeling in their bones" because a thing is bound to happen. They take it as a "hunch," a premonition that the thing is "destined," that it HAS to come. They say afterwards, "It was Fate."

The opposite is true. You do not have this feeling because the thing is on its way to you and cannot be evaded. But by encouraging the feeling, dwelling on it and thinking of the calamity as inevitable you yourself bring it to pass, BY YOUR OWN ACTS.

The main direction of our acts is in accordance with our real feelings, and the deeper the feelings the more intensive, extensive and effective the acts. This is true of all feelings, good or bad.

In other words, you don't have a "feeling in your bones" because a thing is being brought to you by influences outside yourself, but it comes to you because you had the feeling first and then went more than halfway to meet it.

If you will remember this great principle and realize that it works both ways you can bring good unto yourself by entertaining good feelings "in your bones" just as easily and as surely as you have been bringing the bad.

Very few people realize this. They think the only "premonitions" that come true are the evil ones. That is because it is always easier to drift, to slide down hill, to settle into pessimism. It becomes a habit.

Also because the average person is ignorant of the most vital laws of his own nature.

Few people have remade their lives to suit themselves, because few have taken the time or trouble to learn the simple rules by which anyone can do so.

But all who have learned them and then tested them ever so little know that they explain the main, general conditions of every person's life; that they ALWAYS WORK.

You have progressed a long way when you recognize that these deep feelings are the real forces which directly or indirectly create the conditions in your life, but this advance is nothing to that which follows when you take one more step and realize that YOU AND YOU ALONE DETERMINE WHAT THESE INNER FEELINGS SHALL BE.

These feelings build your life, but YOU build the feelings.

You can choose what they shall be exactly as you choose a tailor to make you a suit of clothes. Then you can encourage and discourage them precisely as you do your tailor when you go for fittings.

You need not bother about how the details are going to be worked out and accomplished by your inner self any more than you need to hang over your tailor while he cuts and stitches and trims.

In fact, such curiosity and fretting will greatly interfere with and delay the working out of your desires just as they would with your tailor.

We do not know just HOW the great subconscious mind produces the finished article we have ordered, any more than the layman knows the tricks of the tailor's trade. We only know it DOES, and this is enough for all practical purposes.

One of the easiest ways to test the truth of this, grasp it and begin to get ready to use it as a tool in your life's workshop is to trace the effect of any definite mood upon yourself.

Maybe this attitude is one which originally other people suggested to you. You opened the door of your mind to it and then entertained it in your thoughts, just as you would a friend in your parlor.

Say that at breakfast some member of your family remarked, "Mary, dear, you don't look at all well this morning. Are you ill?"

You weren't ill at all, in fact quite the contrary. You had arisen feeling it was great to be alive and feel so good. But you had done your hair a new way and inadvertently used the talcum instead of your usual pink powder.

"Oh, no," you replied, "I never felt better in my life. Isn't it a wonderful morning?"

On the way to the office you meet a friend who also notices the effect of the talcum.

"You look a little pale, Mary," she says. "Is it spring fever?"

"No, indeed," you answer. "I'm very well, thank you." But the tiny thought at the breakfast table was allowed to take root and already you are not quite as enthusiastic as you were.

When you reach the office those kind friends who characterize so many offices, and who never miss a thing like that, exclaim, "Why, Mary, for pity's sake, what ails you? You look like a ghost!"

By noon you take the boss's advice and go home for the rest of the day, and by four o'clock that little dab of white talcum has brought you a sure-enough, honest-to-goodness headache!

On the other hand, the next time you get up feeling a little shaky or "headachy" do as a friend of mine does in such cases. First, take special pains with your appearance. This is not absolutely necessary if you are very strong-minded, but in rebuilding your life, as in doing anything else, give yourself every chance, make it as easy and pleasant for yourself as possible while you go along.

This friend of mine is pretty strong-minded herself, but she says that when her acquaintances declare how unusually fine she looks that day it prevents the right attitude from wobbling.

Of course she does other things besides dress up and take pains with her hair and face. She keeps the door of her mind tight shut every time

Your Predominant Moods

little old Ache comes a-knocking, and she constantly tells herself how good she feels.

When she gets to the office she takes up some matter that calls for real concentration—something that will pull her mind away from herself.

By noon her headache is gone and she doesn't even know when she missed it!

In a later lesson I will tell you exactly how to cure much more insidious ailments than headaches, and in another just how to treat your subconscious to induce it to do your hard work easily and quickly, but the above stories will suffice to remind you of similar things in your own experience which will help you to see that we have a lot to do with what comes to us.

To the pessimist the wrong things are forever happening. To the optimist come continually the right things, the helpful things, the good things.

If you are in the pessimist class you have probably said: "It's no job for HIM to be bright and smiling. I'd be a little Merry Sunshine myself if some of those nice things would happen to ME!"

And some friend of yours defends you with: "Poor man, you can't blame him for being a grouch. Why, just one thing after another goes wrong with his plans!"

It is the long-sustained, persistently encouraged POINT OF VIEW that determines the KINDS of things that come your way. Right about face, today! Try the optimist's outlook, and see!

You can sincerely and honestly apply the optimist's methods and become an optimist yourself, no matter how pessimistic you have been up to now, if instead of calling the optimist "a poor fool who is jollying himself along" you will let me suggest this little but mighty thought to you:

The pessimist sees things at short range, the optimist at long range; the pessimist sees a limited area of a thing, while the optimist sees it in its entirety; the pessimist sees only a part (that part which is nearest and most immediate), but the optimist sees the whole of that thing—the ultimate, INCLUDING ITS INSIGNIFICANCE IN HIS OWN LIFE.

"This too shall pass," he says in the hour of sorrow.

"It doesn't amount to anything, anyhow. What do I care?" he says when people slander him.

"The difference between the pessimist and the optimist," someone said once, "is that the optimist sees the doughnut but the pessimist sees the hole."

One thing we know: no pessimist ever built a healthy, happy or helpful life. And smile at him as you will, the optimist does all three.

He need not have the most brilliant mind, the best education or the deepest intellect; he has something better than all of them put together and for the attainment of which all the others exist—wisdom.

Before we go into the moods which are to bring you the specific things you want, do this much for yourself: look at your secret tendency and find out whether you are predominantly an optimist or predominantly a pessimist.

If you are an optimist, so much the better. If you are a pessimist, the very recognition and admission of it to yourself will help you, for it will diagnose part of your case, and diagnosis is the first step toward a cure.

The optimist builds for himself a heaven on earth and the pessimist a hell. You take your choice by choosing which one of these moods shall hold sway in your innermost heart, and then by being loyal to that choice, REGARDLESS OF WHAT HAPPENS.

For, remember, it is not true that your moods are really MADE by what happens to you. What happens to you, IN THE BY AND LARGE OF YOUR LIFE, IS MANUFACTURED IN THE BACK ROOM OF YOUR TAILOR SHOP by the moods you permit to dwell there. There are two worlds, the seen and the unseen. We think of the seen as the most real, but it is really only the coat worn by the unseen—a coat that changes as the inner world produces happiness or wretchedness, success or failure, health or disease. Cause is always more significant than effects, for it is the creator of them.

Your unseen world is far more significant than your outer, seen world. This personal unseen world is your own individual domain. No one but yourself can rule it. It is your kingdom and you are its absolute monarch. You and you alone can decide what this great unseen estate shall produce for you out here in the material, everyday world of reality.

You and you alone can give the orders it must obey. It knows no will, no voice, no power but yours.

The wills, voices, suggestions and power of others can never vitally affect it or sidetrack it save as YOU translate these into your language and speak them to your own subconscious mind.

It is because of this that all psychologists now declare there is no suggestion save auto-suggestion; that no suggestion made by another can remain in your mind to affect it unless YOU make it YOUR OWN and hand it on to your inner consciousness.

It is this which makes every suggestion you give yourself so powerful. YOU give the order, wherefore you back up that order with every fiber of your being.

Having ordered it, expected it and worked toward it throughout your organism, IT CANNOT FAIL TO COME TO PASS.

This law is operating all the time whether we recognize it or not. Whatever your moods bend toward, that will you seek, finally find, then touch, and ultimately bring into your life.

Whatever you lean away from, ever so slightly, in your secret soul, that will you gradually GROW away from, and if the mood of repulsion is continued, finally separate yourself from completely.

More will be explained to you concerning this latter law in the lesson on environment, but this much here will help to clarify in your mind the truth of this powerful law of moods.

Whenever doubt or fear enters into these moods the force back of your desire, instead of being magnetized to bring you that thing, becomes deadened, neutralized just to that extent.

But if fear and doubt are repelled every time they come near you the drawing power of your desire will ultimately become irresistible. It will become so, not from any mystical, mysterious cause, but BECAUSE OF THE NATURE OF MAN. "Whatsoever a man thinks on, that does he become." And as we BECOME, we ATTAIN.

As we grow inwardly larger, the cloak of reality will become larger and more glorious. If we become small no power on earth can prevent its shrinking to fit us.

The thing to do if we would get what we want is not to waste time railing against the imaginary something we call fate, but to create the fates we desire.

This we can do by setting to work to change the moods that are operating in our inner world. Our external world will change accordingly.

Any predominant mood works itself out into reality by drawing unto itself many apparently outside influences, much as our country in time of war drafts men from everywhere and compels them to come to its aid.

This is equally true whether the attitude is destructive or constructive. If destructive, fearful or anxious the forces it summons to its aid are the destructive. It can call out only its own workers, just as America can call only American soldiers and Canada Canadian soldiers.

One of the first external manifestations of destructive attitudes will be apparent in your physical health. No person who is depressed, melancholy, worried or afraid can stay well. He may not become aware of this immediately, but soon certain functions will begin to slip a cog. What these are will depend on which organ or system is his weakest link.

One of the next things to appear on the surface as a direct result of any person's destructive moods will be the CHANGE IN HIS PERSONAL APPEARANCE. Voice, movements, gestures, facial expressions and especially the lines around the mouth and eyes will publish it.

This, in turn, will repel the very men and women he needs to help him, till sooner or later he will be compelled to confine himself to association with other fear personalities like himself, all of whom will aggravate his own destructive tendencies by directly or indirectly RE-SUGGESTING them to him.

Conversely, an uplifted outlook will start instantly to rejuvenating you physically and mentally. It will glow so radiantly in your face and shine so brightly from your entire being that successful, constructive people will be attracted to you, learn to like you and gladly help you toward what you desire.

When you stop to think that everything we get out of life we must get through, from, with or by OTHER PEOPLE, you begin to see how important this stage of your progress is.

There are no self-made people really. They are only self-made in the sense that they work to deserve the help of others and, having deserved it, get it.

Looked at in the light of experience and actual facts, then, it is no wonder our predominant moods create things all around us in their own image.

They are not confined to any one avenue, but go out into the highways and byways of our immediate and remote environment, and bring back whatever they need for their fulfillment.

They affect every act and event in our daily lives, these predominant moods of ours. They color and distort, expand or condense all kinds of happenings when we are least aware of it.

They construct from within and attract from without. They have not only drawing power but selective power—these intense feelings of ours—and always their picking and choosing is in accordance with whatever furthers our deepest self-estimates.

If the attitude that predominates in your inmost heart is one of certainty that you will get what you want, a thousand silent, invisible forces are set to work inside and outside your own organism to bring it about. Not only will your body do its work more smoothly, but your brain will evolve ways and means undreamed of before for bringing this thing out into the visible world and straight to you.

Fear of any kind is a depressant to both mind and body, while faith stimulates us to attempt and finally accomplish the impossible.

Fear and all thoughts of failure register themselves upon us inwardly and outwardly in many ways, one of the most obvious of which is noted when fright instantly drains the blood from a man's face.

When it has this effect externally it is easy to picture its restrictive effect upon the vital inner organs, to each of which an abundant blood supply is absolutely essential to health.

Feelings are not feelings alone. They are dynamic forces, setting into motion, in accordance with their own nature, the entire organism of a man, paralyzing or expanding it as the case may be.

A feeling of strength not only releases the strength already stored up inside a man's mind and body, but generates more and more as he uses up his supply. It is this which brings the well-known "second wind." Within each of us lies the real cause of the general conditions that come to us— physical, financial, professional, personal and social. We make our own world, our own character, our own habits, our own environment.

Since we have MADE all these we can UNMAKE them and then REMAKE them to suit ourselves. The moment we recognize this greatest law in human life we can set about to use it CONSTRUCTIVELY and CONSCIOUSLY instead of allowing it to use us DESTRUCTIVELY and UNCONSCIOUSLY as we have been doing in the past.

Never forget that whatever you are feeding into the mill of your subconscious in the form of thoughts and feelings will be actualized in some form in the events or environments of your life.

Just accepting this one great fact will help you immeasurably, for it will enable you to stop this moment the building of disease, failure or despair. If you will pass this knowledge on to others, not by preaching, but simply by handing on this little book, you will strengthen yourself even further by having strengthened them. Our mental attitudes act somewhat like planting-plows, going ahead, laying open the soil and planting therein the seeds that correspond to our general feelings concerning ourselves. Unless you do something to prevent it, your future harvests will be in exact accordance with the planting you have done up to now.

But if you will right now stop watering them with your thoughts, remarks and actions, and learn to plow under, with new moods, all that have sprouted, you will be ready for a new and better crop. The soil is the same. As the farmer raises corn one year on a certain field and the next year wheat, so you are able to change entirely the fruits you will reap from your great Subconscious Mind, by changing the seeds you plant.

In the next lesson I will show you exactly how to go about it to reseed that illimitable field within yourself by REMAKING YOUR MOODS.

LESSON II

How to Remake Our Moods for Mastery

WE ARE THE SOLE MAKERS AND ABSOLUTE CONTROLLERS OF OUR OWN PREDOMINANT MOODS.

If we would remake our lives we have only to REMAKE OUR PREDOMINANT MOODS.

This, once you recognize its necessity, is a simple thing to do—so simple it seems unbelievable, yet so powerful it will affect your life for the better from the moment you try it.

We are so constructed that we rid the subconscious of anything we desire to be free of simply by REVERSING the process that put it there, viz., by REFUSING TO HARBOR AND DWELL UPON FURTHER THOUGHTS CONCERNING IT.

The old mood then dies for lack of cultivation.

Another wonderful fact is that whereas we build harmful attitudes but slowly, we can build harmonious ones WITH INCREDIBLE RAPIDITY.

This is due to the fact that when we build downward we are opposing all the constructive forces of nature, whereas we ally ourselves with all our God-given powers the moment we start building upward.

This is proven most graphically in two aspects—that of habits and diseases. It requires a long time to build a disease into your system,—sometimes years of neglect and abuse. But with conditions just right in the subconscious mind of the patient he can be (and in thousands of cases has been) cured of that disease instantly.

Years or months usually go into the formation of an undesirable habit, but if we apply the law fully and completely it leaves us in an hour, never to return unless we deliberately call it back.

Another illustration showing why it is easier to go up than down, easier to succeed than fail, is to be found in any automobile engine. When it is grinding along in second gear it burns up more fuel, becomes much more heated and yet makes slower progress than when in first.

Now we are all intended to be "in high" ALL the time. Like the auto engine, we are BUILT FOR IT, and when we harbor wrong attitudes we are "in low."

True, we move along, in whatever direction we are headed, but all the good in us cries out against it. Since there is much more of this spiritual element in us than we realize and since it is impossible to kill it, we never can hurt our lives quite as quickly or completely as we can help and improve them.

Every time we lift our heads or hearts we are met instantly by some shining power greater than ourselves. The making of a good resolution—how it strengthens and inspires us!

And the making of a bad one—the threat to "get even," for instance—ever notice how it affects your face muscles, your appetite, your ability to concentrate on worthwhile things?

The TURNING TOWARD THE RIGHT is all that's needed just at first.

Bear in mind that there is NO SUCH THING AS STANDING STILL. YOU ARE ALWAYS MOVING.

You are either weaker than you were yesterday or stronger, more confident or more afraid; and what you are letting yourself FEEL today will affect you tomorrow. If persisted in it will build events for the coming years.

This is an eternal, immutable, inexorable law. Therefore if you would change your future, change your mind, especially the content of your great subconscious mind.

This is much easier to do than you may suppose. You do it simply BY WATCHING YOUR REACTIONS, and gently, deliberately, persistently giving back to the events of life the kind of reaction you want to build your future.

It is never what happens to you that counts, but how you TAKE what happens to you.

For, strange as it may seem, it is never the EVENTS of your life, but the WAY YOU TAKE THEM which creates the MOODS that in the final analysis MAKE your life.

Once the mood has "set" it goes ahead, of its own accord, and builds out into your life the KINDS of things that correspond to it.

Therefore to change your life for the better it is absolutely essential that you change your PREDOMINANT MOODS for the better.

To do this it is not necessary to struggle or make resolutions that would tax your strength. It is not necessary to try to do everything in a minute. "Rome was not built in a day," and the same is true of anything else worth while. You have all your life before you in which to make these improvements, and all the power available for doing them.

Don't be in a hurry and don't be afraid. Don't give yourself a great deal to do. Start easy and add more as your strength grows. It will grow with amazing swiftness. You will not have long to wait. Meanwhile you must NOT be impatient. BUT YOU MUST BE PERSISTENT.

There is an old legend about a boy who had a pet calf. He wanted to develop great lifting power, so he lifted his calf several times each day. He did not skip a single day. And when the calf was full grown and weighed a thousand pounds he could lift it without a quiver!

It is persistence, NOT INTENSE EFFORT, that plants and replants your subconscious; just the gentle dropping of thought-seeds into the soil. You will recognize this if you will recall how your present general attitudes were developed.

Do you want me to remind you, dear troubled one, just how they did grow?

Come with me back over your yesterdays. It will be a very interesting trip and will reveal some things you have never suspected.

First, I want you to note that the attitudes which today predominate in the back of your mind REGARDING YOURSELF did NOT grow up suddenly. They came into being gradually—crystallizing, getting "set" as time went on.

You are quite surprised when you catch occasional, unexpected glimpses of yourself to note the changes that have taken place IN YOU since you looked in last!

These changes, for better or for worse, are going on every moment within us, as definitely and uninterruptedly as the physical growth of a child. We do not notice it unless we make a special effort to do so any more than we note the growth of our own children. But a friend who has been absent only a little while is struck by the change. Everything about us tells the history of our FEELINGS and our self-estimate and others read it whether we can do so or not. The bulletins are there in full view even when we least realize it.

What puts them there? Always and forever one tendency and one alone—THE WAY WE HAVE BEEN TAKING THINGS. Not the events, remember, but the REACTIONS we have been giving to events since they saw us last.

In this manner we slowly but surely build up moods that will take us to the heights, physically, financially, socially and personally, those that will take us to the depths, or those that land us somewhere between.

If your own moods are of the highest, purest, most constructive, you will go high; if they are of the lowest, basest, most destructive, you will sink very low; if they are "so-so," not very bad or very good, just medium, so will your life be.

To see just what I mean, ask yourself this question: "When unpleasant things happened to me how have I reacted to them?"

"Have I rebounded mentally and emotionally in a spirit of challenge, feeling way down inside, 'This can not defeat me!' Or have I developed the habit of falling flat before little troubles, of making mountains out of molehills, of fretting and stewing and feeling crushed?"

"Or have I done neither, but just muddled through, feeling sort of numb and unaffected?"

If you will look back over the years you will see that THE MASSED CONDITIONS OF YOUR LIFE TODAY CORRESPOND, WITH AMAZING EXACTNESS, TO THE MAJORITY OF THESE SUBCONSCIOUS REACTIONS.

Moreover, in the years to come, when you see a man or a woman who has gained wealth, station, honors, friends or power you will not need to put the old question, "How did he do it?"

What is true of you is true of each and every human being in the world. The plan always precedes production. The dream precedes the doing. FEELINGS precede the FACTS. This is the greatest discovery of modern human science.

When you see such a one, you know that this person acquired the habit I am showing YOU how to acquire—of giving back to the events of life as they came and went, REGARDLESS OF WHAT THEY WERE, a HARMONIOUS instead of a HARMFUL reaction.

Every successful life has two sides: the outside RESULTS which the world sees, and the INSIDE REACTIONS which brought about those results.

Every successful person has met with opposition, "hard luck," failure, disillusionment. If you read biography you will see that more than average difficulties have lined EVERY path to power.

But instead of giving in, as the average person does, those destined for success seem literally to sharpen their weapons upon the rough edge of adversity.

If you would rise, if you would attain success, fame, love or any other thing, you must give a new set of orders to your subconscious mind BY NOT YIELDING INWARDLY when trouble comes.

What people DO when trouble comes is important, of course, but what they FEEL is far more important, because these feelings added together plant and replant the subconscious mind while our overt acts often affect only the surface.

To make clear to you what takes place in your inner world and HOW your HABITUAL REACTIONS color the events of your life, a certain homely illustration is the best one I have found.

Have you ever watched on a Monday morning while someone "blued" the family wash? If so, you have noticed how she first "blued" the tub of water by dipping the little package of bluing balls into it till the right color was obtained.

Your subconscious mind is like that tubful of water. Every time an event of importance comes to you, life is handing you what some people slangily call "a package." But whether this event, be it pleasant or unpleasant, brightens or darkens your subconscious content DOES NOT DEPEND UPON THE EVENT ITSELF, FOR NO EVENT CAN REACH YOUR SUBCONSCIOUS MIND. It depends entirely upon YOUR REACTION to that event.

In other words, upon THE WAY YOU TAKE IT, for this aftermath ALWAYS reaches your subconscious.

When you take any experience constructively, you are bigger, better and stronger than you were before it came, NO MATTER HOW DESTRUCTIVE THE EXPERIENCE ITSELF MAY HAVE BEEN.

When you do this you have "brightened" the color of the subconscious content just to that extent—and to that extent it will eventually brighten the external garments of your life.

But when you "give in" to an unhappy experience, when you brood over it, pity yourself or nurse destructive feelings, you are deliberately TAKING HOLD of this unhappy experience, turning around and DIPPING it into your subconscious content and thereby HURTING YOURSELF in the ONLY place where it counts.

"But when unhappy experiences come to me how CAN I be happy over them?" you ask.

You cannot be happy over them, of course, and it is not necessary that you should. Momentary happiness or unhappiness is not what we are talking about, for it is unimportant. We are talking in this course about your life's happiness AS A WHOLE, the most important question, the one significant issue in every person's life. Whether this one biggest thing shall come to you depends on how you treat the little ones, the petty trials, tribulations and disappointments. This was illustrated in the famous answer Michelangelo made to a careless young man. This young friend, a fellow artist (whose name, for obvious reasons, is not known) returned from a holiday and called on Michelangelo at his studio.

He was disappointed to find the great sculptor working on a statue that was practically finished when he left six weeks before.

"So far as I can see," complained the young man, "you've accomplished nothing while I've been away!"

"You are quite wrong," answered Michelangelo, and he pointed out this and that little improvement — the remodeling of a finger here, a curve there, delicate retouchings everywhere.

"But these are only trifles," said the young man.

"Yes," answered the great one, "they are trifles. But trifles make perfection and PERFECTION IS NO TRIFLE."

Whether you are building for lasting health, happiness and success or their opposites does not hinge upon the raw material life's experiences give you to work with. This is surprisingly similar in all cases.

It depends upon whether you are taking things with courage or with cowardice, with the "I give in" attitude or the attitude which says, "A thing like this shall not lick me!"

If you will take this latter attitude, happiness and all other things "shall be added unto you," for ultimately everything gives way before it. It is irresistible. It is in accordance with God-made laws, and God-made laws, like man-made ones, are no respecters of persons.

No matter how sad or discouraged or heartbroken you may be; no matter how many times you have failed in what you attempted; no matter how cruel or disappointing life has been to you up to now, NOTHING ON EARTH can keep you from what you desire if you will start today and REACT CONSTRUCTIVELY to the experiences that come to you.

Remember, your everyday life, your environment, the actualities are after all only the garments worn by your soul. If you really want those of tomorrow to be bright and beautiful, simply see to it that you meet every event constructively.

If you would clearly understand how you have the power to use these events as you will, try this:

Think of yourself as a LITTLE HOUSE whose happiness and achievements depend upon the workings of the machinery DOWN IN THE SUBCONSCIOUS BASEMENT.

Your conscious mind may be likened to the front parlor. Every event or experience of your life enters that front parlor, through the doors of your five senses. Thus do you become "aware" of anything that happens to you; thus only can you have an experience.

These events of life come into the parlor of your conscious, THINKING mind without even knocking. Some are good and some are bad; some pleasant, some unpleasant, but it doesn't matter in the long run which they are, because they cannot affect you save in the form in which they reach your subconscious basement, and that is entirely UP TO YOU.

Every event, experience and happening of your life finds its way down into your subconscious basement as soon as it leaves the conscious parlor, which occurs as soon as a more pressing event or experience is thrust upon you from the outside world.

For instance, each event of yesterday, engrossing as it may have been at the time, gave way to subsequent events and is now only a memory, so far as your conscious mind is concerned. But it is a LIVING FORCE in your subconscious.

Whether it is a helpful or harmful force depends on THE WAY YOU LET IT AFFECT YOU AT THE TIME.

In other words, the events of yesterday went down the back stairs of your house and on into your subconscious basement, not in their original form but AS LITTLE GHOSTS OF CONSTRUCTION OR DESTRUCTION.

But no matter how destructive one of these experiences may have been, no matter how its appearance terrorized you when it entered your consciousness, IT WENT INTO YOUR SUBCONSCIOUS AS A HELPFUL WORKER IF YOU FACED IT CONSTRUCTIVELY.

Everything you contact in life—everything you read, every person you meet, every event—must pass through your own consciousness down into your subconscious and be transmuted there before it can be brought out into your life.

It comes to you as raw material and must be made up by you before you can use it. It is gold, coming to your mint as raw bullion, to be minted and stamped with your own die before being used in the world of affairs.

The events that come to you are putty in your hands. You can make of them anything you will. When you have done so they become living things, working for or against you; good or bad fairies according to the shape you give them.

Always bear in mind that what this shape shall be depends upon the MOLDS you are building day by day in your own subconscious mind.

When you realize that not one thing that ever happened to you could have hurt you had you applied this great principle, and that nothing in the future can hurt you except as YOU USE IT AGAINST YOURSELF, you can rebuild your entire outlook.

Here are the specific steps which will, if adhered to, eventually remake your life:

Rule 1. Whenever an unhappy experience comes into your front parlor, do not let IT do all the talking. Make it see you are master there. Say to it, just as though it were another person, "You are not a very pleasing thing now, but I can turn you into one of the best little workers I've got and I am going to do it!"

Form the habit of saying this from THE INSTANT an unpleasant thing begins to happen, and before deciding on ANY KIND of action. It will steady and sustain you till you can see what to do. But don't stop there. Rule 2. Then to yourself say, "This experience has GOOD in it for me SOMEWHERE, and though I do not see it just now I shall look till I find that good and put it to active use in my life."

Then search till you find it. You will usually discover more than one. In my own life every unpleasant experience has paid for itself many times over and the worst ones most of all.

In order that you may recognize the truth of this reassurance while giving it to yourself I ask that you DO NOT WAIT till some calamity descends upon you before testing it, but glance backward NOW and see how true it has been of the disappointments you have had in the past. You can see clearly and perhaps for the first time the lesson each had for you—a lesson you could have been using all this time had you only allowed yourself to find it!

If you will do this, strength will come to you out of every experience. Breadth and wisdom and character will develop within you, and everything in your life will enlarge to fit it.

Rule 3. Regardless of how disastrous any event seems to be, no matter how many terrible results you believe it is bound to bring you, do not DWELL upon these aspects.

They will come to you in the form of pictures—little moving pictures—in which you are the chief actor and in which you see yourself hurt, wrecked or even killed by this event.

If you let them, they will unwind before your mind's eye, scene after scene, and start in all over again every time the fade-out comes, adding new and more awful possibilities till you have a ten-reel tragedy revolving constantly in your mind. This will not only keep you unhappy but it will certainly prevent your finding the lesson in that experience.

Remake Our Moods for Mastery

It will do three more things if persisted in: it will eventually make you ill physically; it will undermine your mentality; and, because our actions follow our thoughts, it will cause you to ACT in accordance with your fears and thus BRING SOME OF THEM TO PASS.

Rule 4. Start out each day determined to go through with the minimum of friction; with the least possible wear and tear on your own organism.

Decide that NOTHING shall upset or frighten you; that, no matter what comes, you will finish TODAY without giving way to destructive moods.

Though you may feel certain you cannot go on forever upholding this high standard, even if you are sure you will HAVE to give way by tomorrow don't bother about that. Center your mind on THIS ONE DAY, and deliberately refrain from heaping unnecessary burdens upon your shoulders. "Forever" never comes,—no, nor tomorrow,—so take care of today and eternity will take care of itself.

But you will not have to wait for eternity to vindicate your new consciousness. By tomorrow you will see that it was better to postpone the destructive mood or action, for its significance will then be obvious.

Soon you will have formed the habit of reacting constructively, and YOUR WHOLE LIFE will change accordingly. It is this tendency to live Yesterday and Tomorrow instead of Today that causes most of our destructive moods. Today can always be managed. It is only when we pile the memories of past tragedies and the visualizations of future ones upon our backs that we break down.

And this is precisely the type of person who could so easily make his life happy and successful. Such a one has imagination, the rarest mental power there is. Only he turns it against himself instead of making it work for him.

People who are lacking in imagination can never rise very high nor fall very low. Imagination is like an electric current; it works in whatever direction you turn it. Whether it takes you to the depths or builds your life on the heights depends upon the way you press the button.

The rules given throughout this course show you how to turn your God-given power into constructive channels instead of using them for self-destruction as we unknowingly do most of the time.

Rule 5. Refuse to cross bridges till you come to them.

Stop wondering whether So-and-So will keep his appointment, whether Mrs. Somebody-or-Other will pay her bill, whether everything will work out all right in the forthcoming deal, whether other people will understand your motives, whether it will rain next Sunday and spoil the picnic, whether you will make a good showing at the club meeting, whether the children will stay well, whether they will make their grades at school, whether some loved one will return from that journey safely, etc., etc.

Remember the old man who said, "I've had lots of troubles in my life but most of 'em never happened."

If you are given to this sort of thing, step aside and have a good laugh at yourself, for once. Look at yourself and see how funny you are.

Don't let anyone else into the secret. Just go off by yourself frequently and say, "My dear, if we'd spent half the time thinking out ways and means that we've wasted wondering and jumping at conclusions, we'd have been somewhere by now."

Do this till it becomes a habit. Then every time you start borrowing trouble that big healthy habit will step up and give you the wink. You will soon find yourself laughing at the very things which now crumple you all up.

Rule 6. Confine yourself TO THE BUSINESS IN HAND.

This has two wonderfully helpful effects. First, it prevents your imagination running wild and dragging you with it. Second, it will remove the cause of one of the worst sore spots in your subconscious—the realization that you have been letting the quality of your work deteriorate.

I shall have more to tell you about work in another lesson, but this is the place to tell you that, though we are seldom aware of it, one of the most prolific causes of destructive moods is the fact (consciously repressed but forever NAGGING at us subconsciously) that WE ARE NOT DOING JUSTICE TO OURSELVES IN OUR WORK.

Rule 7. Don't let the facts stated just above or any others cause you to waste ONE MOMENT regretting the neglect of your work IN THE PAST.

That is all gone. What's done is done. You can make up for it and everything else and actually PROFIT by your mistakes if you will turn your back on every one of them and THINK ONLY OF THE FUTURE.

A great American once said, "Get rid of your regrets. You are what you are because of what you have suffered. Rightly understood and applied every error can prove a blessing."

Rule 8. Avail yourself of suggestion, the greatest law of the subconscious mind, by keeping yourself surrounded with the little things that help you.

For instance, if you are in earnest about remaking your life, the first thing you should do is copy rules out of this lesson and put them in a place that is conspicuous to you BUT WHERE OTHERS WILL NOT SEE THEM.

I know one young woman who rebuilt her life by tacking these rules inside her clothes closet under the hook where she hung her nightdress. This compelled her to see them at least every morning and every evening when she might otherwise have been too busy to look at them.

A business man of New York City changed himself from a morose, depressed failure to a happy, courageous success by pasting these rules in plain sight inside the top drawer of his desk—a private one which he opened many times a day but which others had no occasion to see.

It is better, especially at first, for you to keep this to yourself, because the law of suggestion, like every other, works both ways. In self-defense the unambitious and unaspiring are inclined to suggest failure to you and this greatly delays the progress of any sensitive one, whether he admits it or not.

This attitude is especially characteristic of the skeptical, critical people in your immediate environment who like to think they know you better than you know yourself. Remember our one big fundamental rule: make everything as easy for yourself as possible; GIVE YOURSELF EVERY CHANCE. Then YOU CANNOT FAIL.

Every business house in America has recognized the efficacy of these "reminders," and many of them have profitably invested thousands of dollars in such slogans as "Do It Now," "Every Knock's a Boost," etc.

The most famous of all such things was Elbert Hubbard's "Message to Garcia," a little essay so full of suggestions for workers that firms all over the world ordered copies of it for their employes. It was translated into twenty-six languages and over forty million copies were sold.

Suggestion is the most potent force in business as well as in personal life. If you would succeed at anything you should avail yourself of suggestions of a constructive nature whenever possible. To be sure of enough of them, do not wait for them to happen—MAKE them happen.

The printed or spoken word is by no means the only ways in which suggestions get into the subconscious mind. In fact everything we see, hear, touch, taste and smell, as well as everything we say, think and do suggests something to us. If not short-circuited the suggestion goes down into the subconscious in its original form.

Whether any class of suggestions get sidetracked and kept out of the subconscious, or whether they go straight into it, depends on the standing orders you have given to your habit-mind.

All good suggestions have the right of way, the main track, as it were, and take precedence over all others as soon as you give orders to that effect.

Give that order right now to your whole self, and henceforth keep plenty of helpful reminders around you.

In addition to these rules, have inspiring slogans, poems and mottoes in plain sight. They are of inestimable value. Choose those which appeal to you personally, whether anyone else likes them or not, and do not try to see any that do NOT appeal to you, no matter how popular they may be or how much they mean to someone else. In these matters "every soul lives alone," it knows its own needs and must make its own selections.

Besides these, be sure to have in full view in your office, your bedroom or your workroom anything else that uplifts you. What these are will depend entirely upon yourself and your experience.

Thousands of busy men keep sweet and strong through all the struggles and vicissitudes of business by having the pictures of their wives and babies on their desks or over their work benches.

A look at her wedding ring has turned many a wife from temptation. She may have been nursing the idea that her husband no longer cares for her. But that plain gold band speaks to her of the beauty and love it once symbolized.

The subconscious mind deals ALMOST ENTIRELY IN SYMBOLS, hence the power of these simple external reminders.

If you are inclined to depreciate yourself, criticize or condemn yourself, here is the best suggestion of all:

Keep plainly in view in your own private room, or where you will run across them frequently, mementoes, favors, badges, trophies or other REMINDERS OF YOUR VICTORIES.

Whenever you are feeling "down in the mouth" run over the list and see how much better you are half an hour afterward!

Rule 9. Avoid just as many inharmonious ideas, events and people as you can.

Your subconscious, once your conscious mind has given the order, will translate even the most unhappy experience into a helpful influence, but that is no reason for abusing it or giving it

UNNECESSARY WORK to do. Be good enough to save it for the main issues.

It goes without saying that you will be piling rocks in your own roadway if you persist in cultivating the things, people or conditions that hurt or humiliate you. Your subconscious can crush them into sand for the road bed, it is true, but if you want to make the utmost speed don't give it needless tasks to perform nor load yourself down with excess baggage.

By this I mean such things as reminders of your past failures. Forget them and let everyone else forget them. So far as possible stay away from the people who know of them and especially those who speak of them.

If old friends or members of your family have the habit of referring to the time things went against you, of keeping green the graves of blasted hopes, gently but firmly tell them it's not the past but the present and the future that count with you.

Rule 10. Avoid so far as possible all pessimistic, cynical individuals. Recognize their condition as pathological in each case, give each one your understanding and NOT your censure. But don't permit them to agitate you.

It is not possible in this workaday world always to avoid unpleasing people, but whenever we run into them we can remember what Marcus Aurelius recommended. He said:

"Begin the morning by saying to yourself, 'I shall meet with the busy--body, the ungrateful, arrogant, deceitful, envious, unsocial. All these things happen to them by reason of their ignorance of what is good and evil." Rule 11. Stay away from political wrangles, all mobs, all quarrels and all "againster" meetings.

These serve little purpose other than that of stirring up the primitive and most pugnacious instincts within us. One such experience can put you far behind in your progress.

If you want to help the world, remember all the good that has come into it has come in spite of fighting, not because of it, and this applies to individuals as well as nations.

Rule 12. Mingle with optimistic, hopeful, inspiring people as much as possible. Seek them out.

Rule 13. Make it a point to attend meetings, lectures, conventions, concerts, churches, etc., where the message of hope prevails.

At all inspiring gatherings you are bound to hear many things that will help you—things you can apply to your own problems, that will be available for your own needs. The rest you can let alone. Even a goose knows enough to take the corn and leave the cob.

Rule 14. When things go wrong in your work, say to yourself, "These are merely annoyances incident to my business. To let them irritate me signifies I am not big enough for my business."

Whatever your work, environment or field of endeavor, bear in mind that there are bound to be certain difficulties INHERENT in it, since it is a human institution.

Rule 15. If you are an employer of any kind, you are sure to meet with stupidity and inefficiency occasionally. Instead of letting these enrage you, remind yourself of another of Hubbard's maxims: "If he had my brains he'd have my job."

Rule 16. If you are an employee, bear the same thing in mind. Instead of becoming blindly angry when the boss calls you down, search for the grain of truth in what he says about you and let it grow into self-improvement. Otherwise you will be forever taking orders from others.

Instead of harboring resentment, planning to get even or feeling abused when you seem not to be appreciated, try to figure out what is wrong WITH YOU and how to COMMAND appreciation.

Rule 17. On the other hand, don't think you are hopeless because you are not perfect.

One of the brightest girls I ever knew was on the verge of a nervous collapse when this rule came to her attention.

She had worked hard and wanted to make a hundred-per-cent record. Whenever anything went wrong, when an error was found in her department, she broke down and was almost ill for days afterward. When she decided to do her best and let the rest go, her nervousness and self-consciousness disappeared, hence her work improved until it was practically faultless. Today she is one of the healthiest, happiest and most successful business women of the Pacific Coast.

In this connection remember also that you can never make any other human being completely, permanently happy.

Perfect happiness is something no individual can give to another and which each must acquire for himself if he is ever to have it. But there are numberless men and women who are wretched all the time because someone whom they feel unduly responsible for—husband, wife, child or parent—is not supremely happy. They forget that happiness is an accomplishment each must achieve for himself. We can no more attain it for others than we could, by taking their piano lessons, make good musicians of them.

Destructive moods finally begin to dominate our lives from one of the TWO MAIN TENDENCIES —too much selfishness or too much unselfishness.

If all your moods center around yourself, your possessions, the way people treat you, the money you have or hope to have or are afraid you won't have, the way things are going to affect YOU, you belong largely to the former.

But if you are so sensitive to the feelings, hopes and rights of others that you are constantly afraid of hurting them, you belong to the latter, and, what is more, you are causing the very ones you love best a good deal of needless anxiety.

I know a family of ten in which all the members keep themselves miserable worrying over each other's difficulties. Each one is amply able to bear his own if he would only stick to his own. But each carries those of every other member, thus weighing himself down with the burdens often instead of one, and making more trouble for himself and everybody concerned by incapacitating himself for his own affairs.

No man was intended to ride through life on the back of another. We only weaken others, especially young people, when we try to relieve them of all responsibility. This is especially true when we try to relieve them of the responsibility of making THEMSELVES happy.

Rule 18. Do not allow yourself to gather a long list of things you "just can't stand!"

Such a mood is like a fly for multiplying! If you encourage yourself today in imagining there are three things you can't and WON'T endure, this time next year there will be a dozen, and in five years a hundred.

Did you ever stop to think that one of the main reasons why old maids (of both sexes) are so unattractive is that there are so many things they "simply can't bear"?

They won't eat this, they can't go out in this or that kind of weather, they never read this or wear that or do something else!

Whenever you get an aversion and begin to raise it for a pet you are taking a step toward fussy, fretty old-maidishness.

Rule 19. Stop kicking at every pin-prick life sends you.

If you want to respect yourself or ever make a life worthy of the name you have got to be BIG. Big things don't come to petty people. But big things simply can't stay away from big people.

You can size up your tendencies and see whether you are growing toward littleness or bigness, insignificance or greatness, by noting whether you ignore some of the bites or whether you hit back every time a human mosquito stings you.

You may feel you are unfortunate, that no one else has quite so much to bear, but the fact is that people with big minds and big affairs have a greater number of these things happen to them than others. Their activities bring them into contact with a far larger number of people, and the envy their success creates in small minds makes them the victims of many things the world knows nothing about. But they rise above them by ignoring and forgetting them.

Those who are big enough to rise above the crowd are also big enough to bear the mud-slinging for which such eminence makes them the target.

If you want to evolve above the dead level you must be prepared get your share of unjust, even false criticism. But realize that, after all, this is a compliment to you, since it is a well-known psychological fact that people never bother to knock those they consider their inferiors.

Begin to school yourself not to mind mud and especially NEVER to throw any back. Mud that is let alone dries, turns to dust and eventually flies back into the eyes of him who slung it.

Rule 20. Be persistent, NOT INTENSE, in following the rules of this lesson.

Remember, it isn't occasional skirmishes but "eternal vigilance" that is "the price of liberty."

ADDITIONAL AND SPECIAL HELPS FOR ALL WHO ARE GRIEF-STRICKEN, REMORSEFUL, HEART-BROKEN OR WOUNDED IN SPIRIT.

If you are in one of the above groups, the first thing you must do is ask yourself this question: "Do I really, deep, deep down in my soul, WANT to be free of my sorrow, remorse, broken heart or wounded spirit?"

At first glance you will say, "What a foolish question! Of course I do!" We will waive that answer and ask you to look again into the depths of your innermost heart.

What do you find there? I ask you, dear one, in all love and sympathy. But you need reply only to yourself. I ask it because you must know the true state of your own mind and be honest with yourself if you desire to overcome the grief that is hurting you.

It is a fact well known to all psychologists that sorrow-sufferers are of two classes: those who long to rise above the burden that bears them down and those who secretly, subconsciously and often UNCONSCIOUSLY want to keep it.

One of the most famous neurologists of America recently stated, "The three main classes of destructive moods are harboring the grudge, dwelling on the past and PLAYING THE MARTYR."

To recognize that you are indulging in the first two is hard enough, but to admit, even to yourself, that you have been getting a good deal of subconscious pleasure out of your own martyrdom is pretty difficult unless you are an unusually big soul.

Arnold Bennett says, "Grief and remorse are two states of mind which feed on the past instead of on the present. Remorse, which is not the same thing as repentance, serves no purpose that I have been able to discover. What one has done one has done, and there's an end of it. As a great prelate unforgettably said, 'Things are what they are, and the consequences of them will be what they will. Why, then, attempt to deceive ourselves into feeling that remorse for wickedness is a useful or praiseworthy exercise? Much better to forget.'"

Bennett goes on to say: "As a matter of fact, people 'indulge' in remorse; IT IS A SOMEWHAT VICIOUS FORM OF SPIRITUAL PLEASURE. Grief, of course, is different and must be handled with delicate consideration. Nevertheless I see, as one DOES see, men and women dedicating existence to sorrow for the loss of a beloved creature. To my idea, that man or woman is not honoring, but DISHONORING, the memory of the departed; society suffers, the individual suffers, and no earthly or heavenly good is achieved.

"Grief is of the past; it mars the present; it is often, though not always, a form of self-indulgence, and it ought to be bridled much more than it often is. The human heart is so large that mere remembrance should not be allowed to tyrannize over every part of it."

To me this seems a little harsh. All grief is not selfish, though it is self--centered more often than we ourselves realize. I have seen what passed for unselfish sorrow but which was in reality the last word in selfishness.

One woman particularly comes to my mind in this connection. She seemed unable, after years of widowhood, to give her mind to anything other than her loss. "HER" loss was always on her tongue and in her thoughts—the loss of HER happiness, HER home, HER husband, HER future, the weight of HER loneliness, HER unhappiness—with never a word about the one who had lost his all.

She even went so far as to criticize him occasionally.

"Grieving for her lost husband," everyone said. But actually she was grieving exclusively over herself.

Another striking case came under my observation—elderly parents, who had married late in life and lost their only child, a bright beautiful girl of ten.

They talked of her uninterruptedly to the days of their own deaths fifteen years later, but did I hear them refer to the tragedy of the child who had given up life at its morning? What she might have been, what she might have done, what she had missed was never mentioned.

What THEY had missed in not having her with them in their old age; how lonely the twilight of their old age was without her; how they had been compelled to forego the comfort and cheer and love her young life could have brought into their own dreary ones—this was the burden of all their laments.

Yet they were quite innocent, as doubtless all are in such instances. It is well for us to take stock of our destructive moods if we wish to be rid of them. By being honest with ourselves we can often save time and trouble by attacking them at their source. By recognizing and going after the cause we can eliminate the effect.

But if you are one who secretly enjoys his grief or any other destructive mood, and if you wish to continue that kind of perverted pleasure nothing and nobody in heaven or earth can cure you.

To help you we must have your earnest co-operation. Without it even God will not help you, for He helps only those who help themselves. Many prefer to pity themselves.

If there is one type of all others farthest removed from Him it must be the self-pitier. People who pity THEMSELVES never get pity even from their fellow men. They supply their own so abundantly everyone feels they do not need any more.

On the other hand, if you truly desire to rise above your sorrow and will persistently avail yourself of the helps suggested in this lesson, you can still find life a beautiful and wonderful thing.

IF YOU HAVE LOST A LOVED ONE BY DEATH

Help No. 1. If you are one of those extremely unselfish souls who suffer intensely whenever those you love are unhappy, the death of a loved one is likely to cause you the deepest suffering the human soul can know.

You will tend to forget your duty to yourself—the duty to be a strong soul. Despairing over what your beloved has lost you may thus deeply harm another of God's creatures—yourself.

Remember, you do not belong to yourself, but to Him. To make of yourself the highest type of human being, to build the finest character, these are duties you owe to the Power that created you, and you can never do it save by courage.

Help No. 2. Try to realize that whatever power gave life has a right to take it away. If this seems impossible because you are not "religious-minded," ask your scientific mind this question:

"Could the Power which rules the universe, which operates upon everything, from the tiniest atom to billions of constellations, IN ACCORDANCE WITH UNDEVIATING LAW, alter its laws for ME? And if so, what assurance have I that it would not do so for others equally unworthy?"

Such a Power would forfeit your respect instantly, and deserve to. Such a Power as that would not be capable of creating a universe. All would be chaos, where now ALL IS ORDER—a condition that ultimately convinces all, whether they will or not, that there IS A POWER SOMEWHERE BACK OF IT ALL, AND THAT THAT POWER KNOWS ITS BUSINESS.

You may say that since God permitted this tragedy to come to you, you get no comfort from Him in your grief; that it is impossible for you to trust Him any more. Yet every death occurs because of the violation of a natural, immutable, eternal law or laws.

If you will look at it impersonally for a moment you will see that just as you cannot trust an earthly parent who is partial to you (since you know not what instant he may be partial to others and AGAINST you) you could not trust a God who would alter his great laws of life and death to please you.

And if you will look one more moment with your reason instead of your poor broken heart, you will see that it is precisely this ETERNAL IMMUTABILITY of law, even to those governing the physical body, which proves that there IS a JUST POWER, an IMPARTIAL TRIBUNAL somewhere.

This realization, as in the case of an earthly parent, commands more admiration, love and trust in the final analysis, than any degree of partiality could ever do.

Help No. 3. In view of the above, then, try to realize that though you may not see it, though all appears disastrous, there is a DIVINE REASON back of the event that grieves you.

Do not lay waste your energies or rack your little human brain DEMANDING to know what that reason IS. Seek to know, search diligently if you wish to, only remember you cannot understand anything or anybody so long as resentment, distrust or rebellion against that thing or person fills your heart.

At the same time, do not try to COMPEL yourself to believe anything antagonistic to your reason. Such a course complicates matters for you. If you cannot formulate your belief at this trying time; if, despite all you can do, you find no answer to your questions, rest awhile from your labors.

The full why and wherefore of life and death are not yet known to us. Some day they may be.

Meanwhile remember that the universe got on beautifully millions of years before we and our loved ones lived, and will do so millions of eons after we have passed on, UTTERLY REGARDLESS OF WHAT WE BELIEVE OR REFUSE TO BELIEVE.

The most we can do here and now as well as for eternity, is to face the great mystery of death as we now face the equally great mystery of life—with courage, not cowardice; with heads up, not down; with hearts as brave as we can make them, and WITHOUT WHINING.

If we will, we can make of our greatest sorrows the most powerful aids to the highest human achievement—the building of a strong and beautiful character. If you cannot believe in the survival of your beloved in any future realm, know that part of him still lives right here so long as you love him. Carlyle said, "To live in hearts we leave behind is not to die."

Help No. 4. If you have lost one you loved and who loved you, though you may never make for him any of the sweet personal sacrifices your heart would now delight in, yet can you still perform for him three sublime services:

First, by relinquishing him to the Powers which created him, that he may go on, if further development awaits him, without earthly shackles.

Second, by being as happy as possible.

What a false loyalty it is that leads us to mourn, to keep ourselves miserable, to ruin our health and lead a crushed existence for the sake of one who loved us!

A glimpse of your own heart will tell you so. If you had been taken first would you wish him whom you loved never to be happy again? The one thing you would ask if you could, would be that he get and keep and cling to all the joy and peace he could find, and whosoever loved you would say the same, could he speak.

They may know, those who have gone on ahead, just how we are feeling—and they may not. If they do, your continued suffering here may be causing far greater suffering over there. But if they do not, is it not at least as disloyal to encourage your grief as to violate the wishes of an earthly loved one when his back is turned?

The greatest gift you may lay upon the altar of your love is to try to be WORTHY of him, of the sweet experiences you shared, of your common happiness.

By the sacredness of all you meant to each other you become a part of each other. Part of you has gone with him to that "Beautiful Isle of Somewhere," and part of him remained behind with you. It lives on in you and can never die so long as you are alive.

To think of this as your talisman, to make a shrine for it in your heart and strive every day so to live as to dignify rather than crucify it, is the highest form of loyalty—and the hardest.

IF YOU SUFFER FROM REMORSE

Remorse is based in self-criticism and often leads to self-loathing. It is a dangerous and evil mood for two reasons.

First, because it is based in the false hypothesis that we are degraded or hopeless for having done certain things.

Help No. 1. No person is hopeless who WISHES TO BE BETTER, and none degraded who TRULY REGRETS HIS MISTAKES.

The fact that you are filled with remorse proves you are above the average, rather than below it, for the average person feels little or no remorse for his unworthy deeds.

Help No. 2. To know how you compare with the average, and especially to test the degree of your own evolution, note HOW SOON AFTERWARD your remorse or regret for a thing begins to appear.

The highly evolved soul regrets his wrongdoing almost immediately while the low-natured may commit murder and never feel a pang of remorse. All kinds and types of soul-development lie between these extremes.

Help No. 3. Always remember that whereas the COMING of remorse is proof of your natural GOODNESS, the HARBORING of it is certain proof of WEAKNESS.

While being SORRY don't forget to be STRONG—and put remorse out of your heart.

Help No. 4. The worse your past acts the more essential is it that your future ones be good and beautiful.

Substitute self-confidence for self-criticism if you would atone. You can instantly acquire the foundation of true self-faith if you will accept the fact that only fine souls are capable of the remorse you are now suffering.

IF YOUR HEART IS BROKEN

Though you hunted the world over, it is probable you couldn't find one adult person who had not, at some time or other, had his heart broken.

It is sure to happen sooner or later to those who are now children. Some day each of us knows what heartbreak is. It is one of the experiences Life has up her sleeve for every one of us. No one is spared, no one is immune.

I am thinking now of the heartbreak that comes from being disappointed in love.

This is the heartbreak hardest of all to bear because of its peculiarly poignant nature and because it is the kind about which we can say and do the least. It is usually impossible to confide it to others, therefore we cannot seek the balm of sympathy so helpful in times of other sorrow.

Because you will necessarily be deprived of ordinary help from other sources in the hour of this greatest of all heartaches, I have compiled here the suggestions most helpful to me and to the thousands of others who have acted upon them.

Heartbreak is an experience difficult to be prepared against. But if you will study these "helps" it cannot take you entirely unawares nor find you quite helpless:

Help No. 1. Admit the truth to yourself.

Even though it seems fairly to kill you, gather up every scrap of courage and honesty you possess and say to yourself in so many words, "He does not love me. I love him but he does not love me."

Do not lengthen the days of your suffering and postpone your recovery by seeking for proofs of his love, once he has told you or shown you conclusively that he does not care for you.

You will recall past endearments which—your bleeding heart tells you—could NOT have been based in other than eternal love. Or present courtesies, actuated only by his pity or sympathy for you, will cause hope to rise again.

Be not deceived by them. Remember truth is greater than all else in the world. Cling to it. It will sustain you in most unexpected ways if you will.

Help No. 2. Call forth your pride.

Facing the truth and respecting yourself, these are the two primary essentials to the solution of your problem. If you do not call upon your pride you are going to make advances that will humiliate you far more than the loss of love can ever do. We can live without this person's love and still hold our heads high. But without our own self-respect we are broken.

Help No. 3. Learn to USE, to CAPITALIZE, to PROFIT BY the knowledge your heartbreaking experience brought you.

Look for it till you find it—it is there!—and let it save you from making the same KIND of mistake again. Someone said, "If a man deceives me once he is dishonest. If he deceives me twice I am a fool."

Think how lucky you are to have discovered the kind of person you were dealing with in time to prevent his hurting you or your future any further.

Help No. 4. Do not make the mistake of refusing to love others for fear of being mistaken in them. It is a thousand times better to love and be jilted than go through life one of those "hold-offish," noncommittal people who accept everybody with mental reservations.

It is not how much we have been loved but how much we have loved that makes us great.

As proof of this, remind yourself that no man or woman ever rose above mediocrity, ever attained fame, a great personality or a beautiful satisfying love who did not first pass through fire.

Something is forever left out of him who has not known the Gethsemane of a vain love. Something of God enters into him who meets it in the right way.

LESSON III

How to Know What You Want Most

I HAD occasion recently to take a little daughter of a friend out to lunch. We went to a cafeteria, a new experience for her, but she took very little food and didn't enjoy that. As a party it was a dismal failure—and for the same reason that many human lives are failures: she couldn't decide what she wanted.

All kinds of good things were there before her, ready for her, and to be had for the taking. But she could not bring herself to choose.

Instead of looking at each display as we passed it, selecting something and passing on to the next, she ran her eye over all the counters at once and finally grew so excited and muddled she picked up two or three things she didn't like at all and let it go at that.

How like us grown-up, even gray-haired children! The first big stumbling block on the roadway of life that meets and all too often stops us is this one. All we know is that we want from life a great many things—yes, lots and LOTS of things, but settling on just exactly WHAT THEY ARE is something few people ever get around to doing.

We look at the world and its fullness in a sort of by-and-large survey, sweeping the horizon with a cursory, casual glance, and say to ourselves, "Yes, yes—now, let's see.." and a decade or two taps us on the shoulder before we awaken.

Instead of waiting for the rattle of old Father Time's scythe to rouse you, let me help you out of that daze right now. Open your eyes and DECIDE WHAT IT IS YOU DO WANT.

You can get every one of them if you will "come out of it" long enough to DEFINITELY, POSITIVELY CHOOSE, and then go after them.

But you will get only the leavings of life if you fail to do this.

The value of "knowing exactly what you want" cannot be overestimated. We are powerful organisms, all of whose energies automatically mobilize ready to go after a thing the instant we absolutely KNOW we want it.

It always reminds me of the way the sun's rays act with and without a burning glass. You may sit in the brightest sun, reading your newspaper, without its taking fire. The rays are spread over a large area, and nothing happens. But move to a spot much less sunny, take a burning glass from your pocket, hold it in the sun over the paper—and it burns a hole through it!

Know What You Want Most

When you do not know just what you want, your energies are out of focus. They spread over everything and nothing happens. All the power is there but you are not directing it.

Definite desire focuses and harnesses a thousand energies you are not even aware of now—and burns a hole to what you want.

When you do not know exactly what you want, you are like a man who "wants to go somewhere" but doesn't know where it is. You are like the people who say, "Yes I'd love to travel"—but who never do so because they can't make up their minds where to go.

Most people are like those in the old song who sang, "I don't know where I'm going but I'm on my way."

All the world lies open to you. You may go where you choose, but you MUST choose or be jostled by the crowd, not merely figuratively but literally. The world always steps aside for the person who knows where he is going, but it takes a good deal of delight in pushing, bumping into and running over the one who doesn't.

To arrive at any destination worth while you must decide on that destination. Otherwise the pulling and hauling, the mulling and muddling of those in your immediate and remote environments will shunt and shove you down first this bypath and then that, according to their own interests.

"But I am afraid to decide for sure," said one woman to me, "for fear I couldn't get there. I've never tried such a thing before and I don't know what might happen. Things I can't foresee might have to be faced and maybe some of them would be too much for me."

This conversation took place in Los Angeles. The answer I made her will perhaps clear up something for you too.

"You have just been telling me that in a few days you are going to motor to San Diego, haven't you?" I said. "You have never made the trip before. Yet you are not dismayed. You know there may be detours and, at this time of year, a washout or two. But you are not letting that deter you. You know that when you reach them you will find some way of getting by them and going on.

"You must do the same in your life. Go as far as you can see and when you get there you will see farther."

To reach the big places every famous person has had to DECIDE to go to them, letting the detours and delays take care of themselves when their time came. OF COURSE some of these will have to be met! OF COURSE you must allow for them, but take along your mental skid chains, have plenty of gas and spare tires—and you'll get there!

Other people are going to the very same places in life that you desire to reach, and DOING IT EVERY DAY. Are they supermen or superwomen? Are they more able than you?

On the contrary, many of them, as you say to yourself, are inferior to you. But they are getting the good things you want, having a wonderful time and reveling in the headway they are making while you watch from the roadside.

The chances are you have as good a car as the average and a far better one than many who skim past you on Life's Highway—only they START while you stand around letting your machine and yourself rust. Make up your mind.

What if you SHOULD make a mistake and find, a few miles along, that you didn't like the scenery? You could turn around, couldn't you, come back and strike out for something that suited you better? At least you wouldn't have wasted your time altogether, as you are doing now, for you would have learned from the effort a good deal that would be useful to you in the future. We learn by doing.

Every successful person in the world made a lot of false starts. Don't be so sensitive that you can't admit an error once in a while too. People aren't watching for your mistakes half as much as you imagine, anyhow, and those who do will forget them as soon as you give them something better to think of.

I know of several brilliant people who have allowed life to pass them by, leaving only failure in its wake, because they were afraid to attempt. "The man who never made a mistake never made anything."

If sensitiveness to criticism has been holding you back, if you have been afraid to begin anything for fear it might fall through and give some people the laugh on you, just remember "He laughs best who laughs last."

There are two things far harder to bear than an occasional laugh—the smile of superiority and the look of pity we finally call forth from the very people for whose good opinion we sacrificed our chances.

Decide what you want, where you wish to go. Have a definite goal in view. Know what you want and WHY you want it. Use all your intelligence and imagination to select just the things you will want AFTER you get them.

You must aim at a target if you expect to hit it. You must get your gun lined up and point it straight AT the very thing you are after. You will bag nothing out of the jungle of life if you fail to do this.

At first glance you will say, "I know what I want, all right. It's the getting it that stumps me!"

But do you? I venture to make a guess that if you were asked to sit down right now and make a list of the ten you want most, you would have a hard time of it. Within five minutes you would come to a standstill trying to make up your mind which of several conflicting desires stands first with you.

A simple illustration of this was given me several years ago by a student of mine, a middle-aged woman of Iowa who wanted to "do something in the way of a school" along the lines of these teachings.

Her ideas were vague. She was interested in psychology but didn't know what branches she wanted to teach. She felt that she would, as she put it, "get a great deal of self-expression out of having something like this to do." When she finally decided to start she could not select what to teach.

At last she definitely made up her mind to use for a basis such principles as are outlined here. But even after that she was delayed for several months more because she could not decide whether to begin in New York or Washington, D. C. She wanted so badly to live in both places. Each offered such allurements she could not decide to forego either, and as a result had to forego both for many useless months.

When she finally settled on Washington all went smoothly and happily. She has never regretted her decision, and her success has long since reconciled her to what she missed in New York.

Another student, a man of thirty-eight, had kept two fine women waiting and himself out of years of happiness because he could not decide which to marry. He was in the same predicament as the poet who sang, "How happy could I be with either, were t'other dear charmer away!"

Each woman possessed certain advantages and each certain disadvantages, from his point of view, just as do all things between which we hesitate. "If only there were but one of them!" he used to say, "and that one a composite lacking the faults and combining the good qualities of both!"

Often some such impossible idea keeps us from deciding on a course of action. But until we stop demanding perfection in people and things all we get from life will be a mass of imperfections.

Make up your mind that New York is not Washington, that the person or thing you are choosing is NOT perfect, that it lacks some things you could have gotten elsewhere, but that, as the ritual says, you are taking it "for better or for worse." Then make the most of it, and, like the respectable married woman, refuse thereafter to flirt with the one you have renounced.

If you do not, if you persist in keeping a sort of "mental option" on both, the thing which happened to this man will happen to you—you will lose both.

Everything in the universe moves. The bird you would like to bring down may sit so long on the same branch you imagine it will be there forever, but I assure you it will fly away when you least expect it.

This, then, is the thing you must do: decide just what you do want. The big, main things in life are like trees—beautiful and satisfying for the most part, but with a few flaws, gnarled branches and other imperfections in every one. You are not in heaven—yet. This is the earth—but a place you can mighty near make into a heaven if you will use one of the least used and rarest things in the world—common sense.

We do not see just how or why a desire begins to fulfill itself the instant it is definite and positive in our own mind. We only know it does. We know this definiteness calls forth our reserve armies and they come marching from every fiber within the body, brain, mind and spirit, ready for exact orders.

This one bit of knowledge is enough to make life over for each of us, whether we ever understand WHY it is true or not. We do not know why two and two make four, but we use this fact successfully. We do not know why a horse hauls our burdens. But that does not prevent our hitching him up and putting him to use.

We can train our desires and make them carry us wherever we wish to go. We need only to get sufficiently acquainted with them to put them in harness and guide them.

Every person you meet is full of desire—the most powerful electricity in the world—but usually fails because he never learns how to put the current to work for him.

It is going to waste. It is always there, ready to be turned into any direction the instant he decides what that direction shall be, the moment he stops throwing the switch back and forth. It will be with him as long as he lives. It is inexhaustible, in fact so much so that the more we use the more we generate. But it must be focused and applied to be of any service to us.

History and biography reveal the fact that every person who achieved great things knew what he or she wanted and WANTED IT HARD.

When you know WHAT you want and want it HARD, you clear a path for yourself. The underbrush that looked hopelessly entangling yesterday disappears. Once you actually START, great spaces will constantly open before you and you will have much smoother traveling than you can now imagine.

You will meet with difficulties, of course, and would deserve no success otherwise, but they are never as appalling when you come face to face with them as you supposed in advance, nor half so overwhelming as the onlookers imagine.

The following specific suggestion will help you organize and crystallize your wants: Rule 1. Tonight, when you are alone, take a paper and pencil and begin to write down your strong desires.

Meanwhile let your mind play with the subject but make no written notes. By that time you will have some definite ideas and will get nearer the truth than if you jotted down the first thing that crossed your mind just now.

Rule 2. Put down all your deepest desires, REGARDLESS OF WHETHER YOU EVER EXPECT THEM TO MATERIALIZE AND NO MATTER HOW UNATTAINABLE, SILLY OR RIDICULOUS THEY LOOK ON PAPER.

If you have magnificent, marvelous ambitions, aspirations, aims and ideals, so much the better. DO NOT PERMIT THIS TO OVERCOME YOU.

Above all, do not take the attitude, "Oh, well, I'll do it, but nothing will ever come of it."

Rule 3. Tell no one WHATEVER about your list.

Rule 4. Do not be disturbed by the fact (which will probably be apparent in a day or two) that some of the things on your list are quite new to you—things you have never before been CONSCIOUS of wanting. When this stage is reached you have begun to get down to some of the real secrets of your subconscious—to the things you have been wanting very much but for some reason would not admit to yourself. Some of these will be selfish, some unselfish, some primitive, some very spiritual and beautiful.

We will have a weeding-out party when the time comes, but for just now don't deny a single big desire that wants to write himself down. That would not annihilate him. It would only push him out of sight and behind you, from which place he would continue to push YOU without showing his hand.

The best place for any desire is out in the open (of your own mind, but not paraded before anyone else's). If it is ugly, a good look at it will do more to cure us than all the preaching in the world. If it is beautiful the same light that pitilessly exposed ugliness will reveal additional beauties, and we will be strengthened to live up to our ideals.

Rule 5. Keep this list in your mind throughout the course, for we shall add something to it, take away others, frequently refer to it and constantly study it. These lessons are to show you HOW TO GET ANYTHING YOU WANT, therefore this list of your wants is the order sheet we will work from.

Rule 6. DON'T KEEP WONDERING WHETHER OR NOT ANY OF THESE WANTS WILL EVER BE REALIZED.

If you follow the rules laid down in these lessons, NOTHING UNDER HEAVEN CAN PREVENT YOUR GETTING THEM.

Rule 7. DON'T KEEP DOUBTING YOUR-SELF, NAGGING YOUR TEACHER, OR QUESTIONING THE GREAT LAW YOU ARE TRYING TO OPERATE.

For reasons I shall further explain to you in a few minutes, I do not, after promising you these things, fling all burden back on you with the abili, "You must have implicit faith or nothing will come to you."

How could a reasonable being be expected to have "implicit faith" in ANYTHING before it produced results?

The laws I am to teach you will work WHETHER YOU BELIEVE IN THEM OR NOT, just as the sun will rise and set whether you believe it or not, for the same Creator made both.

Do not indulge in self-distrust or self-depreciation.

Rule 8. Do not interfere with your own progress by encouraging or listening to the apprehensions of skeptics.

When you meet such a one simply remember that if he had ever TRIED these laws himself he would be defending instead of deriding them. And since he has not, he is, as they say in court, "not a competent witness," for he does not know what he is talking about.

"What a man is not up on he is very likely to be down on," said Hubbard.

Rule 9. Do not allow your mind to dwell upon, much less enlarge upon, the 'insurmountable obstacles" you imagine lie between you and anything you now desire.

Rule 10. Whenever something "tells you" (as something or other is bound to do) that your chances are very slim, don't let it frighten you.

This is nothing but the cowardly, fearsome side of your own nature, the primitive, lazy, animal side that doesn't want to be bothered—the same weak self that has ruined millions of good men and women by whispering each morning, "Oh, let's lie still. Why get up? What's the use? One more nap won't hurt anything. One more tardy mark at the office won't do any harm"—the same weak traitor that taunts you years later by saying, "You've wasted so many years now you could never catch up!"

This inert side of you is merely good-for-nothing. It doesn't want to bestir itself nor be bothered by the stirrings of your great self. But it is a "false alarm" and will lie down and behave when you show it you mean business.

It has run—and ruined—your life for so long it forgets YOU are the rightful master and that whatever you say has GOT TO GO. You have spoiled it till this useless, worthless, whining, sniveling coward actually has the audacity to advise you!

When these suggestions of weakness come from others, just remember the warning is merely a self-defensive pretense from THEIR weaker side, too. There is only one thing the weak side of a man hates worse than stepping aside for his own strong self, and that is stepping aside for the strong selves in others.

The world of weakness is in a grand old conspiracy against the world of strength—but it is all bluff, and goes down and out in the first round when your true self really gets into the ring.

Rule 11. When the thought flashes into your mind, "Is it possible that I am a fool for thinking I can actually get anything I want?" hold yourself steady, knowing you are merely meeting an ancient enemy whom you can defeat any time you really want to.

For a little while it will come back in various forms, masks and disguises. One of these says, "Isn't it really too much to expect? Does it stand to REASON that I could? Why, with MY HANDICAPS, against SUCH ODDS, in the face of SUCH CONDITIONS, how could I?"

But do not be deceived. It is the same old sneak in another false face trying to tempt you into inertia.

Another one—one of his most effective—is this: "Aren't we too old for that? Now, this would be fine if we were only young, but, you see, AT MY AGE (there's his biggest shot!) what can we do? This is splendid for young folks, but for old codgers like me—Ah, .. well, .. it's TOO LATE!"

Millions of wonderful men and women have fallen for that one. It ruins more lives than all the wars and shortens more than all the diseases combined. It has more casualties to its credit than any other one thing in the world, so you can't blame it for being a little unreasonbly attached to its opinion.

It defeats millions, BECAUSE THEY ARE AFRAID OF IT, yet ANY ONE PERSON CAN DEFEAT IT ANY MOMENT HE WANTS TO!

Another is the one about your health. "Are we really STRONG ENOUGH to try for this thing? BE CAREFUL NOW, dearie, or you'll overdo yourself! Go easy or you'll break down and THEN where would we be?"

This has almost as many victims as the one just mentioned. It chloroforms a lot of good people, leading them around by the nose, making them think they can't get what they want without "ruining their health"—when the fact is that GOING AFTER what they want would put more pep into them than all the coddling in the world, add from five to fifty years to their lives, BESIDES GETTING THEM THE THINGS THEY WANTED. But old Willie Weakness has another favorite disguise which he falls back on when all these fail. He is very proud of this one and with good cause, for thousands of wonderful people who have seen right through the others go under when he springs this one. "How about your duty to friends and family?" suavely, sweetly suggests Willie. "If you go after these bigger things it might mean leaving home for a while. It might mean you couldn't spend so much time in the family circle. Why—just think of it!—you might actually have to DEPRIVE them of some of the comforts and luxuries they now enjoy. They're depending on your steady salary, and though of course it ISN'T what you might get if you ventured forth, it's SURE, and—well, better forget it!"

Willie doesn't tell you the rest of the story—how much MORE you could do for those you love if you'd stop listening to his snivelings and begin to take counsel of your GREAT SELF.

Your Great Self will tell you, though, if you'll listen; if you'll take your ear away from Willie long enough to catch what the God in you has to say. It will tell you the truth—how much MORE your family and friends will admire and love you when they see you are no longer a coward; how much more you could do for them if you aimed a little higher.

Those who truly love you will be GLAD to make a few temporary sacrifices for the common and future good of all, and those who don't are certainly not worth the forfeiture of your future.

A good general rule is this: LOOK OUT for any and every NEGATIVE thought, mental picture or idea that comes creeping into your mind trying to get you to DOUBT the possibility of getting this thing you want. Every one is a SNEAK THIEF, a LIAR, a TRAITOR—masquerading in first one

Know What You Want Most

excuse and then another—and every one is a BOASTING, BLUFFING, BULLYING BRAGGART made of smoke.

You can walk straight through them any moment you want to. But you must really WANT to, which brings us to a very interesting discovery:

Rule 12. Be honest enough to yourself not to try BLUFFING YOURSELF.

If you don't really want these good and great things which you've been thinking you wanted, stop lying to yourself right now. You will make little progress until you do, in fact you will get deeper and deeper into the muck, maze and maelstrom of mediocrity.

Your subconscious is a great wholesaler mind. It won't take orders from your pretenses any more than a big wholesale house will do business with individuals.

When an individual wants anything from a wholesale house he must order it through the proper channels and in the proper way. So it is with you in ordering what you want from your subconscious. There are ways to do it and ways NOT to do it, all of which will be made clear in this course of lessons. One of the ways NOT to is by fibbing to yourself.

You have been getting a lot of things you didn't want and missing a lot you did want because you went at it wrong. Meanwhile your subconscious has been doing the best it could for you, sending you what you ordered, whether you ordered it by mistake or otherwise.

Your subconscious is like your grocer in one way. He takes your orders and fills them. He doesn't know what you've been telling your friends about the fancy things you tried to get for dinner. He simply accepts the order YOU send him and DELIVERS THE GOODS. Your subconscious doesn't know or care what you pretend to have ordered. I only knows what you did order—and this you always get.

Rule 13. Don't be a mere "Wisher—be a "Wanter."

If you expect to get things you have got to WANT them—HARD. This is a course of lessons in "How To Get What You WANT," not what you weakly "wish" you had. "Wishy" folks are wishy-washy, but wanters are the rulers of the earth. All great men and women have been great wanters. They knew WHAT they wanted, WHY they wanted it, WHERE to go after it, and they GOT IT.

They didn't spend their time, thought, energy, money or efforts drifting around. They took the shortest routes regardless of how rough they were, and ARRIVED.

Every great name in history is the name of someone who was, first of all, a great Wanter—the kind of person who "wants what he want when he wants it."

But every failure has been Wisher.

Rule 14. Be DEFINITE in your wants, and dismiss all that are not definite.

Don't encourage in yourself the mental fogginess that comes dreamily yearning for something other. Many people live in a self-manufactured atmosphere of discontent, of general dissatisfaction with their limitations, conditions, circumstances and possessions. They never quite decide what it is they don't like about all these things; they never decide exactly what it is they do want.

They only feel that something is wrong, that the machinery is out of order, but make almost no attempt to find out where the trouble lies.

Two friends of mine illustrate the difference between this type of mind and the one which concentrates, focuses and WANTS. Each bought a car of the same make and model in the same month. One always investigated when something went wrong, and was not content till he fixed it or had it fixed. He would not tolerate even a rattle, but looked for it till he found it, and tightened the screw, bolt or whatever it was. He listened to the purr of his engine every so often, and if a cylinder was missing he had it attended to.

Result, his car is in a splendid condition, runs like new, and for all practical purposes is as efficient and dependable as a this year's model. He was offered a very good price for it recently—much more than the standard appraisement—because of its perfect condition and appearance.

The other man cultivated the opposite habit. So long as his car would run at all he refused to do anything for it. It might wheeze, jerk and splutter, but unless it came to a dead standstill he worried along. Naturally he and those who accompanied him had little pleasure when driving, whereas everyone exclaims over the smoothness and reliability of the other man's car.

His machine is now broken down and can be sold only for junk.

Rule 15. If you want to get things you must take stock occasionally and find out what your present conditions are.

Don't go thumping, bumping along through life realizing something is wrong somewhere, without doing something about it.

Know What You Want Most

Before you take another step in this course stop long enough to think of what you want that you do not have, and also what, specifically, you would like to be rid of.

Look the matter in the eye, fearlessly, honestly. To attain the fullest measure of present enjoyment, to be able to travel speedily and pleasantly toward your desires, and finally to market your abilities for the highest possible price, you must not neglect to rid yourself of the things that hold you back.

Rule 16. If you think the thing you want above all else is not to be had in your present environment, investigate and make SURE.

You will usually find that either it can be secured where you are or that you can alter, adapt or adjust your present environment to attract it.

But if such is not possible—if, for instance, you have exhausted the possibilities of a musical, artistic or educational training in the community where you are—you should face the fact and begin to prepare your mind for whatever change is essential to the fruition of your Great Desire.

Rule 17. If you find that the people you live with, work with or associate with discourage you, depreciate, nag or ridicule you or your high ambition, you must do one of two things: leave them (which you should do if possible) or, if that not practicable at this time, spend little time with them as possible, be kind and tolerant, and keep your own counsel.

Rule 18. Try to see as much as possible of people whose tastes, ideals, aspirations and talents are akin to your own. No matter how timid or retiring you are by nature, it will pay you to rise above it and FIND YOUR KIND.

You need not push yourself or be forward to accomplish this. It can be done easily if, instead of dwelling on what you can get FROM others, you think out how you can GIVE most TO them. Soon you will have every opportunity for the kind of companionship and encouragement you require.

Rule 19. With regard to things you want not merely to get but to DO, try to grasp the truth in the following eternal law: DESIRE TO DO A THING IS PROOF OF YOUR ABILITY TO DO IT—THE ATTEMPT, ON THE PART OF THE TALENT, TO GET ITSELF EXTERNALIZED IN THE WORLD OF REALITY.

In other words, intense desire to DO does not come accidentally. It is never, as you may have supposed, a freak feeling. It is not the first step, but the second. It is not a cause but an EFFECT. In this case the cause is an INBORN, GOD-GIVEN CAPACITY.

Talents of all kinds are choked, strangled, repressed and smothered constantly by millions of people who do not know this and who imagine their longings to accomplish a certain thing are will-o'-the-wisps instead of the divine promptings they really are.

You only desire as you are able to acquire.

Rule 20. Take your desires and WANTS seriously. Be in earnest about them.

After all, the big difference between the genius and the failure is not so much in their abilities as in THEIR ATTITUDE TOWARD THEIR ABILITIES.

The genius encourages his wants. The failure develops the habit of inhibiting his. The genius uses his wants as cores, starting points around which he builds the rest of his life; he makes everything else adapt to his supreme Desire. The failure allows "circumstances," friends, relatives and the fluctuations of chance to build his.

The genius looks upon his wants as sacred things. He is in dead earnest about them. He gives himself to them and they in turn give back to him fame, money, love and success.

The failure looks upon his desires as impossibilities, jokes or vagaries. He doubts them in secret and often ridicules them in public.

I always like to think of John C. Calhoun who, when a young man, said, "I shall study law, and the rest will have to take their chances."

It sounds a little vain, doesn't it? But it was really the healthy kind of self-confidence that begets much of the success and achievement in this world.

Rule 21. Do not take the attitude that anything is too good for you.

The moment you do you will begin to deteriorate, until eventually what you get will not be half good enough for you. The way to deserve the best is to believe in it and work toward it. Don't worry, you won't get it or be able to keep it till you are good enough for it.

Once one of Napoleon's sick soldiers remonstrated when Bonaparte ordered some unusual delicacy for him. "Isn't this too good for me?" he asked.

"Nothing is too good for a soldier of France!" answered Napoleon.

You are one of God's own soldiers, sent here to fight a good fight, to do your best, to grow into your best, to become the best—and nothing He put into this beautiful world is too good for you.

Rule 22. Once you have decided on a thing, give it YOUR VOTE, not occasionally but ALL THE TIME.

Do not impose limitations of ANY kind on your expectations, or on your visions of the future. If you want a million dollars set your mark for a million and don't waste a moment entertaining any thought opposed to it.

It is these opposition-thoughts that keep you away from what you have been wanting.

Be loyal to the forces within you or they cannot produce their maximum for you. They are all-powerful, but for that very reason supersensitive, highly organized and susceptible to EVERY SUGGESTION you give them. They must have your complete trust to do their swiftest, supremest work.

True, they will do the best they can against this handicap, but they are like you and me—they can produce ten times as much and do it ten times as quickly when the one they are working for trusts and relies on them.

Rule 23. Once you have decided on a thing that you really WANT, stop thinking or saying to yourself ANYTHING that reminds you of your present lack of it.

Above all, do not dwell on the fact that this present lack and your future hopes are widely separated, or that there is any contrast between them.

All great achievements are made in the mind first—by MENTALLY bridging the gap between the present and the future. If you keep thinking of the gap instead of the bridge you will never bridge the gap.

Would Brooklyn bridge ever have been built if the engineers had devoted themselves to picturing the gap, of visualizing the untouched, unoccupied air between Manhattan and Brooklyn, reminding themselves that the bridge was NOT there?

They did the exact opposite. Whenever they thought of that space they visualized a bridge across it till it seemed as real to them as the actual structure was when finished.

You must do the same or you will never build the bridges that carry you from the Unpleasant Present to a Glorious Future.

Rule 24. When you have decided on a thing and know exactly what you want, let it alone for a few days. Do not try to think or plan or WORK OUT the details, ways or means of going after it.

Give your conscious mind a little vacation. Take about three days off the subject. Let your mind lie fallow. Get a very clear picture in your mind of what you want and file it away, figuratively speaking, in your great subconscious gallery.

It will materialize just as blue prints do if properly treated.

Rule 25. On the other hand, BEWARE OF TAKING TOO LONG VACATIONS from the thoughts of what you want.

If, after this three-day vacation, you find that, in spite of all you can do, your mind refuses to return to plans for a thing it is probable that you DO NOT WANT IT AT ALL.

If, on the other hand, you find it impossible to put the plans out of your mind even temporarily, the probabilities are that you have more talent in this particular direction than you have realized—perhaps genius.

Rule 26. Do not be afraid of overworking your body or brain during the first few days' planning.

Edison has slept an average of four hours out of each twenty-four during most of his life and has reached seventy-five in splendid mental and physical health.

There is more recuperation in work we like than in most of the leisure we take, and far more than is found in the average vacation.

We can produce, enjoy and thrive on a prodigious amount of work if it is what we like. We do not even require the change of work that is the next best thing, and as for "dropping it" in the midst of an important phase, as our friends often recommend, this is agony to the genius.

A genius is one who cannot be kept away from his work. The same tendency will reveal itself in greater or less measure wherever talent is being tapped. If you feel impelled to get away from the work connected with a thing, you do not really want that thing.

You may want what it would bring but you do not want the thing itself.

Rule 26. Another interesting test of your ability, talent or genius along any given line can be made by noting how soon, how frequently and with what degree of heaviness you GET SLEEPY when thinking out the details of a thing you want or when planning how you are to get it.

If you find yourself getting drowsy for no apparent reason every time you settle yourself to think out ways and means in connection with this thing, you do not want it. You only WISH you wanted it.

This is especially true if you fall asleep or become even moderately sleepy in the forenoon after a good night's rest.

You must use your common sense in making this test. If you work hard during the day, eat a large meal and lie back in the Morris chair with your feet before the fire to work out your plans for a certain thing, it does not necessarily signify a lack of talent for that thing.

A genius, however, would withstand even this severe test, or rather, he would avoid it. When a man has found the thing for which he has actual genius he doesn't jeopardize it by big meals nor demand comfortable surroundings in which work. He often completely forgets to eat or rest or sleep.

Rule 27. Note how many extraneous, superficial, PLEASANT things you forget, overlook, fail to avail yourself of, when planning toward this big thing.

Things you truly, deeply, desperately WANT make you forget the clock, creature comforts, vacations, and the non-essentials of life.

Rule 28. If you want still another test of whether this thing really means a great deal to you, take note of how many EXCUSES you find for laying it aside—only you will call them "reasons."

If you are constantly finding many of these reasons (each of which seems to you good and sufficient) for doing no more today, waiting till you can talk it over with somebody, or otherwise delay it, don't fool yourself— you are only WISHING for this thing.

You do not deeply, subconsciously want it, and your own subconscious mind knows it.

In cases like this the subconscious, knowing you do not really want to do it, provides these escapes for you. As fast as one serves this purpose it gives you another. In nothing more than this does the subconscious reveal to us its unlimited power.

The subconscious works in whatever direction you really WANT it to work. If you truly WANT to do a thing it will furnish you ample reason and full power (exactly as Edison's has done for him) for working year after year on four hours' sleep. If you do NOT want to do it, your subconscious will give you numberless apparently legitimate reasons for avoiding it.

One of its favorite methods is to help you lose or break your tools. Or it may convince you that you can't go on till you get others, or something new in the way of materials, etc., from town, from the stockroom, or (if you dislike it extremely) from another city or state.

"Too bad," you say when you get back, "the retailer didn't have it. He had to send to the wholesale house for it."

It is this expertness at perfectly sincere alibis which finally convinces any employer that you are not INTERESTED in your work. He knows that WHAT WE WANT TO DO WE FIND A WAY TO DO, regardless of everything.

He also knows that no matter how honest and truthful you are when you tell him So-and-So or such-and-such prevented your getting what he sent you for, it is really YOUR FAULT if it persists in happening. If some unforeseen catastrophe is alway intervening to prevent the completion of your work, he knows that the intervention is coming partly FROM WITHIN YOURSELF.

If he is a student of the human sciences he will realize, as we do, that you are often unconscious of this fact and, therefore, innocent; that your Unconscious mind is doing it and that you are not aware of the motivation behind these occurrences. But this does not alter the facts nor make you a good investment for him.

"Willingness," says every employer, "is worth more than anything else to us, provided the individual has ordinary intelligence."

Because he knows that wherever willingness is, there will your subconscious mind be also, and with its tremendous capacities back of your work you will FIND WAYS to do it.

Your subconscious will organize, arrange and ultimately contact for you whatever is necessary to the accomplishment of any deep desire.

But where one is not willing, where his deep desires are not involved, the most brilliant mind and the best muscle in the world are worth little. It is also for this reason that we should all find the vocation, the life work we truly love.

If we drive ourselves into that for which we have no liking, all the training, experience and forced effort in the work will never make us produce anything worth while.

If we goad ourselves day after day to work at something we hate, we are pushing ourselves uphill with the brakes on. Eventually the thwarted Great One within us takes its revenge. Ill-health, failure, nagging unhappiness and premature death are some of the penalties we pay. Our deep, subconscious desires are not to be lightly ignored.

Rule 29. The above rule can be applied to persons as well as to work, to places and to everything we think we want. If you are engaged to marry someone and are often irritated when it comes time to dress for him or her, better wait awhile.

This irritation, especially if it has existed for some time and more especially if it grows worse instead of less, is a danger signal. If the one to whom you are engaged has several times postponed the wedding day for what she felt were good reasons, she does not deeply love you. If you were relieved each time this happened, the growing indifference is mutual.

If something always comes up to make it impossible for you to keep your appointments with a certain person, you subconsciously want to avoid that person. If things interfere only enough to make you late, you are not enthusiastic.

Know What You Want Most

You will recall how easy it is to be early when we are to meet those we love, how we make preparations far in advance, planning what we will wear, getting everything ready, even laying it out so there will be no delay. All this effort at preparation comes actually WITHOUT effort, doesn't it?

But when you don't WANT to go, "everything goes wrong," as you explain afterward. Your hair won't go up as it should, your gown needs a hook, the clean laundry hasn't been opened, you just miss the street car, etc., etc.,—all perfectly good excuses provided by your subconscious to save you from the undesired.

"Surely you don't mean that my subconscious mind is responsible for the lost hook on my gown or the string around the laundry?" you ask.

And I don't. What I do mean (and what you will recognize from a thousand personal experiences as the truth) is this:

If you had truly WANTED to go, your subconscious (which is the storehouse of memory and remembers everything) would have tapped you on the shoulder and reminded you, in plenty of time, that the hook WAS off your gown; that the laundry was NOT opened; that the street car would soon be due.

It has done just such things for you a thousand times in the past—in fact whenever you completely WANTED something.

A young school-teacher whom I knew intimately many years ago and who lived in the same house with me was engaged to marry. I realized from scores of indications that she did not want to marry the young man, but she continued to think she did. She had promised her mother at the latter's death bed that she would do so, and as they had long been betrothed, promised to make the following Christmas the date.

She had arranged to go to her home in the adjoining state for the wedding, which was the inspiration for a reunion of her large family, some members of which were coming from abroad for the ceremony.

As the Christmas holidays drew nearer and nearer she became more and more restless and nervous, due—she supposed and declared—to the extra work of fittings at dressmakers, attendance at "showers," etc.

All this time she refused to think anything except that she wanted to marry this young man. She tried to prepare for the journey but put things off and off. This finally necessitated the combined efforts of all her friends in the house to help her get ready. There were a dozen of us and each constituted herself a committee of one to see that M.. made the train when school was out Friday afternoon.

Seemingly the fates had ordained that she should go. Not a thing was lacking. We all went down to see her off, with rice, flowers and all the rest of the trimmings. Her grip was in her section, the train due to leave in two minutes, and all of us standing outside her window, chatting and laughing, when she suddenly left her seat, dashed to the door and down the steps, crying, "I have forgotten all my love letters and valuable papers in the secret drawer of my desk! I must get them. I could not trust them to anyone! I will take the next train. I will manage somehow.." and nothing we could say to reassure her would convince her that her securities could be sent to her in safety.

She returned to her empty room, took out her valuables, sat down by the open grate and without thinking what she was doing threw the love letters into the fire.

Something seemed to stay her hand when she tried to rescue them from the flames and she let them burn.

Their ashes, she explained afterward, suddenly symbolized the state of her love for her fiancé. Before morning she had broken the engagement and next day wired her family to have a jolly Christmas without her.

This case was unusually interesting from the fact that the young man ALSO MISSED HIS TRAIN (for the same subconscious reason) and when neither arrived the relatives at the station supposed they had eloped.

Rule 30. Watch your MEMORY in connection with anything you think you want. No matter how poor it is in other ways, it will be amazingly accurate and keen with regard to everything that pertains to anything or anybody you TRULY ADMIRE or want.

When you are forever forgetting a man's name you subconsciously do not like him. Did you ever have any trouble remembering the name, initials, house address and telephone number of the new girls you are crazy about?

Rule 31. If there is someone who is always forgetting his appointments with you or explaining what perfectly good reasons made it impossible for him to see you, make up your mind to the fact that he does not really desire to see you.

A word to the wise is sufficient. This person may be and often is sincere in his excuses. Things DO happen, but they frequently happen to save people who are too honest to lie to save themselves.

The subconscious finds a way to save you without lying if you are too honorable to avail yourself of false hoods, and one of its best ways is by causing you to forget.

> "Darling," he said, "I never meant
> To hurt you"; and his eyes were wet.
> "I wouldn't hurt you for the world;
> Am I to blame if I forget?"
> "Forgive my selfish tears!" she cried,
> "Because you meant to hurt me, sweet.
> I knew it was that you forgot!"
> But all the same, deep in her heart
> Rankled this thought, and rankles yet,
> "When love is at its best, one loves
> So much that he can not forget."

If you will develop a pleasing personality you will find that people, instead of forgetting their appointments with you, will come ahead of time, sometimes a day or week in advance of the actual appointment. This is sincere and unintentional, too, the result of the opposite kind of desire.

The subconscious exists only to serve you and it will figure out and produce for you ways and means to get anything you really want if given half a chance.

The great difficulty with us is that we so often hamper it, put up barriers that retard its work. Then it writes in secret and ultimately finds an outlet, frequently in the most unexpected directions.

Rule 32. After you know what you truly, deeply, honestly want to have, you should avail yourself of every possible means for keeping that longing up to white heat.

We are strangely and wonderfully made. We can rule or ruin our lives by the neglect or the encouragement of our own highest desires. They burn brightly at times. Then it seems almost as if something outside ourselves comes along and turns down the flame, as mother used to turn down the wick in the old kerosene lamp.

This ebb and flow is natural to all living things. Do not let it depress you.

On the other hand, do not allow the ebb time to continue too long. This is entirely in our hands. We think we are at the mercy of our feelings when the opposite is true. Our feelings, as we proved in the previous lessons, are the product of our own thoughts. A feeling changes in accordance with the thoughts we feed into it.

Now that you know this, you can overcome laziness, inertia and feelings of dullness by generating their opposites. This you should do whenever you find yourself getting a little neglectful of something you really do want. To keep yourself up to full efficiency in your efforts you must keep your desires keen. The best and easiest way to do this would be by re-reading this lesson, and then re-reading it again until you feel the old enthusiasm coming back.

Each lesson in this course is printed in a little book to itself for just such purposes as this. You should carry one with you every day, in your pocket or handbag, if you want to do great things with your life.

Desire is the real power back of all achievement. It is to the human organism what steam is to the local motive. The train will not move until the water in the boiler has generated a certain amount of steam pressure. If that pressure falls below a certain point the locomotive slows down and soon stops.

It is precisely so with us. If we forget our desires, fail to believe in them or forget to work toward them they cool down, the powerful forces in our brain and body become dormant and soon we come to a standstill. All the potentialities and potencies are there, just as they are present in the locomotive that is standing still on the rails. Lacking desire all these energies are useless, for the steam of human energy is generated almost wholly by desire.

To move forward and upward it is not necessary to PULL THE TRAIN. We need only to keep enough desire generated. It will do the rest.

We can generate desire as easily and as scientifically as steam is generated in the locomotive's boiler. But instead of pouring water into a tank and stoking coal into a furnace we pour the material for this power into the subconscious, thought by thought, image by image, mental picture by mental picture.

All thought tends to express itself in action. These constructive thoughts soon give us the urge, the energy, the vitality and the enthusiasm to DO something toward the realization of our desires—and we are off again for a good long run in the direction of our goal!

Rule 33. Do not become agitated or think yourself merely vacillating because your list of desires changes day by day. You could not expect to see all that lies in your great subconscious the first time you took the lid off, nor hope, at first glance, to see its contents in exactly the right proportions.

After the things you were never before consciously AWARE of wanting have written themselves down on the list, another surprising experience will come to you: you will find yourself taking OFF several things you have been telling yourself and your friends you wanted very much.

When that day comes you are over the worst, for it is our unconscious self-deception which causes most of the conflict within us. These conflicts are like quarrels between the workers in a business house and, as in any business, they cut down output, cripple morale and decrease production.

Do not think of your list of wants as fixed, "set" or unchangeable. Remember that instead of making it ironclad we must strive to keep it flexible so we can constantly adapt it to fit newer and better standards as we find out more about our real desires and as we grow in mental and spiritual stature.

Keep it with you and DON'T FAIL TO WRITE DOWN THE CHANGES THAT COME TO YOUR MIND.

The chief aim at this stage is to get your true desires, that is, YOUR STRONGEST WANTS, into the list. Those in conflict with them you will lop off gradually of your own accord, as fast as you distinguish the greater from the lesser, just as you would cut away the small branches that interfered with the development of a favorite tree.

Rule 34. Look over your list and ask yourself whether the attainment of anything on it would rob anyone else of his rights. By this I mean the good old plain American rights of life, liberty and the pursuit of happiness.

You can attain whatever you desire, regardless of its nature, by following the laws taught in this course, but if you wish to be happy AFTER you get it, I advise you to remove from your list and sincerely renounce anything that you know would deprive any other human being of his chance for happiness.

Rule 35. In closing, let me give you one of the best rules of all: Whenever considering your list of wants try to remove from your mental eyes the spectacles of emotional, personal or primitive bias. Try to estimate every item on your list from the standpoint of its power TO PERMANENTLY SATISFY YOU, its value in the building of CHARACTER, its probable potentialities for bringing you LASTING HAPPINESS.

And now after you have applied these tests you find a very interesting, significant and inspiring thing has happened, namely, that as your list has dwindled in size it has doubled and trebled in strength, until now you know what you don't want at all, what you only wish for and what you want MOST.

Your subconscious mind, in response to your desire to know what you really wanted, has dug up the truth which "shall make you free" and discarded a mass of falsities that had been holding you back.

Instead of continuing to be "a house divided against itself" you will stand, full-armed with the knowledge that is power, ready to go after these things you really want most of all.

You will no longer diffuse your power over the entire landscape but will, like the burning glass, focus it on a few things and literally burn your way to them.

You will stop gazing over all the counters in Life's cafeteria, or, in your hurry, taking the things you don't want.

You will know WHAT you want, WHY you want it and WHERE you are going to use it when you get it.

The forthcoming lesson will give you the next step in your journey to the Land of Heart's Desire, by showing you HOW TO SET THE FIRST GAGE FOR WHAT YOU WANT.

LESSON IV

How to Set the Next Gage for What You Want

I WAS visiting recently in the home of an up to date woman who decided that the gas stove which had been in use in her kitchen for some years should be discarded for a more modern and convenient electric one. But she encountered the opposition of her cook.

"I don't believe it will ever be satisfactory," said the latter. "I don't see how it could. It doesn't stand to reason that a mere machine could do all the things you claim for this new-fangled stove."

My friend did not try to convince her but took her down to the store and asked the demonstrator to explain how it could be operated. He told her of the almost human powers of this remarkable invention—how you set the gages or indicators for preparing anything you want and it will produce the exact degree of heat for the exact time you indicate, no more and no less; how you can set the stove's clock, just as you do your alarm, so that the heat will come on at the very moment you desire, stay on just the number of minutes you choose, and turn itself off at the end of that time. For instance, if you want baked potatoes for dinner on the day of your club meeting, it is not necessary to rush home three-quarters of an hour ahead of time, or upset your nerves and spoil your speech worrying about them. You put them into the oven when you leave at three o'clock, set the heat regulator at just the right temperature for perfect browning, set the clock for turning on the heat at the right time and for turning it off so many minutes later, and when you come in, there they are—done to perfection!

If you also want spinach there is a boiling oven, and broiling plates too—all ready to work for you simultaneously, scientifically and accurately, in your absence. The demonstrator explained all this in detail. The cook was doubtful but agreed to try it. A book of instructions came with it. All the time she was reading them she exclaimed, "It's too good to be true. It simply CAN'T be as easy and simple as all that!" But she carefully read the directions and conscientiously followed them. In less than a week her favorite topic of conversation was the wonders of that stove! So it will be with you. If you will carefully read and conscientiously follow these directions you may set the gages and indicators for anything you want, go on about your everyday affairs, and some day it will materialize.

The stove does this because it is constructed along scientific lines, in accordance with great eternal, immutable, natural and divine laws—laws which the brain of man discovered and now applies to the solution of his problems. Each of us is constructed by the Maker of these divine and natural laws. WE ARE BUILT IN ACCORDANCE WITH THEM—and operate successfully ONLY when these laws are understood and applied. Imagine a machine ten thousand times more versatile than the electric stove, equally simple to operate, equally accurate, equally dependable—and you get some idea of the God-made mechanism you are. The saddest thing in life is that most people are like the cook, refusing to believe in their own possibilities, thinking these promises too good to be true, and clinging to outworn methods. They want things, all kinds of things, just as she wanted her cooking done, and they want to get them with the least effort, just as she did, but they cannot bring themselves to utilize the great new discoveries. You may have imagined that the human race hates work worse than anything else in the world, and it does—with one exception. That exception is THOUGHT. Like the cook, the average person will struggle with unnecessary toil, exercising his muscles long, arduous hours rather than exercise his mind ever so little. How many times you have seen people doing work they hated, in the hardest, slowest way, wearing themselves out, making themselves old and keeping themselves in poverty, when a little THINKING would have enabled them to shorten and lighten it, thus improving it to the point where better pay and emancipation would come from it. This course of lessons is for the purpose of explaining the possibilities of your great subconscious mechanism—a mechanism that can secure for you anything you really want and with far less effort than you have been expending up to now, provided you will only read the instructions and then APPLY THEM. In the first lesson we explained how your moods set this great inner mechanism to working for or against you, according to whether they are destructive or constructive; that these moods of ours are great currents of power which can, by right thought, be turned on constructively; or, by wrong thought, turned so as to burn down our houses with us in them. In the second lesson we explained just HOW to keep the current turned into constructive channels; and that we do not do the work ourselves any more than the cook furnishes the fire for the baked potatoes in the electric stove. We simply WATCH THE SWITCHES AND KEEP THEM TURNED THE RIGHT WAY by giving the harmonious reaction to the events of life. In the third lesson we explained how DEFINITE DESIRE generates a high voltage and focuses it on the thing you want; how not to dissipate your current; how to make up your mind, just as the cook must, as to EXACTLY WHAT you want most. We can't eat everything for dinner, no matter how much we would like to. We must make a selection, and then work toward

Set the Next Gage

its realization without thinking about all the things we decided to forego this time. We found that, just as in the case of the dinner, some of the things we would like and could get are not good for us, some are not worth cooking, and some do not combine well with the other things we want more. In this course we are going to explain the four gages which, when properly set, will produce anything in this world you really want; the four steps by which we arrive at any destination we wish to reach.

Definite desire sets the first gage. In this present lesson we are going to show you how to set the second gage for exactly the things you have decided on. Precisely as in the case of the cook, the unthinking, skeptical or antiquated type of mind may say upon reading these instructions, "It is too simple, too easy, too childlike. Why, it CAN'T be possible that there is a machine as marvelous as this right inside me. It's too good to be true." But every human being who follows these directions and APPLIES each simple rule will see for himself, and soon be as joyously enthusiastic as the cook. We do not know or need to know just HOW the inner self operates. Its activities obey certain laws, and we know what these are. If we harmonize with them we will succeed; if we oppose them we will fail.

The laws of your subconscious and of all else about you—from those that rule the digestion of your food to those entailed in your most complicated achievements— are God-made, unchanging, immutable.

They operate as inexorably as do the laws of gravity, electricity or chemistry, and your refusal to adapt yourself to them will no more nullify them than your non-belief in the laws of gravity can keep you from being hurt if you drop from a ten-story window, nor than your refusal to believe in the laws of chemistry would keep you from death after you took sulphuric acid. The laws explained in this course are eternal. They do not change. They always work. They can be used by anybody at any time, in any place, and for any purpose, precisely as the laws of electricity when applied to the stove will cook poison for you as quickly and certainly as they will wholesome food. Your belief or non-belief cannot invalidate these laws, any more than the cook's refusal to believe in the electric stove prevented it from producing results for her when once she actually set the gages in accordance with instructions.

The big thing that belief does is to cause us to GRASP, MASTER AND APPLY THE INSTRUCTIONS MORE QUICKLY, ACCURATELY, ENTHUSIASTICALLY and thereby to GET RESULTS MORE QUICKLY.

Bigotry, skepticism and doubt stay your hand while you are in the very act of setting your gages; they induce you and your conscious mind to experiment with the mechanism (to lift the hood, as it were), to stop and start it and in other ways turn it off and on, and thus interfere with speedy results.

Your ACTIVE OPPOSITION to these principles, though it can never alter nor abrogate them nor interfere with others who use them, will naturally make it impossible for YOU to get results from them, for the simple reason that ACTIVE OPPOSITION will keep you from really setting your gages. Though you might declare to us or pretend to your friends that you had turned them on, you would not actually have done so, for active opposition keeps you ACTING in its own direction—which in this case would be the OPPOSITE action from turning on the gage.

A perfect example of active opposition would be seen if the cook had refused to set the indicators on the electric stove. Obviously she could not have achieved results. Whenever you refrain from setting the gage within your own powerful mechanism, or when you do not set it in accordance with the rules, you will be just as sure to meet with disappointment. Whenever you follow the directions you will be equally certain of getting results. The reason why predominantly destructive moods bring destruction to our lives is that our predominant moods AUTOMATICALLY set the gages and FULFIL EVERY REQUIREMENT FOR BRINGING TO PASS IN OUR LIVES THE DESTRUCTIVE THING WE ARE DWELLING UPON.

A long-cherished mood of any kind sets in motion the VERY FORCES that are essential to its materialization in the outer world. Until you know what these are you will not be able to recognize them and of course have not recognized them heretofore. But they always follow certain lines and develop stage upon stage in perfect unfoldment. This is accomplished, first, by putting us in the frame of mind to keep the current turned in this direction; second, by forcing us sooner or later to actions that fit it; third, by printing our real feelings upon our externals; and fourth, by making us susceptible to all outside suggestions which coincide with it.

Since the suggestions of others are always IN RESPONSE TO, IN ACCORDANCE WITH and of the SAME NATURE as the feelings we have externally expressed to them, their suggestions will complete the circle and simply replant the subconscious with the same kind of seed as

Set the Next Gage

the original mood—precisely as any shrub, tree or flower will reseed the ground underneath it season after season if left to itself.

The above indicates the four main stages or developments by which any chronic mood gets itself materialized.

A recognition of these facts is wonderfully self-revealing, but what we all need is something beyond that—the exact rules and steps whereby we can turn this powerful current TOWARD what we want instead of mistakenly throwing the switch in the very direction we do NOT want. This course supplies that need. Just as the book of instructions tells the cook exactly how to set the gages for what she wants her stove to produce, we will give you the exact rules for setting your gages for anything you want your subconscious to produce for you. It will do it for you with the same certainty and dependability as that exhibited by the electric stove when it performs for the cook, IF ONLY YOU WILL STICK AS CLOSELY TO THE RULES AS SHE DOES. I explain all this to you, dear friend, in order that you may know there is an open road to whatever you desire. It is there whether you can bring yourself to believe it or not. To travel on it to your desired destination you must select your destination (which you have done in the previous lesson); and you must start your car properly, which this lesson is going to explain in detail.

I do not tell you, as you have been told hundreds of times before, that what you want lies over yonder, but that before you can reach it you must somehow find the ax called Absolute Confidence and blaze your own trail through the forests of Doubt.

He who can find that much confidence does not need me nor anyone else. He will find his own way to the land of Heart's Desire, as did all the great who achieved before this science was formulated. But he who cannot yet believe must be led gently and lovingly by the hand around the first turns and corners and over the foothills till he can see his own highway stretching away before him. This is my mission and the unique mission of these lessons.

"I am so glad," hundreds of students have written me, "you do not demand that we have full belief before we begin, for how can I BELIEVE I am going to get a thing if there doesn't seem to be certainty of it? "How can I EXPECT I am going to get this thing I want so much when I never yet got the things I wanted most? How can I have FAITH when there is nothing reasonable to base it on? My whole experience in life has been so disappointing I simply haven't confidence in myself or in my ability to get what I want." My reply to all who feel so, is this: Belief and trust and optimism will HELP A LOT TO SPEED UP THE DELIVERY OF WHAT YOU WANT, BUT THEY ARE NOT ABSOLUTELY ESSENTIAL to your getting it eventually.

Non-belief is of your conscious mind, and your conscious mind is something entirely apart from your subconscious. It knows very little about its operations and activities.

You and that conscious mind of yours do not get this thing and bring it to you, anyhow. This is all done by the subconscious, which begins to produce certain things for you WHENEVER YOU DO CERTAIN THINGS TO IT, JUST AS A CLOCK STARTS TO RUN WHEN YOU WIND IT, just as a car starts when you step on the starter.

You don't do it. You merely do certain things TO your car, and because it is constructed in accordance with LAW, it responds.

The same is true of your great subconscious. Backing it up with confidence will make it work more quickly, for the simple reason that confidence MAKES YOU ACT MORE QUICKLY, ACCURATELY AND EFFECTIVELY TO SET IT IN MOTION, just as belief in your ability to start your car makes you start it more quickly. Just as confidence in your car saves you the delays of puttering around or of stepping on the gas tremblingly, so confidence in your ability to do a thing helps you in two ways—by SAVING TIME and by APPLYING MORE POWER. A thing that is attempted with enthusiasm is already half done. Confidence that you are going to get what you want helps your subconscious get it for you because it flings into the front trenches all the bodily forces, generaled by your best brain forces.

Fear that you will not get it chokes and shackles every cell in your body and brain till they lag and drag along behind.

Even so, however, these body and brain soldiers are under the command of General Subconscious and have got to obey him, just as he has got to obey YOU. It is a law of your being and always works when you set it in operation, whether you believe in its mechanism or not.

If your belief in your ability to get what you want is great, so much the better. You will not only get in it far less time than would be required otherwise, but you will have a better time while you wait.

But if for any reason you can't force yourself really to expect it at all; even if skepticism in its worst form possesses you, yet YOU CAN GET WHATEVER YOU WANT.

Instead of demanding that you HAVE FAITH AT THE OUTSET, all I ask of you is that you read these simple directions carefully and follow them persistently.

THEY CANNOT FAIL. They have brought to thousands of skeptical people in this country the things they wanted but never expected to get; they have worked miracles in the lives of the sick and wonders in the lives of the poor and unsuccessful. They will do the same for you, because they are in accordance with unchanging, eternal laws. Every man can use them quickly and miraculously if he have enthusiasm, slowly but surely even if he lack enthusiasm—but no man can nullify them. Your subconscious never looks beyond or behind your orders. It is your servant—a servant with unlimited power, but of absolute loyalty and UNQUESTIONING OBEDIENCE.

Whenever you really get your order over to it, it sets to work instantly, and will some day deliver it to you (unless you cancel the order), whether you believe in its powers or not; just as heretofore it has been producing the wrong things in accordance with the orders you unknowingly gave it when you weren't even aware of its existence.

If, up to now, life has brought you mostly disappointment, if everything you tried has failed you, you could not be expected to have absolute confidence in the efficacy of these rules merely because I said it was there.

Therefore I do not ask it. I shall give you, step by step, the rules for getting anything you want. All I ask is that you try them. They will work for you if you APPLY THEM, as they have for the thousands of our students who have already used them during the past few years, and will remake your life, as they have remade theirs. Believe anything you prefer. Simply try them. Confidence in them will come when they begin to produce results—which will be immediately. After that, bigger and better and faster results will come as you apply them more expertly, more frequently and more enthusiastically. To be most effective, confident expectancy must be based on EXPERIENCE. Then it generates itself, thus saving you the trouble, and leaving your subconscious free to attend to the actual working out of ways and means. Confidence attained in any other way is short-lived and as unsatisfactory as a car that is forever having to be cranked. I have found in my many years of dealing with ambitious reasonable people that it is better to produce results before demanding unquestioning confidence in these new teachings.

It is a somewhat slower process, but the only one capable of building a solid foundation. If the individual is to be permanently helped, I believe it is imperative and only fair that he be excused from blind confidence until he has achieved results which warrant confidence.

If one's teachings are worthless without faith, the teacher either has not a complete grasp of the principles involved or is getting only temporary results. The results, if any, in such cases are not from the principles laid down by the teacher but from the faith of the student himself. In other words, if you are told that without perfect faith in certain principles NO GOOD can come from applying them, it is obvious that your own faith, and NOT the principles taught, is the determining factor. In such case you are applying not so much the principles taught as the PRINCIPLES OF FAITH, whose results are well known. The teacher who is sincere will not promise to teach you scientific principles of attainment and then fling the burden back upon you through such an alibi.

A truly scientific principle is eternal and unchanging. It is ever operative, and as effective in producing results for the non-believer as for the believer, IF HE APPLIES THEM. This is not a denial of the great law of faith, but rather a declaration that faith has principles of ITS OWN so great and glorious they deserve to be known AS SUCH and given full credit — not exploited to furnish horsepower for other so-called principles which would be useless without it.

Faith deserves all the honor and glory we can give it. But faith in a lie will not make it the truth, nor will lack of faith in the truth make that truth false.

Faith is the greatest force in the world because it is the supreme energizer, the attitude which instantly turns on the POWER that connects us with the sublime. Faith is a magic substance, one drop of which, when added to any human effort, will make that effort hundreds, thousands, millions of times more effective, because it concentrates ALL our forces in one direction, removes vacillation, intensifies, revivifies desire — in other words, RELEASES OUR GREATEST POWERS.

The law of faith is itself a scientific principle and can be briefly explained as follows: FAITH ALWAYS SPEEDS UP THE RESULTS OBTAINABLE FROM ANY OTHER SCIENTIFIC PRINCIPLE BY MAKING US APPLY THAT SCIENTIFIC PRINCIPLE, RULE, LAW OR FORCE MORE QUICKLY, EXPERTLY, FREQUENTLY AND FORCIBLY.

THE GREATEST THING FAITH DOES IS TO INCREASE THE VOLTAGE IN THOSE MYSTERIOUS CURRENTS WHICH LINK US TO THE DIVINE. Faith can be compared to a vast Niagara. You can use its power everywhere, all the time, in every act and endeavor of your life; or you can refuse to avail yourself of it and do everything by hand.

Faith helps us always and immeasurably in applying any law because it places our entire being in HARMONY with that law and leaves no room for opposition. It gives us, moreover, aside from its assistance in the matter at hand, the realization of how much we can accomplish once we center ALL our forces on anything—in other words, a CONSCIOUS FAITH is based in and backed up by reason.

This kind of faith we never lose. It grows stronger the longer we use it, and so do we. But we do not demand that you have faith in these principles until you try them.

In this lesson we shall give you the rules whereby you may ultimately attain RESULTS, whether you believe you will or not. Simple though they are, they operate upon forces that are all-powerful.

It is not necessary for you to understand the intricacy of these forces in order to put them to work for you, any more than it is necessary for you to understand all the forces and principles operating within your electric stove in order to make it produce results; no more necessary than for you to be an engineer in order to run your automobile; no more necessary than for you to be an electrical engineer in order to use electric lights in your own home.

But you must, just as with these other mechanisms, FOLLOW THE RULES. Your automobile is built upon very complicated principles, but every one of these is at your disposal and will PRODUCE RESULTS for you if you will only learn the few laws for their operation, and APPLY them.

Henry Ford himself cannot run one of his own cars any more effectively than you can if you will master the simple rules of driving. Vast laws, principles and powers lie behind your electric lights, yet you can, by pressing certain buttons, light your home as effectively as can the greatest electrical engineer in the world. The following rules will do for you just what the pressing of an electric button does in your home; just what the few movements do for you in driving a high-powered car; just what setting the gages on the electric stove does—BRING TO YOU AND PLACE BEHIND YOUR DESIRES THE VAST, UNTOLD DIVINE PRINCIPLES AND POWERS NECESSARY FOR THEIR FULFILLMENT. They no more explain these vast principles than the electric button explains electricity, and they do not need to. The great thing is that THEY ALWAYS WORK if you use them according to directions.

Come with me on an imaginary journey. We will go a million years back to a place called The Beginnings of Human Language. There we will find our remotest ancestors struggling to form words to express the feelings that surged up from their subconscious minds.

The brain was little developed at that time, but the subconscious was full of ambitions and longings—the forces that have brought man up to his present stage of development. Man's conscious THOUGHTS at that stage were few and far between, but his FEELINGS and MOODS—those wonderful, powerful things which, as we have seen in previous lessons, make and unmake our lives—these were fully organized. They were developed to the point where to give VOICE to them was an imperative need, an intense, burning desire, a great craving which finally PRODUCED WORDS.

Every word you use, therefore, represents a feeling. This accounts for the indescribable effect upon you of certain words. They are not "mere words" to your subconscious mind.

They are the CHILDREN of your own subconscious mind and that of the race.

For this reason your subconscious invariably responds to certain words in certain ways, and to other words in other ways. It recognizes them as a mother recognizes the voices of her children and distinguishes between them as a mother can distinguish.

Rule 1. Any mood or feeling which you encourage, entertain or cherish is certain to get itself EXTERNALIZED, MATERIALIZED some time, and one of the first STEPS or STAGES toward this materialization is shown in YOUR WORDS.

Words, therefore, are WORKERS OF THE SUBCONSCIOUS. Each and every one came into existence from the subconscious to help it in expressing and materializing certain feelings, moods and conditions.

Entertain any mood for a while and unless you are dumb YOU ARE CERTAIN TO PUT IT INTO WORDS.

If it is a mood you do not want other people to see, you will at first say its words only to yourself; that is, you will simply THINK the words over to yourself.

But very soon you will be SAYING them to yourself, and usually aloud. The conscious mind deals in images, pictures, visualization, but the great subconscious has for millions of years dealt with words. The spoken word is now the code it uses most. Today we have a word for almost every known feeling—a language through which we can reach this great Feeling Mind and set it to work.

Your subconscious is a marvelous establishment, a huge factory full of forces we have as yet only glimpsed. We do not know exactly all that goes on inside it and we do not have to. But one thing we do know: that the instant we communicate with it through its favorite code of words it sets to work for us IN EXACT ACCORDANCE with the words we have used in our message to it, and EVENTUALLY PRODUCES THE FINISHED ARTICLE which our words ordered. A very simple example will suffice to illustrate how the subconscious prefers words to any other form of order, and why, if you want your order obeyed in the shortest time, you should avail yourself of words. The head of a boarding house where I lived during one of the college years was a very motherly woman, but not inclined to humor us with desserts or other things we especially liked. Our hinting and praising and cajoling did little good. We had given up trying to get anything more than meat and potatoes, when someone discovered that we could get anything we wanted out of her if we'd tell her daughter and let her deliver the message as her own.

Our subconscious has a beloved child and that child is the avenue through which it prefers to receive its orders and messages. That child in each of us is the little girl whose name is "Words." "Written" and "Spoken" are her two first ones.

Therefore the next gage in your subconscious is to be set through the help of this young lady. When you send your orders into the subconscious through her you will not be disappointed.

Rule 2. Let your desire alone to find the right words for expressing itself. Do not try to hurry it. Do not try to think of any yourself, but make of yourself an open door, as it were, for receiving and registering whatever words seem to FIT your desire.

By this I mean the words that SUIT you, that express, to YOU, the thing you want.

Do not FORCE yourself to us second-choice words in connection with what you want. Wait for the right ones to come to you. They will arrive.

You cannot have a desire very long without its crystallizing into words. But the ones most effective with YOUR subconscious must be selected BY your subconscious. Calling things as well as people by the right names is important. The "right names," or words to be used in ordering the things you want and all the words in connection with them, will usually come to you spontaneously after you have dwelt for a little while on any particular thing you really want.

In this, as in all other methods used with the subconscious, you should not agitate yourself or try to speed it up. It knows better than you possibly can just how to go about getting what you want, and nagging is neither necessary nor advisable. Therefore, relax your mind until just the words that seem to express what you want, come to you.

In most cases these words have been in your mind and on your lips thousands of times before. You already know what you want and since reading Lesson III you know what you want MOST.

These desires will begin, if they have not already done so, to frame themselves into words, to boil themselves down into a FEW words, and some will condense themselves into just one word. The subconscious is a wonderful efficiency expert. It never wastes time or effort on red tape. It tends to formulate a symbol for everything, much as shorthand writers make symbols expressive of certain ideas. The success of Coué and his method is the most spectacular and convincing proof of the POWER OF WORDS. The Coué method consisted of one thing and one only: having the patient or student say, "Every day in every way I am getting better and better."

The fact that hundreds of cases of disease, unhappiness and inefficiency were completely cured simply by saying this phrase over twenty times a day is surely all the proof needed by a thinking individual of the great power of words in setting the subconscious to work.

The Coué formula was no doubt the best general one that could have been devised for universal application. But it did not cure all those who recited it. I am convinced that this was due to the fact that its phrasing did not appeal to all; therefore it did not REACH THE SUBCONSCIOUS MIND of every person. There were many who, for one reason or another, did not like it, did not "take to" it, as we say. Such a person could not be cured by the formula no matter how hard he tried nor how faithfully he was using it, for the simple reason that something blocked its passage and prevented its getting into his subconscious mind.

It has been repeatedly stated that those who were most like children in their attitudes, whose mental processes were most simple and elemental (such as the average French peasant), were the ones most often cured by the Coué method.

It is easy to understand how this would be true, because this is the type of mind which not only would accept more help in formulating its desires into words, but would have the least individualized and the fewest preconceived attitudes toward its desires. Greater and far swifter cures can be made by the highly intelligent, strongly individualized person, for the reason that such a one possesses a far stronger, far more crystallized subconsciousness; while those of the keenest brains, highest forms of mentality and most distinctive individualities can secure the surest, swiftest results of all.

A high degree of intelligence, a definitely individualized personality and especially a positive, successful conscious mind, all these are indicative of a subconscious mind which is unusually powerful, remarkably balanced and thoroughly organized. The only thing needful in these cases is that the individual make his own formula—one that does express what he wants to come true—and then USE it! It is sad that the people with these greatest potentialities do not avail themselves more frequently of the tremendous potencies of their subconscious minds, yet why they don't is easily understood. The conscious mind has worked so well and so successfully that they imagine it has secured all their results for them. Being successful, they have had no occasion to go over its head, beyond or behind it for what they wanted. They are on such intimate terms with their conscious minds that they are partial to them, as one is to a pal, and, as in such instances, often give him credit for some big service which has really been performed by a loving mother or other relative off in the background somewhere. Today more and more successful men and women are recognizing the part their subconscious minds have played in their success.

Rule 3. If you have not yet seen a formula or affirmation that seems just to fit your ambitions, you must make YOUR OWN formula.

Do not copy Coué's, mine or anyone else's. Do not make any special effort to have it pretty, didactic, dramatic, fancy, clever, polished or any other thing.

Take time and build a phrase that, TO YOU, fits your own list of desires; that boils them down, yet contains the general idea of them all. Or, if you prefer, make a formula for each one of the big desires you have down in your list of Wants.

I believe it will help you to understand just what is meant by "making your own" if I cite two instances from my own experience which show that each knows what affirmations help him most, and that it is too personal a matter for anyone else to arrange for you.

A very quiet, retiring, devout little woman told me that although she had studied the power of affirmation for many years she had had almost no results. She had practiced a certain formula day after day for years. She was desperately in earnest and apparently had done her part.

I asked her what she had been affirming all this time and she repeated to me a dry, theological phrase—one that her minister had used in a sermon years before. She admitted that this phrase didn't especially appeal to her, in fact that she really didn't care for it, only it sounded inclusive and rather awe-inspiring at the time and she "supposed one was about as good as another, just so you stuck to it, said it often enough and never stopped trying."

Her difficulty was the same each of us encounters when we try to FORCE anything that we really DON'T WANT or don't LIKE upon the subconscious. It knows we really don't want that and goes on about its business, waiting, waiting, as any good servant does, for you to order what you DO WANT. I asked her if she had ever thought of any formula or phrase that strongly appealed to her, and she at last confessed that she had. "Only," said she, "I never admitted it to myself, much less repeated it, it seemed so PROFANE.

"Every time I want something, I would LIKE to say, 'I'll get you IN SPITE OF—!' but of course I never say it. I've often wondered if it wasn't this wicked thought which kept me from getting the things I wanted." "If you have that old word in your subconscious," I told her, "it is because your subconscious, for some reason or other, has fastened on it as a powerful, vital weapon.

"It does not mean to be profane, only to GET RESULTS. It evidently needs this word in its business, just as your carpenter may need certain tools you personally can't or wouldn't use.

"If you want to develop beyond it, better let him use it to build something better and thus grow out of the need for it. The fact that you have refused all these years to use this word is proof enough to Him Above that there is no blasphemy in your mind."

She was some time bringing herself to accept this theory, but when she did she made real progress.

The other case was of an opposite nature, and needed opposite treatment.

He was a man of the roughest exterior, the loudest voice and the most uncouth manners of any student who ever came to me. He had lived in a mining camp most of his life, far away from the "refinements of civilization," yet he had been strengthened, uplifted and, as he believed, directly inspired toward his financial success by an involved yet spiritual affirmation from one of Browning's poems. Rule 4. If something someone else has written suits you better than anything you can think of yourself, take it and use it, by all means. We sometimes buy a house built by another person in preference to building one ourselves. We often find a ready-made gown that pleases us better than anything a dressmaker could produce for us; and we often see our own ideas better expressed in an epigram than we were ever able to express it ourselves.

So it may be with your formula. If you have discovered that Coué's "Every day in every way" appeals to you more than any you can think of yourself, don't hesitate to use it, and don't be afraid or ashamed to do so.

If you find any other anywhere that helps you, use it also. Don't make the mistake so many do of refusing to use a thing because you didn't think of it first.

Remember, nothing is new under the sun, not even Couéism. Coué himself says he got his method from a little pamphlet published twenty years ago by an old doctor of Rochester, N.Y.

Rule 5. Having devised a formula or phrase that, to you, states just what you want, MAKE ITS ACQUAINTANCE BEFORE USING IT.

By this I mean, "break it in," as the cowboy does a horse, before trying to ride it. This is for the purpose of letting your conscious and subconscious minds get acquainted, for just as sure as they do not you will lose the co-operation of one or the other. Remember, these two great minds are almost strangers to each other, yet for full efficiency they must now work together in harmony.

Your conscious mind frames your formula from the material furnished by your subconscious desires. It is your conscious mind which at this moment is getting the instructions I am giving you. These two should agree on your formula if you are to get the fullest and quickest benefits from it. The refusal of their conscious minds to co-operate with Coué's formula prevented those who were not cured from receiving its benefits. Therefore both your minds should like and ENJOY the formula you arrange for yourself. This is easy and in fact inevitable if you let them alone to work it out and give it time to take root. Give these two minds of yours ample time to get together, to see something of each other, to adapt themselves to each other a little, as new neighbors would, before attempting the fullest intimacy.

You will be the best judge of the proper time to begin to use your formula. If you have been fully aware for a long time of just what you wanted, or if you have been telling yourself in so many words what your wants were, your conscious and subconscious minds are already in unison on this important step and you can proceed at once. In this case what you have already been repeating to yourself as your greatest wants may constitute most, if not all, of your formula. But if all this is new to you, if you have never heard of the power of words over the subconscious, if you have never tried to formulate your desires, if your own words frighten you; if, for any reason, you do not find it easy and PLEASANT and NATURAL to express your desires in words just yet, by all means wait until these new ideas have had time to adjust themselves to you. Wait till you feel at home with them.

Rule 6. When you feel perfectly at ease with and enjoy the statements of your own deepest desires, when you realize that they are not strangers to you but the most real and vital part of you, BEGIN TO EXPRESS THEM IN SOME FORM.

Again, in order to get the fullest results I leave you to choose whatever FORMS or METHODS of expression appeal to you most.

To the ear-minded the easiest was at first will be to speak it right out, to say it aloud, to "talk it to yourself."

To the eye-minded it will seem much more effective at first if written down. If you are a naturally talkative person, you will probably find verbal expression easiest and pleasantest to begin with.

But if you are one who prefers to express himself on paper, who writes better than he talks, you will feel more at home with your formula at first by writing it down several times a day.

If you are neither of these, but think out ideas habitually which you never express either on paper or by talking, you will derive the greatest benefits at first by letting yourself THINK your formula over and over.

If you do not so much think things out as FEEL them, then you will get the fullest and quickest results from your formula just by giving yourself time and opportunity each day to FEEL the meaning and significance of your formulated desires.

If you find none of the above suggestions is exactly suited to your particular requirements, but feel it necessary to exercise your own independent judgment in order to meet your needs, do so by all means. Examine carefully the suggestions offered, then draw your own conclusion as to the formula and method best suited to your own case.

Rule 7. If you are satisfied with the results you are getting from the one preferred form of expression, you need not add any other. But if you find the results are not all you want, it will be well for you to tap deeper regions of the subconscious by GRADUALLY EXPRESSING YOUR FORMULA IN EVERY WAY THAT YOU NORMALLY EXPRESS OTHER THINGS. You have all these abilities, of course, locked away, and one or more of them may be the very method you have been needing.

It is now well known that art is produced only when the artist has been denied full expression through the more commonplace channels. The highest forms of literature, music and acting are invariably productions that come out to the world through the little side doors because the big main ones in the artist have been closed up.

Before going on to the next rule let's see what you have now done toward setting the gage for this second step: You have framed the formula which CONTAINS THE BOILED-DOWN ESSENCE OF YOUR DEEPEST DESIRES.

You have put it into the words that MOST APPEAL TO YOU.

And you have decided which FORM OF EXPRESSION COMES EASIEST AND MOST NATURAL TO YOU. Rule 8. Do not fail to PRACTICE your formula EVERY DAY and as many times a day as you can do so without interfering with your regular activities.

Learn to sandwich it in between other things—especially when waiting for street cars, elevators, telephone answers, the return of your change at cashiers' windows, and the hundred other times each day when you are delayed for a moment in the traffic of life. At such times, instead of growling, working yourself up into a nervous state or saying the things that aggravate the situation, grasp this opportunity to concentrate on your formula.

In one year's time such a habit would enable you not only to make great headway toward what you want, but it would remake your disposition, your facial expression and your chances in life.

I have found that the capitalization of these off moments serves a triple purpose, in that it KEEPS US REMINDED of the good and strong in us instead of the bad and weak; it holds the switches IN THE RIGHT DIRECTION; it remakes our PREDOMINANT FEELINGS; and besides all these, produces other helpful effects some of which are too deep and far-reaching to be explained here, but which helpfully and permanently affect our whole lives.

Rule 9. In addition to these, avail yourself of a well-known and effective plan, by expressing your formula or affirmations the moment you are awake in the morning.

NO MATTER WHAT TROUBLES YOU MAY BE FACING, let the formula come first. Say it, write it, think it, feel it or otherwise dwell upon it for a few moments before permitting yourself to go on to the consideration of anything else WHATSOEVER. Do the same thing at night as soon as you are ready to go to sleep, saying your own best-beloved statement of desires over and over till you lose consciousness. The subjective state which lies between wide-awakeness and sleep is the ideal one for digging out weeds and planting good seeds in the subconscious. Whatever we say over or think about to ourselves at this time goes straight to the subconscious and begins to produce results immediately. This one thing alone accounts for much of the world's misery. Most people use these subjective states for reiterating the very troubles they fear.

If you will follow these rules you will be far better able to meet and vanquish anything that menaces you.

If you will follow this plan every day for a month you will find the number of things which do arise to threaten you will have decreased; also you will be surprised to note that many of the things which now irritate you have no longer any effect upon you.

Rule 10. In addition to these unexpected halts there are others which are forced upon you in your work and activities; there are also certain things you must take time to do every day of your life, and which you do so easily they use up no mentality.

Use these for planting in the soil of your subconscious the formula containing your big order.

Think of the hours you have mentally and spiritually wasted during your life up to now, just putting on your clothes, lacing your shoes and washing your hands. Think of the months it would count up to if we computed the time the average woman spends in doing her hair and the average man in shaving!

Naturally we must not neglect these things. Time thus spent is profitably invested, but it could be used for two purposes simultaneously. We do all these by habit, that is, without thinking or feeling, and little if any mental energy goes into them.

But it goes somewhere. The mind is never idle during one waking moment. What it usually does at these times is more harmful than helpful to us. It is a favorite little time with many people for getting themselves into a stew wondering if this or that or the other unpleasant thing is going to happen! We should train ourselves from this day onward to use these moments for affirming our personal formula. This kind of repetition will print its orders so clearly upon the subconscious we will see good results immediately.

Rule 11. When you are expressing your formula do not encourage yourself to think ONE WAY OR THE OTHER about whether you are LIKELY to get the thing you want. This rule is very necessary, for a very interesting reason, which I shall make clearer to you as we go on, but I can tell you this much now: the subconscious never gets your order as clearly when you are wondering about it as when you issue it whole-heartedly. I do not ask you to go so far just yet as to have faith or confidence, but I do ask that you refrain from crossing your own wires. When you are trying to keep these two things side by side in your mind it has the same effect as though you called up your grocer and while reading your order to him you tried also to read a book or carry on a conversation with someone in the room. You would assume perhaps that you could snatch a few sentences of your novel while he was writing down the separate items of your order. But you would be sure to give them less distinctly, less clearly, less definitely than if you had laid the book aside and devoted your mind to one thing at a time.

This is also illustrated in an experience all of us have had at some time—that of trying to write a letter in a room where others were conversing; in spite of ourselves we will almost invariably record on our page some word we were listening to instead of the one we meant to write.

Or we have been trying to talk to one person while listening to another, with the result that we became confused and did not express ourselves clearly.

Rule 12. If you really want you formula to give you the utmost service, do not tell it to anyone.

This is a necessary precaution because your subconscious is interested in no one in the universe but you, and also because you can never do justice to your deep desires when trying to express them to others.

Others always misunderstand your inner nature to some extent, and you become so well aware of this that you do not get back to complete co-operation with it again for some time.

Bear always in mind that the subconscious of every human being is different, in its inmost content, from that of anyone else, and that no one else in all the world can do as much with yours as you can yourself.

All effective suggestion is, as we now know, AUTO-suggestion, that is, self-suggestion.

Furthermore, it does no good for others to know or try to know just what goes on in your secret soul. They can help very little except as they help you to help yourself, and these lessons will do that. Let others see your RESULTS, never the inner mechanism. Rely more on the God within you and less on the people outside.

Rule 13. There are two main classes of affirmations or formulas. You should choose the kind which appeals to you most.

One states that you have RIGHT NOW the thing you want, that you are RIGHT NOW what you desire to be, that you are doing RIGHT NOW what you want to do.

As an example of this I have submitted the following in my classes and it has helped thousands of people: "I am well, happy and successful." The other kind of formula, and one which the average person finds more helpful, is:

"I am getting healthier, happier and more successful all the time." The latter form helps a greater number of people for the reason that it does not ask the reasoning, arguing, fact-loving, conscious mind to accept or believe anything contrary to its own senses.

That you are getting more happy, healthy and successful all the time is a probability your conscious mind will agree with, and thus it will lend its co-operation instead of its opposition.

Another form of affirmation that has been wonderfully successful places the emphasis on a different word each time, namely: "I am success,

I AM success,

I am SUCCESS."

The more conscious type of mind would derive a greater good by saying:

"I am more successful,

I AM more successful,

I am MORE successful,

I am more SUCCESSFUL."

A mind so recently awakened to the powers of the subconscious as not to be able to accept so much at once can derive fullest results by the following: "I am growing more successful, I AM growing more successful,

I am GROWING more successful,

I am growing MORE successful,

I am growing more SUCCESSFUL."

The above formulas can be applied to health, happiness, wealth, love or any other thing in the world you desire. There is greater efficiency in a short formula, for the obvious reason that it can be repeated oftener, but chiefly because it is more inclusive. You will doubtless feel that health, happiness and success include almost if not everything you want.

There is another great advantage making your formula inclusive like the above examples: it leaves the subconscious free to work out the details, to use its own methods, and gives it nothing to do but PRODUCE RESULTS. However, all this must be decided by yourself for yourself. If you feel after making your formula that you can improve upon it, do not hesitate to change. Your subconscious only wants to serve you, to bring you exactly what you want, and the more clearly you express what you want the more quickly and completely can it DELIVER THE GOODS.

Rule 14. Never make any statement regarding your own future or that of anyone else the full responsibility of whose materialization you are not willing to assume.

In other words, never say anything about yourself or others unless you are willing to see it come true and are willing to accept your full share of responsibility for it. Suggestion is a powerful force which acts directly upon the subconscious mind. WORDS are wireless suggesters that go straight into it, setting it to work INSTANTLY in accordance with whatever the NATURE, MEANING, SOUND and INTENT of those words signify to YOU.

Learn to refrain from the use of all inharmonious, negative, destructive or even colorless words.

Try to frame every thought in the most harmonious, constructive, colorful words you can. And here is the last and best plan of all, with regard to the spoken word: If any thought or feeling you wish to express cannot be put into any but destructive or harmful words DO NOT EXPRESS IT AT ALL.

LESSON V
How to Prepare for What You Want

Whatever we prepare for, we get.

The more quickly we prepare for it the more quickly we get it. The more completely we prepare for it the more completely we receive it. The more perfect our preparation the more perfect the materialization. Do not waste your time, thought or energy looking for exceptions to this, for you will not find them.

On the contrary, you will discover, perhaps for the first time, that the REALIZATIONS of the people you know match the PREPARATIONS they made in advance.

You will see that these two sets of things, in ALL the lives you know, coincide too nearly to have "just happened."

Whenever you see a man with a suit that looks "as though he had been poured into it" or a woman wearing a gown that fits her perfectly you know for a certainty that each had several fittings, "try-ons," before such accuracy was attained.

You can know the very same thing when you see the general conditions in any person's life.

He may complain that these are farthest from what he ordered, that these things he is surrounded by (the things that happen to him and the things he possesses) are the exact opposite of what he had arranged for.

And no doubt they are very different from what he MEANT to order or what he thought he was ordering.

But look closer and you will find that they REFLECT precisely what that person HAS BEEN PREPARING FOR IN HIS OWN SECRET MIND.

Life doesn't pay much attention to what you TELL OTHER PEOPLE you are after; it pays no heed to what you PRETEND or imagine you are ordering. But it pays the strictest attention to what you actually GET READY FOR—and delivers the goods accordingly.

"Ah, but you are mistaken," you say. "Why, I know a man—several of them in fact—who have made every preparation for success, and failed. Also I know of several people who just stumbled into success."

And so it may seem to you, for you see only the shell of any human being. The INSIDE INDIVIDUAL, the REAL person, you seldom get a glimpse of. That real one in each of us lives far beneath the person visible to others, and is often so different from our external nature that no one suspects what we really feel.

We all are Dr. Jekyll and Mr. Hyde, more or less. And the one you THINK is the real you is often secondary. This is always true of the kinds of people you have just mentioned. These men who, you say, have always prepared for the best but got the worst, what IS the truth about them? That they APPEARED on the outside to be making great preparation for the best in life.

But this was the LESSER personality. The greater, the REAL one, was getting ready all the time for EXACTLY WHAT HAS HAPPENED.

These other people—the ones you say "just stumbled into success without preparations or capacity for it"—what are the inside facts about THEM? That no matter how little you thought of them or how little you realized it; no matter how it seemed to you "on the outside looking in," these people WERE making preparations which you never suspected, and for THE VERY THING that has come to them—not only for success but for THE VERY KIND of success they achieved.

There are no accidents. Everything in the universe occurs in accordance with law. If you don't know it, it is merely that you do not see or understand the law. And of laws, there is none more certain than that YOU GET WHAT YOU PREPARE FOR.

People often cry, "Why doesn't success come to me and my friends—us estimable deserving people—instead of those unworthy ones who are not half so good as we are?" They won't believe it, because they like themselves so well, but here is the true answer:

"Only those deserve me who are willing to woo me, to love me, to seek me and, above all, to PREPARE for me," says Success.

All these requirements have been fulfilled, you may be sure, by every person in the world who ever succeeded, whether you have been aware of this or not. You doubtless often consider these successful people less worthy than yourself, but worth consists of many elements.

Success is a loyal friend to all who study her laws, her peculiarities, her demands, and who take the trouble to FULFIL them. She will have nothing to do with those who talk about her behind her back, who turn their mind's eye constantly upon her rival, Failure—and she flatly refuses to go where there have been little or no preparations made for her. This lesson is for the purpose of explaining the law and the LURE of preparation. It is irresistible. Prepare for a thing and sooner or later you will find that thing walking into your House of Life. It may wait years, or it may come tomorrow—but come it surely will. No matter what the neighbors say, get ready, "set thy house in order" for achievement and she will one day appear at the door. If Success seems fickle to you, if she has refused to come to you, it is because you have thus far never really prepared for her, and she knows it!

All the talk in the world, all your hard work and "just deserts" will not induce her to pay you a visit if you have left out the special PREPARATIONS for her which she demands.

Hard work and just deserts are wonderful things and they are absolutely necessary, but they are not ALL that is necessary. To induce Success to come to you, you must work, yes—and work effectively—but you must make the special arrangements for her coming which she is so partial to, otherwise she will continue to pass you by.

Much less work will win her if you will take the trouble to find out and produce for her the things she is especially fond of. She is like a very busy man I know. He is noted, in fact famous, and very popular. Everyone invites him to dinner. He has a very kind heart and hates to refuse, though he knows he will be frightfully busy and really cannot spare the time when the date arrives. He accepts nearly every invitation, but seldom appears. His secretary calls up at the last moment with the message that he is unavoidably detained. "There is one kind of household I always favor," he said to me once, "the little ones where the woman has no servant, where she does all her own work and where she personally has made all the preparations, even to cooking the dinner. "I cannot disappoint people who go to so much trouble for me with their own hands," he explained. "But these big houses where my hosts have put themselves to no bother, where a retinue of servants have been ordered to arrange all the details—these are places I often fail to reach."

Does this reveal anything to you? Next time you see someone whom you consider less deserving than yourself riding on the top wave of success, realize that you are looking at one who has, WITH HIS OWN HANDS, HIS OWN HEART and HIS OWN EFFORTS, PREPARED FOR THAT VERY THING. Bear also in mind when you see the failure that somehow or other he has NOT made those preparations.

Despite all he says, he has not given HIMSELF to the wooing of Success. He has invited her, of course—but that being done he has devoted himself to SOMETHING ELSE while waiting for her to arrive. How seldom you hear of a "guest of honor" being unable to attend the luncheon or reception! We get there somehow, don't we, when the preparations have been made for US, personally? Well, Success is just like you and me. If she has not arrived yet, the chances are a hundred to one that although you have invited her, you have been making your real plans and preparations for her enemies, Failure, Unhappiness, Ill-health and Self-Pity. Let her know SHE is the main show, so far as you are concerned, give some of your best personal attention to making the banquet ready for her—and she WILL ARRIVE.

The other thing we hear so often from the disgruntled is, "That successful chap was given certain opportunities that were the making of him—all kinds of chances! No such luck ever came to me!" These people fail to see that opportunities are EVERYWHERE, ALL THE TIME—more than any of us can use—but are of no value to him who is not prepared for them.

"When opportunity comes," says W. A. Heath of the Federal Reserve Bank of Chicago, "is of little consequence. The thing is, what are you PREPARED TO MAKE OF IT when it does come? Opportunities are always to be found, ready and waiting, but men who are READY for opportunities are found very rarely." Mary Garden says, "Thousands have written asking me how they may become successful at singing, but most of them seem to think if one has talent no preparation is necessary.

"Even genius needs more preparation than the average person realizes, and as for talent, it is useless without preparation.

"Every hour of the day the young singer should be thinking, planning, dreaming. He should be studying the art, the musical world, his or her own personality, every turn of the road to be traveled. The singer must live with his art and dream day and night of his career if he would succeed." If the thing you say you want most does not come to you in your night dreams, day dreams and every other kind of dream, it is not one of your deepest desires, and you should begin to prepare yourself for those things which DO come to you in your imaginings.

"After the singer's training is complete," continues Miss Garden, "she should expect to give three years more—the first for finding herself, the second for perfecting herself, and the third to get on the stage. "If she cares so deeply for her art that she can think of nothing else for very long at a time, and will prepare herself under the best teachers, she will find the opera companies to receive her, the opera lovers to hear her and the opportunities to make as large a place for herself as she is able to fill." Robert W.

Stewart, head of the Standard Oil Company of Indiana, is now one of the highest-paid executives in that great organization, due to the simple fact that he was ALWAYS READY for opportunity. He always prepared to win, even in the smallest affairs.

He left no stone unturned, no matter how insignificant the matter was nor how uncertain the outlook. He used to live in the little town of Pierre out in South Dakota. If you ever saw this drab, forsaken village you would probably say there was no chance for a man in such a place, no use to go to a lot of trouble preparing for Opportunity in that spot!

But young Robert Stewart organized his law cases, little as they were, with the same care and thoroughness as if he were handling the biggest cases for the biggest concerns in the world—which he is now doing.

Once, for instance, he was given a case that involved damages for a fire which was alleged to have been caused by sparks flying from a railroad engine quite a distance away. The amount at stake was small and young Stewart's fee still smaller, but he spent twice the sum for railroad fares to ride back and forth on that train till he got his evidence!

Later, when his ability as a "preparer" had become known and he was attorney in a case where the question was one of adulterated goods put out by a certain concern, he didn't rely for his facts on the testimony of paid experts, but donned overalls, got a job in the factory at small wages and studied processes at first hand for many weeks, till he KNEW what he was talking about—and of course won the case.

Every successful man could relate many such stories from his own experience. Don't be afraid that your preparations will be in vain. The whole world is crying for PREPARED PEOPLE. It will pay almost anything for them.

It is a well-known fact that although men are always standing in line for the small, underpaid jobs that require little or no preparation, many of the highest-salaried places are frequently vacant because men big enough to fill them are not to be found. Lots of men would like to have them but cannot take them because when the big opportunity knocks at their doors they are not ready.

I know many people, and so do you, who want the biggest, reddest apples on the Tree of Life but who never think of shaking it. They want the rarest fruits to fall into their laps—and won't even hold their laps!

Life's tree is loaded with the things you want, but if you spend your time standing under it in the shade you will get only the windfalls.

There will always be flaws in the things which fall at your feet—wormholes, frostbites or something—because the folks who CLIMB THE TREES take all the plums. Inspiration is a wonderful thing, but unless it is backed up by preparation it won't carry you very far. Inspiration isn't supposed to pull your load. It is mighty important as a self-starter, but when it gives you a push in the right direction you are expected to do something for yourself. If you don't, you will have fewer inspirations, more perspiration and less realization as time goes on.

You hear about a man who "rises to an emergency"—and you wonder how he did it. Invariably such a man has prepared himself in advance for just such a tight place. The subconscious mind is the habit-mind. It can easily be trained to new and different habits, and one of its best is that of BEING READY for the thing you want. "But if I prepare and it never comes?" ask the ninety-nine out of every hundred.

Poor, skeptical, short-sighted ones! Don't you know that no person in all the world ever grew BIG ENOUGH for a better place without finding a better place BIG ENOUGH for him?

The occasions when one can do a big thing without preparation are so few and far between that they will never build a successful life. The things we do efficiently and brilliantly apparently without effort are seldom done on the spur of the moment at all. These are always done by the subconscious or UNconscious mind, which is able to accomplish it for you because—when you least realized it—you had been filling it with the power necessary to this brilliant performance.

Last year a remark made by a fifty-year-old salesman in an Eastern city was printed all over the country.

He had gone into the office of a man who was the buyer for one of the largest building concerns in America, and came out twenty minutes later with a million-dollar order.

The other salesmen gathered around him in awesome amazement and exclaimed, "And you did it in TWENTY MINUTES, didn't you?"

"Yes," he replied, "twenty minutes, PLUS THIRTY YEARS!"

But his commission on the order amounted to a splendid income for that thirty years, so he didn't mind.

Rule 1. KNOW that "psychological moments" are sure to arrive in your life—and BEGIN NOW TO GET READY FOR THEM. On this subject Purinton says to all who are in business: "Study your job and the job of the man higher up than you, for by doing so you are preparing yourself to go up higher when the psychological moment arrives.

"Those who do not believe they can get the things they want or who refuse to get ready for them are never prepared for these magic moments. They remain in the mediocre class all their lives, or at least until something awakens them to the great truths. The subconscious mind must be given preparation by proper methods."

By preparation I mean FILLING your subconscious with your desires, FAITHFUL PREPARATION for getting, recognizing, using and capitalizing the thing you want, by faithfully feeding your subconscious with expectant, constructive success-thoughts about the particular and specific thing you are interested in. The ways for doing this are so many you will have little difficulty in finding them, but the KINDS of things necessary to do so are few and so well known to all successful people that any intelligent person may learn them and apply them. If he will, he can make the achievement of what he wants absolutely CERTAIN.

Rule 2. A certain amount of training for what you desire to do is naturally essential, and if you really want this thing you will ENJOY the training it necessitates.

Your hand must be trained—don't forget that but your head must be trained more, and if you really want the great things of life, your heart most of all.

Give yourself the technical training or whatever is necessary in the way of TOOLS. Don't expect to be a successful lawyer without studying law or a doctor without taking a medical course. Don't expect to sing or paint or play or act or sell or speak or preach or do anything that is WORTH DOING unless you have studied your subject—that is, STORED YOUR SUBCONSCIOUS mind with the fundamentals.

If this study connected with the thing you say you want is distasteful to you, you do not really want it, and you had better turn to something you fully desire.

Do not think, as so many have, that conscious training, cramming of technicalities, facts and figures into the conscious mind is the main preparation toward acquiring anything. It is the FIRST step, but not the BIGGEST, BEST or LONGEST.

The greatest step is taken toward what you want when you begin to TRAIN THE SUBCONSCIOUS.

To take this step toward what you want, first KNOW WHAT YOU WANT; second, AFFIRM THAT YOU ARE GOING TO GET IT; third, consciously STUDY toward it; fourth BEGIN TO DWELL UPON this great thing you want, by letting your inner mind have charge of it.

Rule 3. Encourage yourself to seek and to create the atmosphere and attitudes that go with this thing you want.

For instance, if you wish to be a minister, a missionary, a social worker, or do anything unusual in this field, place yourself as frequently as possible in this atmosphere.

Do not wait for the actual arrival of the time when you will be in this work yourself, but seek out the places where this ideal dominates. Seek out the people who are doing the biggest things in this field, and gradually make their acquaintance.

Do not rush them, do not force yourself into their company. Remember the rule stated once before, and one which will be stated many times hereafter—that it is by GIVING TO, not in trying to GET FROM, people that we win them to us. This method is not only FAIR but invariably successful. Make yourself useful, helpful, inspiring—and pretty soon you will have made yourself indispensable, for these are qualities the whole world admires and responds to. People will seek you, make a place for you, give you opportunities—and the rest is easy. Before you try to do anything for them or with them, however, make yourself ONE OF THEM at heart. Learn what it really is they are doing, what the movement actually stands for, what its history has been. Familiarize yourself with its great personalities and study their lives, as well as the subject itself. Otherwise, you will be at a disadvantage when you meet the representatives of this great movement. Furthermore, it will make you UNINTERESTING to them.

"I love you because you love the things I love" is something to remember. In this connection, let me give you two widely different illustrations from life:

A beautiful young college woman came to me some years ago and said she had ambitions to be a missionary but did not know how to go about realizing them. She had been brought up in a dry-farming region in Nevada, far away from any church, and did not contact Christian people or Christian ideals until she entered the University of California. Immediately she became deeply interested and, as was natural to one of her spiritual nature, wanted to do something to help. She had decided as a freshman that she wanted to do this work but when she came to me in the last semester of her junior year she had gone no further toward preparing for it than three attendances at church every Sunday. The whole idea had been so new to her she did not know where to begin, and she was too timid to admit that the facts about the Christian religion so familiar to all the other girls were utterly unfamiliar to her. She had been afraid to make any move for fear of exposing this ignorance.

Right here is the best place to say that if you want to get anything worth while you must not be above confessing lack of information whenever necessary to GET information. Such a one will always remain ignorant while he who asks and admits he doesn't know will grow into knowledge.

The ignorant man doesn't fool anybody anyhow—except that he is usually considered more ignorant than he really is—while the man who is frank about what he doesn't know is the one we tie to.

A national convention of the Y. W. C. A. was soon to be held in a near-by city, and I recommended to this young woman that she attend every session she possibly could, not as a participant at all but to listen and look and ABSORB everything she could. "What can I LEARN that way?" she inquired. "I will be just a spectator, I won't know what it is all about. I want to get at the inside facts. I want to know what they are doing and why, and who everybody is, and how I can get into it too." She had thought so much about her conscious training and knew so little about the necessity for the far more important development of the subconscious, that she was much surprised when I said: "Go there and throw yourself into the atmosphere, just as a man who is trying to swim goes into the water; let it submerge you, sweep over you, swallow you up. Don't try to figure out, first thing, what everyone is doing and why. Give the ideals, aims, hopes and aspirations connected with it a chance to soak into your soul. "Stop THINKING or STUDYING or WONDERING or ANALYZING or JUDGING about it. Just let yourself FEEL what is going on, sense the bigger things back of the speeches, motions, business and committee meetings—in other words, GET INTO THE SPIRIT. "If the spirit does NOT carry you along, you will know for sure you are not meant for this work, in which case more training would be useless." I recommended that she join the University Y. W. C. A., enroll in classes devoted to the history of Christianity, that she familiarizes himself with the Bible, and that she read all she could find on the lives of the great modern preachers. But most necessary of all in her case was a sympathetic agreement with all that Jesus taught. If she gave herself fully and enjoyably to these a solid foundation would be laid, and the rest could be added later. But if she felt impelled to withhold the best of her CONSCIOUS SELF from the Master's teachings her subconscious would never yield up its fullest efficiency. All these things furnish THE SUBCONSCIOUS with the raw materials it must have for manufacturing the finished article for you later on. The other example is as far removed from this one as could well be imagined, but is an equally clear illustration of the fact that subconscious preparation for a thing is needful regardless of what the thing may be. It will also show that the AMOUNT and intensiveness of preparation you should make to get any particular thing will depend on how far you are removed from it to start with.

A young Norwegian servant girl of intelligence hut of little education, of good character but crude personality, told me the one thing she wanted most of all was to marry well—preferably some American of means, education and refinement—and to have a lovely child.

That this young woman—ambitious, intelligent and beautiful in character though she was—had a long way to go to prepare for such a marriage, you will agree.

She had practically to remake her personality and acquire an education.

Within five years after her arrival in this country and within four years after she applied my instructions this young woman who could not speak a word of our language when she landed, who knew nothing about our ways, customs or standards, had mastered English, attained a good education, developed a pleasant personality—and acquired a successful young husband, and a beautiful baby boy! To the people who had known her as a servant girl only five years before, her brilliant marriage was no doubt a mystery. But not to us who also knew the laws. She had taken herself and her big desire seriously.

She had studied the very rules you are at this moment reading—and she APPLIED them incessantly, uninterruptedly, earnestly.

Nothing is impossible to the subconscious mind of the ambitious man or woman.

Rule 4. Make your preparations as COMPLETE, "HEAPED-UP-and-RUNNING-OVER" as you can. Never be afraid of building too strong a foundation.

When rewards are slow in coming or when those attained are not as great as you had expected, rest assured that insufficient preparation is partly if not wholly the cause.

As soon as your preparations are adequate, as soon as you have really done YOUR PART, the results will begin to come.

Don't be discouraged, don't slide back and give up. Don't slump and say, "Oh, what's the use? Maybe there's nothing in this, anyhow!" Instead, get a new grip on yourself, go on with your preparations—and you will see. It is precisely because the law of preparations IS eternal, impersonal and accurate that superficial, slipshod preparations never accomplish much.

Thoughtful, serious, earnest preparation--in short, REAL preparation—ALWAYS brings the desired results, or better ones. The following illustrates the law of adequate preparation in a very graphic way. It is from the lips of Harriet Luella McCollum, who lived on a Kansas farm till past middle age, yet who is today one of the most fluent, entertaining, inspiring and helpful lecturers in the world. She says:

"My own work will illustrate the road which you may have to travel, no matter what line of endeavor you may choose or have chosen. "Before I entered public work I was using the formula to develop an ability to do the work I had chosen—teaching psychology. "I was timid, nervous, reticent, retiring, dreaded public opinion either in praise or condemnation, but I realized that if I was to do the work successfully which my higher self said I should do, I would have to reverse my psychology, and I did so.

"After sufficient preparation, as I thought, I went into a town, advertised my lecture and otherwise prepared for it. I expected at least five hundred people to attend. To my consternation when I arrived at the lecture hall at the appointed hour only three women were there, seated on the front row. No more came in.

"That was my entire audience. I slipped into a little room alone and asked myself if I should give the lecture—or quit right then. The answer came, 'Three are as important as three hundred; do your best!' "And I did. To make it businesslike I took up a collection. I told my audience of three that we would have another lecture that night, and asked them to bring their friends. They brought two others. My audience was increasing. I had five. My combined collections amounted to thirty cents—exactly what I was worth. I had not prepared sufficiently.

"My life has been a long story of earnest endeavor, never giving way to discouragement. I constantly endeavor to realize my ideal. I always keep in mind that some day it shall be realized, and do not fret because the way is long, for THE BLISS OF GROWTH is one of the big JOYS of living. "And when even small progress can be discerned one is encouraged to push on toward the goal. Among the benefits of working toward a goal is not only the satisfaction of successful performance and the good accruing from it, but also the development of a well-rounded personality."

Many people of less energy and courage have called this woman "lucky," but they should spell it with a "p" if they expect to find one of the reasons for her big success. Rule 5. Don't try to win what you want by waiting on "luck."

Frederick D. Underwood, president of the Erie Railroad, recently said, "Sometimes there may be a little in what the world calls luck. But don't wait for it. It comes but rarely and never holds very long." A discussion as old as time has been waged around this question of luck. Those on the outside are inclined to say a man's success is due to luck, but those on the INSIDE, those who really know the man, will tell you he made his own luck. Good luck that comes frequently and makes itself at home is always home-made. Bad luck, of the chronic kind, is also "home-brewed," and the "still," like most others, is out of your sight.

"Luck," says a prominent writer, "has a way of favoring THE PREPARED. It may give you a start, but it can never take you far. In the 'long haul' it is one's own power that has to do the work." All the luck in the world can't do much for the man who hasn't gotten ready for it in advance. The man who is known as a "preparer" is always lucky.

Woolworth, creator of more than one thousand five and ten cent stores and a multi-millionaire, said: "There are more opportunities in the world today than ever before. The door of opportunity is open to everyone, and no one can close this door but one's own self. No matter where we are, we can create our own opportunity, and we do so most surely and swiftly by preparing for it. Nothing can then keep it away."

Rule 6. No matter how dark the prospects or how unattainable your desires seem to be now, GO STRAIGHT AHEAD MAKING YOUR PREPARATIONS. Let me tell you a love story. Some years ago when I was still seeing students in private consultation, a teacher thirty-two years old told me her story and her desire for a home and husband. "I have no opportunities to meet men," she said. "When one associates only with children one does not have the chances for matrimony that come to business or professional women. For economy's sake I live at the Y. W. C. A. and there doesn't seem to be any modest way to make the acquaintance of eligible men.

"Some of my teacher friends have had successful marriages, and many of the business girls I know are happily mated. But I'm probably destined to be just one of those 'old maid school-teachers'!" I took her over the very same ground we have covered in these lessons, explaining to her how these laws could be made to bring her the things she wanted most. When we reached this stage—the law of preparation—I asked her if she had ever made any real plans or preparations for finding or winning a mate.

"Of course not," she replied. "Why should I? There has been none in sight, and no prospect of any. Why waste my time?" "This is exactly where you are wrong. There is one thing that is NEVER a waste of time, that cannot be lost, that ALWAYS brings its rewards, and that thing is preparation.

"Don't you realize that you are, as a matter of fact, always getting ready for something, and that when you are not doing anything TOWARD what you want you are, by idleness, wrong moods, disbelief, pessimism and other things, REALLY PREPARING TO KEEP THE CONDITION YOU DON'T WANT?" "Just what shall I do, then," she asked, "to prepare for what I want?"

"First of all, begin to VISUALIZE YOURSELF in the role of a happily married woman, and never, from this moment, allow yourself to DWELL on the picture of yourself as 'an old maid school-teacher.' "This is one of the greatest psychological laws. All achievement is built in the mind FIRST.

"Your thoughts and visualizations are your mental blue-prints. Without these mental images no great thing ever materialized. Just as a skyscraper is the tangible actualization of the mental pictures which existed originally only in the mind of the architect, your every tangible possession is the result of visualization.

"In other words, make your plans. Second, make your preparations, and by this I mean the VERY preparations you would make if you were engaged right now. Don't neglect one. Go right ahead, precisely as you would if you expected to marry within a year."

"Even to starting a hope chest?" she laughed. "Yes, even to the hope chest—only make it EXTRA BEAUTIFUL, EXTRA COMPLETE AND AS PERFECT IN EVERY WAY AS YOU CAN."

"Won't all this time and money and effort be wasted?" she insisted. "I believe in saving every cent I can."

"Don't stop with the hope chest. Begin to use some of the money you have at interest in the bank for a few pretty clothes—not expensive, extravagant ones, but dainty, modest, womanly-looking things. Not many of them necessarily, but enough to avoid monotony."

She could see how the clothes might help but refused to "spend all that work and money on an old hope chest that no one would ever see!"

"Why, I know a lot of girls that get married without ever having thought of a hope chest!" she said.

"And so do I," I told her—"and you might. I'm only telling you how to do your part and then some—good measure and running over—if you want the QUICKEST, SUREST results. People who are in earnest leave nothing undone. This accounts for their always getting more and getting it faster than others." Three years went by and I returned to lecture in her city. The young woman, changed almost beyond belief, called to see me. She looked ten years younger and was much happier, though she still had no "prospects," she said. Her clothes were attractive and she had, she confided, a much larger bank account than when she had seen me last. "Even school boards and principals prefer attractively attired teachers!" she explained.

"I've done everything you told me except about that awful hope chest!" she laughed. "And if you still insist I am now ready to do even THAT."

"I do not insist, and I do not say it is impossible for you to achieve your Big Desire without it. Certainly, you are on the road," I answered. "But it would help. Not of itself so much, but because IT WILL DO ALL KINDS OF THINGS TO YOU. It will crystallize things you are not now aware of at all—just try it, and see."

And she did. The story of that hope chest—it reads like a novel! To begin with, it helped her in her visualizations, and brought out vividly the pictures that had seemed vague and far away before. It kept her concentrated on all sorts of preparations she would never have made otherwise. It brought the same picture to the minds of her friends, all of whom were curious, naturally, and became more so when she refused to make any explanation to them. Pretty soon everybody who knew her was saying, "Margaret's getting ready to be married. Isn't it lovely? And it must be to somebody wonderful, to look at the exquisite things in her hope chest!" "What shall I tell them when they INSIST on knowing WHEN I'm to be married?" she wrote me. "Tell them," I answered, "that it will be as soon as your chest is full."

Months passed and Margaret's "engagement" became the mystery of the day. As such it naturally monopolized much of the thought and conversation of her friends. "What shall I do if he doesn't appear?" she finally wrote me six months after the chest was started. "I know I shall die of chagrin. I will have to resign my position. I couldn't stay here a day if anyone should find this out. Please write me what to do." "Stop showing the white feather," I wired. That was seven months ago. Recently I received this letter. You may read it over my shoulder: "I am on my honeymoon at Lake Louise, a most heavenly spot in the Canadian Rockies, with the nicest husband! How it happened was this: I attended a series of psychology lectures, to brace me up and remind me of your teachings. There I met a splendid young businessman who was interested in just the same things I am. "We used to sit together in the classes. When they were over he called on me regularly. Finally friends told him I was engaged, and he said, 'That is something I am well aware of—for I'm the man!' You see I'd told him all about it as so as he asked me to marry him, and instead of being disillusioned he said he 'admired my thoroughness.' We later told my friends. They laughed a lot, but I've noticed several of the girls busy on fine embroidery lately, just the same."

Rule 7. At first you may feel some doubt or uncertainty. Little fear-thoughts may come knocking at the door of your mind. When they do you should gently but persistently turn them away. If you do this they will return less and less frequently and finally stay away altogether.

On the other hand, if you will do this, better and more effective thoughts BUILDING TOWARD what you want will come to your mind more and more often.

Some of these will suggest ways of reducing your time of waiting and eventually point out short cuts. Practice in constructive thinking builds toward the construction of whatever you are thinking about.

One of the big reasons why outsiders never can see just HOW one's good luck comes is that they cannot see the inner thought-machinery go round.

Things move more rapidly for you the more diligently and the more INTENSELY you think the right thoughts. Entertaining the wrong attitudes for a while can put you back, but you can always resume your forward progress by getting back on the track of right thinking.

If you will stick to your good thoughts when the pull seems hard you will always find that this was merely a stiff grade with a chance to coast for a long distance down the other side, once you get to the top. Rule 8. Don't be content with going through the motions. "As a man thinketh IN HIS HEART" is the vital thing—not what he does with his hands or tongue or pretenses.

INTENSITY is the dynamo which opens new paths toward what you want. The distance you travel and the rate of speed you make depends on your DEGREE OF INTENSITY.

In other words, it is YOU and your great, God-given forces that create your world and the things that happen to you. If you are not making your preparations WITH SINCERITY, you are like an electric light bulb when the power is turned off—all the mechanism there but no light.

Very little effort, when accompanied by a lot of the right spirit, often accomplishes wonders. More effort, combined with more and deeper sincerity, can do the impossible. It is their inability to see this INNER VOLTAGE which makes others think our achievements accidental. The same blindness to inner conditions also makes it hard to explain to them why the rushing, hurrying, "busy" person, as well as the idle pessimist, often fails.

Don't mistake busyness for business. Much of the business of succeeding is done after the doors are closed at night and before they open in the morning!

Rule 9. Don't be in a hurry.

If you try to speed up delivery of what you want by hurry instead of by QUALITY in your preparation you will only delay it. It is always better to build solidly as you go and avoid setbacks, for setbacks always come to the man who has "forced" results by hothouse methods.

If you sacrifice stability to speed you will have to go back sooner or later and make up for it, and this demotion is a far greater humiliation than waiting—sometimes so crushing to sensitive souls as to make it hard for them to hold up their heads again. Sarah Bernhardt's favorite teacher, who had more to do, she said, with her success than any other one person, fully understood this. "Looking back over many years to my early days as a student at the Conservatory in Paris my heart fills with gratitude to my best-beloved teacher there because he would not allow me to compete for a prize when I had been there only three months. He was afraid I would win and that my rapid success would be a detriment to me in the end.

"Later when I had been awarded a first prize by a committee which came without our knowledge to see us rehearse, he refused to let me be told about it. He said to them, 'If you give her first prize, which, I admit, she deserves, she will be almost certain to leave the Conservatory too soon. She has within her the fire of genius, but she needs a great deal more development. She must have more preparation.'" Rule 10. When you recognize that you should do certain things in order to be properly prepared for what you want, DO NOT HESITATE, DELAY or POSTPONE the doing of them, much less REFUSE to do them. Some day (and this is what rewards us for all the preparation) we will be weighed in the balance. If we have done our part the scales will show it and we are sent up higher. But if we have not, we will go down a step or two. A chain is not stronger than its weakest link.

How to Get Anything You Want

When I was a little girl I got my first lessons in a log schoolhouse in the Rocky Mountains. In those days the wildest kind of show we ever put on for our fond parents was a spelling match. This generation won't know what that is, but some of you fifty-year-olds will.

The one who "spelled down the class" was noted for the good old-fashioned preparation he made under the kerosene lamp at night.

The man who "goes to the head of his class" anywhere in life has to be READY for it in advance. Later when I attended a grammar school in town, the same old inexorable law used to keep bobbing up when we least expected it. After putting somebody into the scales it would send him up a grade or back a few. We found we could manage sometimes to get into the next higher grade by cramming, bluffing the teacher or being lucky as to questions—but STAYING there was another story. Here we'd be in another room under another teacher, with a whole year dividing us from our slackness in the grade before—but our sin always found us out, and back we went, "to make it up." Also, every once in a while some plain, green gawk would come in from the mountains, from the country schools of the mining camps or lumber mills. I remember one who started in at the third grade. I'll never forget the shock it gave us fourth-graders one day when this freckle-faced, red-haired boy, whom all of us had teased and ridiculed from our heights of learning, was promoted right over our heads and put into "high fifth."

He had been in school about ten days. He had said very little, and was the most surprised one of us all when the principal dropped in one morning and said, "Red, come with me."

Everybody giggled—everybody, that is, except Red. He wondered what he'd done and how big the stick was going to be. But he went. Everybody heard about the principal's speech and told it at recess.

"Children," he said, when he marched Red into the Fifth, "here is a new member. We find that although he has had only three months of schooling a year and dug the rest out of his books by himself, he is too far along for the third grade or even the fourth, so we're going to try him here for a while. We may have to promote him to the sixth."

When we get into Life's great Grown-up School it is just the same. You will have nothing to complain of in the world's treatment of you if you get ready for the best.

Rule 11. If you want something worth while don't look for soft snaps.

Prepare for What You Want

A thing you can get with little preparation isn't worth even that little, usually. The job requiring little effort pays little, keeps you little and reduces your chances as time goes on. There are so many after these easy places that you will always face lots of competition, and as you grow older they will put younger men in your place.

But the more preparation demanded by your job the less the competition. This will be especially true if you train your mind (which few will do). More especially will you outdistance competition if you develop your subconscious mind, for that is something others can't imitate, and which makes you unique no matter what line you are in.

The man who has trained his conscious mind is hard to replace. Callow youth can't outstrip him, for brains, unlike bodies, are keener at fifty than at twenty.

But the man who learns how to delve into his subconscious and make preparation THERE, gives up his place only when he passes on to the next world. His personality, resourcefulness and depth of vision make him indispensable. For him age does not exist.

Imagine anyone displacing Thomas Edison, Carrie Chapman Catt, John Burroughs, Ex-President Eliot of Harvard, Henry Ford or William Gillette! Eleanora Duse at 64 and Bernhardt at 75 (though of a profession supposed to depend upon youth) could not be touched by any younger star.

LOVE for a thing, backed up by PREPARATION, can do ANYTHING.

If you love this thing you want—in other words, if you REALLY WANT IT—you will enjoy most of the preparation. Not all of it, of course, for some drudgery goes with every great achievement.

We have times and moods when something less exacting looks alluring, no matter how much we love our work, but for the most part you will enjoy it.

Rule 12. If you want any opening with a future to it, you must expect to build in the PRESENT—today, right NOW.

James Logan, the rich and successful general manager of the United States Envelope Company, says:

"It was from my job in a book store that I got my real start, for in it I got my first big idea. After I had been there awhile this thought struck me: 'If I keep books all my life I shall never get very far, BECAUSE a man can learn to keep books in about three months, so there will always be plenty of bookkeepers. I had better try to learn something that is not so easy.'

"I asked the owner if I could spend half of my time out in the store, selling, provided I didn't neglect the accounts. I didn't ask for more pay—only for more work. The head clerk kicked, but the owner backed me up. "When I had learned how to sell books and was fully prepared, I asked the owner to let me go out at odd times to sell books and office supplies.

"This was a new idea to them. They had always waited for the trade to come to them. "I proved to be a good salesman. I had two positions offered me in banks, but I said no. The jobs were genteel but too easy, too little was required and the pay correspondingly low. I wanted a harder job, for I knew that was the only kind that would pay more, and more pay I was determined to get. Eventually of course I got it.

"There may be such a thing as luck, and I would enjoy the good kind as much as anybody, but I never leave anything to luck until I have established control over everything that can be controlled. When one is doing as well as he knows how he is getting ready for the good luck and he is sure to have it." If you want a soft future take the hardest knocks NOW. You will be younger tomorrow.

Rule 13. Do not allow other people to talk you out of doing the work you love. If you LOVE a thing well enough to love the WORK it entails, you can rise to heights in that work, no matter how little other men see in it. Logan, whose story was quoted above, knew banking had no future for HIM because he didn't love it enough to give it complete preparation. This always depends on the individual preference. But Percy Johnston, who at forty became president of the Chemical National Bank of New York City, one of the largest financial institutions in America, says: "A man can attain success if he is willing to get all ready for it. I began preparing myself for a banking career at the age of twelve." Here are some of his mottoes on the subject:

"Always the man or woman who succeeds beyond his fellows is the man or woman WHO PREPARED. This kind of person meets opportunity more than halfway."

"Leadership calls for preparation and knowledge of human nature." "Don't ask what is the easiest way it can be done, but what is the BEST way." "The only pull worth having is the pull your preparation gives you." "Learn to select your risk." Every time you learn anything you are storing something away that you will certainly use, in some way, later on. And every time you fail to learn from experience or look beyond your present place you are PREPARING TO LOSE the place you have.

Rule 14. If you want to test yourself and know, in general, whether you are making the right preparations for the future take note of two things: how far AHEAD you are living IN YOUR MIND, and HOW MUCH you are doing OVER AND ABOVE WHAT YOU ABSOLUTELY HAVE TO DO TO HOLD YOUR PRESENT PLACE.

We must make the most of today, but we must NOT stop there; we must also KEEP OUR MENTAL EYES ON THE FUTURE. How far ahead on the road are your eyes fastened—at tomorrow, next year or a decade away? When interviewers ask me to what one thing of all others I feel I owe my present happiness I say, "The habit (cultivated in spite of laziness and inertia) of LIVING in the Now, but LOOKING twenty years ahead."

"Wisdom," says John Blake, "is a plant of slow growth. After it is planted it must be watered through the years. But it always bears fruit and usually golden fruit at a time when a man knows how to spend wisely and profitably the leisure which is the harvest of bygone years."

Rule 15. Do not waste time bewailing the conditions of your life, but prepare for better ones.

It has been well said, "One half the time spent in bemoaning conditions, if spent in PREPARING FOR conditions, would REMAKE conditions."

Taking yourself or what you are doing pessimistically never helps, and always hurts.

One of the cheeriest men in American industry is one of its most famous and successful—Charles M. Schwab.

Schwab has had two outstanding habits since boyhood—he always wears a smile and he is forever getting ready for something BETTER.

When as a very young man his superintendent took him to meet Andrew Carnegie the superintendent said, "Andy, here is a young fellow who knows as much about this mill as I do."

His phenomenal rise started right then, and never stopped—because he wasted no minutes fretting but invested them growing mentally for the next step up.

Rule 16. "Whatsoever a man soweth, that shall he also reap."

This great eternal law operates everywhere at all times throughout our lives, but nowhere is it more noticeable than in this very matter of preparation.

Very few people grasp this last amazing fact—that there is no such thing as standing still, and that no moment passes without our planting SOMETHING.

What our harvests will be in the Tomorrows depends on the seeds we are planting Today.

Don't think that because you cannot see it you are not bringing something to pass every hour of your life.

WE ARE ALWAYS (by our refusal to act, no less than by our overt acts) PREPARING FOR SOMETHING.

Sins of OMISSION bring their results just as surely as do those of COMMISSION.

Since we are moment by moment laying the foundations for the future, and since what it shall bring to us depends upon these foundations, let us build them strong and sure.

Frank Crane says, "Some day, or to be exact, some minute, you are going to need every ounce of your strength, every volt of your energy and every faculty of your mind. Are you READY?

"Life is determined largely by crises.

"Success in business can often be traced to some one single act.

"Also success in love.

"Our happiness, our character and our fortune depend markedly upon single instances.

"This is not as unfair as it seems, because our ability to succeed in a given crisis is based upon the thoroughness with which we are prepared for it.

"The young pianist, for instance, has his opportunity. He has to play a concerto at a grand concert. Thousands of people are watching him. The orchestra is ready. The conductor stands with his baton raised. Now is his chance.

"He must put every atom of skill into that intense quarter of an hour. It is that which will make him or break him.

"But how he carries off that occasion depends ENTIRELY upon what he has been doing for hours and days and weeks preceding. All those long periods of practice, all those long and wearisome and nerve-racking exercises were a mighty getting-ready for this occasion."

It is the drill that makes the soldier.

Drill makes the expert fireman.

Crises comes to all of us—moments when our whole future or life itself turns on the reaction we give to that instant.

But a crisis is no time to think or reason. We must draw upon the thinking we have done previously, and especially upon the stuff we have been feeding into the subconscious.

"Physiologically speaking," says Crane, "a man gets through a crisis better by using his spinal cord than by using his brain. In other words, he can fall back on the power of habit and the accumulated skill of practice much more safely than he can depend upon his immediate judgment."

The most striking fact concerned is this: Every person DOES fall back upon his spinal cord and habit-consciousness whenever he faces a crisis, and what it brings forth will be in EXACT ACCORD with his previous reactions.

Your subconsciousness will bring forth every atom of assistance it can.

If it is enough, all is well. If it is not, you have not fed into it the materials necessary for building the right response.

A man who expects to ride a horse over dangerous country or even for his daily canter through the par must feed him to keep him strong enough to carry his weight.

You must give your subconscious the right thought-food if you want to go through life successfully.

One of Abraham Lincoln's most famous sayings was, "I will study and prepare myself and when the opportunity comes I will be ready for it."

LESSON VI
How to Find the Open Doors to What You Want

> To him who knocks each door unlocks,
> And he who seeks shall find;
> Nothing can keep thee from thine own
> Save thine own slothful mind.

"BEHOLD, I set before you an open door which no man can shut."

That beloved writer, Orison Swett Marden, quotes the above from the Good Book in one of his own good books, and I pass it on to you as a great and glorious fact.

Whatever you really want is waiting for you, and the door leading to it is always and forever open. No man can close YOUR door, and none but YOU can pass through it.

These doors swing always out ward, to larger and larger vistas, to wider and wider fields, to greater and greater heights. Your House of Life is a hall of many mansions, each more beautiful than the last but less lovely than the next.

Whether you choose to occupy only a few of the first small ones and confine your existence within their restricted limits or whether you will pass onward, outward and upward, constantly expanding, developing and growing, till you revel in the beauties and comforts of all, depends entirely upon you.

It does not depend on what you HAVE, but upon what you ARE.

Some of the people who are richest in money exist in wretchedly pinched quarters inside this House of Life, while some who are considered poor are living gloriously in theirs, so happy in its joys, its outlooks and its furnishings that they hardly feel the lack of other riches.

No man can make these people poor. Without a place to lay his head, such a one is rich. He is rich in the THINGS THAT COUNT. The man who possesses only money is never really rich.

However, to be either of these extremes is not necessary nor desirable. The man rich in mental and spiritual development can attain leisure for fuller development and be able to help greater numbers of other men and women if he possesses enough of this world's goods to enable him to devote himself to others. The man rich in money is not necessarily poor in reality, and need not remain so if he is. The most profitable investment for such a one would be to begin at once to devote whatever time, money and energy are necessary to finding his way out of the spiritual two-by-four closets in which he has been living, and into the large, sunny rooms that have been emptily waiting all these years.

To find these wonderful rooms in our House of Life, to achieve more fully, to get what we want, we must learn and apply the great truth that SEVERAL DOORS LEAD TO THE ROOM OF OUR EVERY DESIRE, BUT EVERY ONE IS APPROACHED ONLY FROM THE ADJOINING ROOMS.

There are no alleyways, short-cuts, no windows to be scaled from the outside, no way to reach or keep what we want save by passing through these adjoining rooms.

We can speed up our passage almost unbelievably by the right kind of preparation, as we have shown in the preceding lesson, or we can travel so slowly that we never get beyond the anterooms near the front hall.

That is entirely up to us. The hinges are built for one-way passage only. These wonderful doors swing OUT OF the room you first occupy, and once you have passed through them to something bigger and better you can never go back. Achieve something worth while and never again can you go back and be less than that achievement. By it you have grown and are ready for something bigger.

These doors are of different kinds, sizes and shapes, but each one is a DOOR OF OPPORTUNITY. "Knocks" will not open these doors, a "pull" cannot keep one open very long. PUSH is the thing that does it quickest and swings it widest. Men constantly refer to their chances for advancement as "openings," which they truly are.

These swinging doors of opportunity are always found ajar. They are not locked, bolted, barred or even latched. But to find them and swing them wide enough for you to pass through, YOU must do three things, as follows: LOOK FOR THEM, RECOGNIZE THEM, then PUSH THEM OPEN.

You can stumble over the biggest chance of your life if you are not on the LOOKOUT for it; then it cannot help you unless you RECOGNIZE it; and after all this is attained it can do you no good if you fail to ACT UPON IT. These are facts few people seem to know, and many of those who do know them do not know JUST HOW to go about it to take these three steps.

To make plain the surprisingly simple methods whereby you can do so is the aim of this lesson—an aim that has been accomplished with such clarity that hundreds of men and women throughout this country give it the credit for their success in the everyday world of practical affairs. In the previous lesson we explained Preparation as the foundation for these three steps. When you have built this foundation by GETTING BIG ENOUGH for something better than you now have, be sure there will be plenty of "openings" for you.

It is only the man who is NOT equal to them who lacks opportunities, and even he is surrounded by many he must forego because of his own inadequacy.

Each one of us must admit that we have had many more opportunities than we took advantage of.

To him who is prepared, chances are literally EVERYWHERE.

Get all ready for a thing and nothing under heaven except your own death can keep it away from you. I will give you two widely different illustrations of this law. Have you ever known a super-sensitive, "touchy" person—a woman perhaps who is always expecting to have her "feelings hurt," who is looking for slights, snubs and other wounds?

You who do not have this experience have often wondered why these hateful things were always happening to her. But you need wonder no longer, and you need not waste your time or energy trying to save her from a repetition of them.

She brings them upon herself, and only she herself can ward them off. How does she do it?

First, she is prepared—fully—every time she goes out, for this very thing. She plans how she will act when it happens and what she will say when the blow falls.

Second, she is on the lookout every moment for something of this kind. She is keyed to the highest pitch of expectation and, just as with a violin string, the more taut this tension the less is required to set up a vibration.

She is so concentrated on looking for something of this nature that she misconstrues the most innocent remarks, looks and actions as criticism of herself.

By assuming this she CAUSES those who were entirely innocent even of thinking of her to ridicule her. They would stop if she ceased looking for it.

Being prepared and on the alert for criticism she has studied all of its manifestations and is able to recognize them instantly. She scents it if two people suddenly cease talking at her approach; she recognizes the supposed meaning of their glances while she is with them, and is painfully suspicious of whatever tones, smiles or words are used when she leaves. If these are gleeful she attributes it to the fun they are supposedly having at her expense. If she hears or sees nothing indicative of this she concludes they are evidently too clever to betray themselves. And if by any chance her name is mentioned she catches it clear across the room. Though their conversation be carried on in whispers so low that nothing else is distinguishable to her, this one word rings out clearly.

She has now taken the four steps which form the foundation for what has occurred—expectation, preparation, concentration and recognition.

She expects to be slighted, so she makes preparations for it. Being prepared to meet it, she keeps on the lookout for it, and by keeping on the lookout for it she recognizes it when it isn't there as well as when it is.

All these lead inevitably to the next step: She DOES SOMETHING ABOUT IT—in other words, ACTS on it.

This action starts it all over again—by RE-CREATING the conditions, RE-SEEDING the soil in her own subconscious. This keeps her chronically in the MOOD, and the mood keeps the seed alive and growing, not only in her own mind and body but, by suggestion, also keeps planting it in the minds of others. You can see plainly how this happens. When she hears someone mention her name she instantly decides it must have been IN CRITICISM, and in one way or another, directly or indirectly—but inevitably—she displays her resentment, pique, anger or hurt.

All these are destructive moods and cause even one's best friends to become disgusted after a while, until they too begin to grow tired and to avoid her. They naturally make explanations to others as to WHY they were compelled to do it and this suggests the condition to a still larger circle.

Those who were not her friends and who may perhaps have said or done things to wound her are only further antagonized by the reaction she gives to the gossip, while those who were neither friend nor foe are gradually moved to the opposition by her own actions, suspicious tendencies and too sensitive nerves.

These ACTIONS on her part complete the vicious circle and start all the trouble over again.

What we EXPECT we PREPARE for; what we prepare for we LOOK for; what we look for we are sure to find, and, by reason of sharpened sensibilities, certain to RECOGNIZE.

Then when we recognize this thing which we have anticipated for so long, we ACT.

This action is the ripened fruit of Expectation.

You can go one step farther back and see that our expectations are caused by our dominant moods.

For those of you who would like a moment's review, I will go back to the real root of it all—the things that make our moods—our THOUGHTS.

Now because WE control our own thoughts, it is not difficult for any intelligent person to see that we directly and indirectly control our own lives and practically everything that happens to us.

He who diligently seeks will find. He will find because there are several potential doors to each thing we want and he will always discover at least one of these doors.

If he seeks the good he will find the good. If looks for the bad he will find the bad. The good always find good in everybody. The bad always find the bad.

Both good and bad qualities are in us all. What we bring OUT of ourselves and other people is the important thing. We always and forever bring out of people, out of life, out of our environment, out of ourselves, out of our future—ON THE WHOLE—the very things we are on the lookout for.

"Look-out" is the mother of "Bring-out." What we bring out is the measure of our success or failure.

I once knew a man who held a position where it was necessary for him to meet and deal with several thousand people a day.

These thousands came nightly to a large auditorium where each naturally wanted the very best seat he could get, and it was this man's business to see that everyone got fair play. "Equal rights to all and special privileges to none" was the motto and he did his best, in the face of odds, to see that it was carried out.

Despite the unpleasant things that could have happened and those which certainly would had a "touchy" person been in charge, this man kept ninety-nine out of every hundred happy, contented and in a constructive frame of mind toward him. He looked for the best in everybody. Though ten minutes before he might have had to make them vacate the crowded aisle or get up from a nice soft seat on the stairway to stand or be turned away from the auditorium altogether, in obedience to the fire ordinance, he always EXPECTED them to see why he had to do it and to like and respect him for it.

He LOOKED only for this kind of response from everybody. He RECOGNIZED it as soon as it came, and ACTED upon it to the extent of ACKNOWLEDGING it.

Find the Open Doors

He LIVED these rules, and acquired not only immediate rewards as he went along but by doing so ultimately opened a still wider door for himself to larger opportunities and greater achievements.

Make good, and SOMEWHERE, SOMEHOW the world will find it out and give you something higher up.

The slogan which, more than any other, helped me to see this and to get ready for bigger things was given in a speech to us high-school students out in the Rocky Mountains one afternoon many years ago by Dr. Frank H. H. Roberts of the University of Denver. He said:

"Make every occasion a great occasion, for you know not when Fate is taking your measure for a higher and better position in life." A thousand times since that day I have gone to appointments with audiences and persons and met situations that were not up to my hopes. Many of these times I have been very deeply immersed in something much more to my liking and sometimes I have been tempted "just for this once" to prepare for it hastily, cut it short or cancel it altogether.

But as sure as I waver, this slogan comes to my mind and I pull myself together, make the best preparation I know how, and go in the spirit of one who is to meet not the person or audience or situation alone, but Fate herself.

That I have met her face to face on more than one of these occasions and have found her strangely missing when I supposed she and I had a rendezvous, is the way of life.

Looking back now I can see, as anyone can who will look, the very days and hours when she took a hand in my affairs and swung wide some great door that I had vainly sought for a long time.

Only yesterday there came to me through the mails something that looks insignificant to everybody else, but which is to me the crack-line opening in a door I have sought for many years. Just enough light comes through that crack to reveal to me the wide and wonderful possibilities in the room to which it leads, and to convince me that they are worth all the work and waiting. At the risk of making this lesson and the preceding one sound like a matrimonial record, I must tell you another true love story which proves the truth of the slogan above quoted. About two years after hearing Dr. Roberts and this "every occasion" slogan I repeated it to a young woman friend of mine and she put it to use too. Like every normal person she was hoping some day to be married. But she was plain to the point of ugliness and had not much to recommend her in other ways. But she had one thing—persistence.

I met her eleven years later in Chicago and though I had forgotten all about telling her my "success slogan" she reminded me of it and said she was living by it just as nearly as she could.

She was plainer than ever, but now she had learned what went best with her particular kind of plainness. She still was not intellectual in the least nor did she pretend to anything of the sort. She stuck to the things she was interested in and made herself master of them.

I know where I am most effective," she explained, "and I concentrate on that. I also know what I can't do or be, and I let those things alone. I may never find a nice man to marry me, but I will have had a grand time looking for him, anyhow.

"Merely living is a great game if you play it with all your might as I am doing. I haven't had one single beau, but I'm not discouraged."

I asked her for more details, for I knew I was looking at one of the few young women I had ever known who was seriously, earnestly absorbed in self-improvement and who had a definite purpose. "Well," she answered, "to begin with, I do all the things I've just told you. In general, that is. Then in particular I have selected a line of work which brings me in contact with a large number of the finest men in the city of Chicago. Some day I shall find the one who is meant for me.

"I never go ANYWHERE without looking for him. I never go anywhere without being ready to meet him. I never go anywhere without EXPECTING to meet him.

"Every time I dress to go to work in the morning, to a lecture or theater in the evening or to church on Sunday I try to realize HE may be there, and I do everything just as I would did I KNOW he would be.

"In other words, and between you and me, I always try to dress and act and talk and conduct myself as though my 'intended' were watching me. I think of every occasion as 'a great occasion' because of this."

Ten years later I talked with her again and yearned for the success on which her heart was still as firmly set as ever. I knew that if she was, WAY DOWN DEEP, still looking and preparing, THE man must appear some day, but oh, how I longed for him to come quickly!

She was then nearing forty — still plain but, as a result of her years of effort and care, a truly distinguished looking woman.

In trying to live up to her ideal she had developed a very attractive personality. This had won her an ever-widening circle of friends among the finest of the people she contacted in business.

Find the Open Doors

The last time I passed through Chicago she introduced me to her home on Lake Shore Drive and to her handsome, devoted husband!

"We were married the very day before my fortieth birthday," she explained. His explanation was even more interesting.

"I was fifty myself and had never married because I considered matrimony an unsafe risk," he said, "Most of the women I knew were undependable—putting up a fine show when an eligible man appeared in the offing, but slumping back when alone with women, and failing generally to 'live up to the sample.'

"I watched Rona for several years, with no idea of marrying her. When I began to admire and like her I started testing her to see when she would deteriorate like all the rest. I contrived a hundred unexpected times and ways to see her—after a hard day of work when she was tired, after she had, to my knowledge, lost a good deal of money to a worthless relative, and a good many other times. "But she was always the same—100 per cent. After keeping tab on her for two years and a half I couldn't wait any longer to tell her how much I cared for her, and this is the sequel." One of the most dramatic things to me was that this man was on the very verge of proposing to her at the time of my previous visit when I was so anxious for her to find happiness quickly. Fate was waiting just around the corner, and we never suspected it!

She was nearing the great door she had looked for so long—and found it largely because she did not despair, but KEPT LOOKING, with the enthusiasm and earnestness of old.

Harriet Beecher Stowe said, "When everything goes against you and it seems as if you couldn't hold out a minute longer, NEVER give up then, for that is just the place and time the tide will turn." These great laws apply equally in the world of business and every other field of human endeavor.

Hundreds of office workers have asked me why they were not getting as much pay as they should, and why they were always refused when they asked for a raise.

They have been especially anxious to know why others who had been with the firm a shorter period were often promoted over them and given higher salaries.

As this happens to an average of about a million people every working day throughout this country, it is an interesting subject.

If you are not getting more pay now than you were a year ago you are violating the very rules that lead to financial advancement.

Take a good, straight look at yourself and see.

First of all, I have said to them as I now say to you: What have you been doing to PREPARE for higher pay?

Do you know more? Have you studied your job to see wherein you could do MORE and BETTER and QUICKER work than you were doing last year?

Remember, your merely having BEEN THERE a long time is no reason whatever for any firm's raising your pay. In fact it is a reason for lowering it if you are NOT IMPROVING. For the man who is not going forward is sliding back.

If you are doing your work this year no better than you were last, you are not doing it as well.

This may not sound right at first, but read it again and then think it over.

Second, when you went to ask for your raise you did not EXPECT to get it. You fully expected to be turned down and even had your answer ready and your conduct planned for that very thing. In most cases you had, all rehearsed and waiting, the speech you would make to the rest of the force when you confided to them your experience with the boss. Third, if you found no ways to improve your work and thus to secure a raise, it was because you did not LOOK for them.

There is not a job in the world nor any piece of work, however small, that is at this moment being done as well or efficiently or quickly or economically as it COULD BE.

Keep your eyes open for some or all of these and you will find them. Fourth, you have been stepping and stumbling all over these weak spots in your job without RECOGNIZING them.

Furthermore, all kinds of ways for promoting yourself have been right under your nose and you also failed to recognize THEM.

Fifth, if you have recognized ways for improving your work but have DONE NOTHING ABOUT IT, still it will do you no good. One or all of these things you have failed to do if you are not getting a bigger pay envelope than you were this time last year.

Look yourself over and see in which one or two of these requirements you are naturally weak. Do you merely "hope" for a raise without ever expecting to get one—with the dejected spirit that says, "Oh, I HOPE so—but"?

This kind of bluff never fools your great subconscious factory one minute. It knows that the "but" and the tone of your voice tell your true mood and give your real order—which it proceeds to deliver.

Do you really look and search for chances to be promoted, but never get around to DESERVING a higher place? Do you tend to look for a loophole somewhere, through which you may squeeze yourself into something better? It can't be done. Every loophole is being watched, just like the entrance to the big league ball games, and anybody who tries to slip through gets caught and sent back.

People who are brainy enough to build a successful business are not so blind, especially concerning human nature, as to leave holes in the fence!

If this is not your weakness, perhaps you are of the opposite kind—a plodder who works his head off for a big concern without protecting his own interests sufficiently to let the right man know of his existence.

As between the over-prepared man of reserve and the under-prepared man of nerve, the prizes all too often go to the latter. True, he cannot keep them if he does not buckle in and hurry to fill the new place—but one needs some of both.

GET READY, then don't fail to let the boss know you ARE ready. "Let your work speak for you" is a wonderful motto. You will not get far nor stay where you get unless it does. But it talks only one language and there are others. Every business concern wants two things in every one of its workers who meet the outside world— efficiency and self-confidence.

If you lack the self-confidence to stand up for yourself and your own advancement, the boss knows you will never be able to GO OUT AND GET BUSINESS. It is the one who can BRING IN BUSINESS, not merely do it afterward, who gets the best pay in the long run. If you have prepared for and looked for opportunities but have found none, it may be possible that you have what is to you a blind-alley job. Either it has few possibilities or you do not happen to have the type of mind that is adapted to this particular kind of work.

James J. Hill said, "Two men may be in the same office working side by side in the same line, one a decided success and the other almost a failure. But this does not necessarily mean that the successful one is more brilliant or able than the other.

"In fact I have often found that the failure was a failure in that particular place because his mind did not happen to be built for this kind of work but for something far better." If you have done your level best in the way of preparation; if you have then looked for and taken advantage of every opening to better yourself; if you have brought the attention of those in authority to your conscientious work, your willingness, loyalty and resourcefulness, yet still have made no progress—it is certain you have "worked out your mine," as the Westerners say, and should look elsewhere.

But never fear, your preparation in this place will be rewarded in the next. It will stand you in hand when you least expect it to. It has already developed you, whether you now realize it or not, and the larger place is waiting for the larger man it has made of you.

You will be better able to find the next opportunity and to utilize it. John Blake, that writer of inspiring short talks which appear in many newspapers daily, said:

"If you picked up a diamond in the rough you would probably toss it away again. Without training you would not know it was a diamond.

"Every day you pass by, unnoticing, opportunities that other men instantly recognize and bend to their uses.

"Your neglect is not your fault. Without preparation you cannot expect to recognize your opportunity. For many years people regarded anthracite coal as useless black stone—too soft for building material, too hard for fuel.

"One day somebody discovered that in the proper stove it would burn better than bituminous coal, and make no smoke. From that day it became a valuable commodity.

"Don't expect opportunity to come and introduce itself to you. Don't expect it even to knock at your door.

"You must learn to look for it. You must learn to see in some particular position a chance of advancement that other positions lack, although these others may pay far better wages just now.

"You must learn to see in some calling an interest that will enlist your enthusiasm.

"The men who get important places and hold them are the men who not only are searching for opportunity, but have learned to recognize it when they see it. "You cannot be a lucky gold hunter unless you find out where the gold is likely to be, and what it looks like in the quartz or gold-bearing sand.

"And opportunity, which is far finer gold than any that is buried in the earth, is still harder to recognize, but fortunately NOT ANYTHING LIKE SO RARE."

Here are a few keys to some of the greater doors of opportunity:

Key 1. TIME. Invest your time, don't merely "spend" it.

He will go farthest and fastest who best utilizes his time.

Every person has more or less spare time—enough to remake his life if he would use it properly. No one need lack for opportunity as long as he has a few hours a day to use as he chooses. The first great difference you will find between the failures and the successes is that the failures have not considered their time worth much, while the successful have always seen in it their greatest capital. Whenever you hear a man talking about having so much time on his hands "to kill," you are looking at one who is headed straight downhill.

But when you find someone, of any age or station, who puts a premium on his time, you are looking at one who is going to climb.

No matter how long your working day may be, you have certain hours each day or week that belong to you. If you will organize your time outside of office hours you can increase your ability, chances and bank account. Time-wasters never find the big doors of opportunity. One of the chief reasons for Franklin's fame was his determination to use all his time for worth-while things.

He tells in his Autobiography how he pledged himself never to waste a single moment. Of course this was a little extreme, but holding it up as a standard for himself had much to do with his becoming one of the most outstanding men of the day in which he lived.

Nothing in the world can hold you back if you use your spare time wisely.

This habit brings many incidental blessings as well as the wonderful direct ones. Here are a few:

It keeps our minds on something worthy and keeps them away from the trashy thoughts that soon infest the idler's head. (Ever listen to the conversation of a street corner loafer?)

It keeps us out of temptation. ("The devil finds work for idle hands to do.") It keeps us away from those who would harm us. (Those who prey upon mankind avoid the time-savers and concentrate on the only ones who are good "prospects"—the people who place no value on time.)

It keeps us out of wrong environments. (The worst places in the world are those where most time is thrown away by the most ignorant people, and the best are those where intelligent ones gather to improve their time and their minds.)

Ask any criminal how he got his downward start and he will tell you it began with the misuse of his spare hours.

Ask any successful, happy man how he got his start and it will not be five minutes until you hear something like this: "I began to use my spare time for self-improvement. I read and studied. I especially studied myself and my abilities."

In my younger days I wrote on a big newspaper that made a specialty of studying the life stories of great men and women. In interviewing them I made the discovery that they had, without a single exception, capitalized their spare time.

Not one of them had money or opportunities to start with. On the contrary, they had less than the average. But they rose to the heights.

Each had made a practice of throwing no more time away than was absolutely necessary. Each had thought of his time as his great opportunity and by employing it properly found many other chances waiting when the time came.

Regardless of where you are now, you can go pretty nearly as far as you please if you will start TODAY to invest the hours you have been throwing away.

If you cannot plan any special program just at this moment don't let this keep you from doing something helpful with the time which must elapse until you can decide on a schedule. Begin this very evening to apply your precious hours to something worth while.

Read a dictionary if nothing else is available. You will be surprised how much you can learn in ten minutes that you never supposed was in it!

Make up a definite program as soon as possible, but meanwhile don't throw hours away.

If no better plan suggests itself go out alone for a long walk this evening and THINK OUT what you want to become and to have, and the best way to start toward it from the spot where you are right now.

If you have been in the habit of "killing" this best friend you have every few evenings by dropping into a trashy movie, a pool room or the home of shallow, selfish, superficial people, sit down all by yourself and answer this question:

"How much better off am I for all the cheap shows I have seen? Did they ever open for me a door toward better things?"

You will realize they have slammed many a one in your face. Are you better off today for the golden evenings you have whiled away with ambitionless excitement-seekers?

On the contrary, you have lost many a dollar, many a good night's rest and many a good chance by doing so. How much farther along the road of health, happiness and success are you as a result of listening to gossip, talking about people or exposing the weak points in the other fellow's armor?

But you have fallen back many a mile for it.

How much gain in health, happiness or success can you credit to the habit of drifting with "the crowd" evening after evening?

You want more money, more recognition, more opportunities. Ever have anybody step up and say, "Here's a raise, John. I saw you out late with that gay crowd last night."

Ever get a letter in the mail which read, "Dear George: I have been watching your record. I see you haven't missed a vaudeville or one of the Follies in over a year. I don't believe you have missed a single jazzy thing of any kind lately. Come over and accept a good position with my firm at a substantial raise."

Ever have this experience: Meet some big employer as you came out of a pool room at eleven P. M. and have him say, "Why, hello there, young man! I'm looking for some body of brains, vision and efficiency to take charge of a department at a fine salary, and I figured here was the place to find one."

You fine young women who want a nice home and husband and children some day, did you ever have a young man who's working for the best in life (and who will get it because he capitalizes his OWN spare time) say to you, "I want you to marry me because I notice you never spend an evening at home. The minute dinner's over out you fly till goodness-know's-when, and I've decided you'd be a wonderful wife."

I can hear some of you saying, "If we stayed home every night and studied our heads off we'd NEVER get married! You have to keep going to meet anybody!"

Yes, to meet just anybody. But to GET one who is SOMEBODY and have him for your very own you've got to be SOMEBODY yourself, and you can't be if you spend your spare time like the anybodies.

Key 2. SPIRIT.

Approach every person, situation and condition—everything in your life—in the RIGHT SPIRIT.

By this is meant the spirit of fairness (not trying to get anything that is not rightfully yours); the spirit of tolerance (for everyone, regardless of what his faults may be); the spirit of kindness (toward all mankind); and the spirit of truth (the best of which you are aware). You will see from this rule and the one which immediately follows that the doors of opportunity are of many kinds, each important to our full development and progress.

You cannot expect those leading to better things to be thrown open to you if, in your own soul, you have closed the doors of your heart to your fellow man.

I have known many ordinary people to go high and far, to attain the best that life holds, owing almost wholly to their loving-kindness and tolerance.

Sam Walter Foss, one of the most beloved American poets, rose to fame upon the homely songs he sung to voice his love for common, everyday folks. The thing for which Abraham Lincoln became most famous and for which he will be loved longest was the love and tolerance he bore toward all mankind. I have known many others of great and glowing mentality who missed not only greatness but the very necessities of life because they thought only of themselves.

Approaching life in the right spirit will cause hundreds of doors you would otherwise miss to swing noiselessly open for you.

As you pass through them to deeper, wider, fuller life and a nobler future you will sometimes FEEL them held open for you by unseen hands to which your own—perhaps years ago—were stretched out in mercy, generosity or friendliness.

Key 3. PERSONALITY.

Study your own and develop it. You have certain personality traits and tendencies—some good, some negative and some neutral.

Try by every means at your command to discover what these are, not with a view merely to satisfying natural curiosity about yourself, but with the determination to weed out the negative, bring out the neutral and cultivate the good.

Personality will open one of the widest of Opportunity's doors.

Through an attractive personality, more quickly than by any other means, you may rise to fame and fortune.

If your personality is unattractive you do not find this big door which leads so straightly and surely and swiftly into better things, and may be compelled by long and arduous effort to seek out smaller, remoter ones to reach the room of your desires.

You have sometimes wondered why friends, promotions and business opportunities which you felt you had EARNED by hard work passed you by.

This is because hard work never brings the greatest things in life. It helps. It is one of the great essentials, but there are others of even greater importance, and one of these is personality. The people who work HARDEST often get the least pay and make little progress. We know today that hard work, unless backed by head work and heart work, will never carry one to the heights. Because we must live with, work with, associate with and deal with OTHER PEOPLE it behooves us to know all we can about THE power of all others which repels or attracts people — one's own personality.

Attractive personality makes others like us, want to be with us, promote us and help us.

Have you ever stopped to ask yourself what your acquaintances think of you?

Do they like you, dislike you, or simply forget you?

Do you think you make a good "first impression" or the wrong impression?

Did It ever occur to you that every individual you meet affects you in one of three ways within five minutes after he begins to speak to you, and that this is also true of every person who meets YOU?

I call these the Five I's. You can remember them by printing this little table on your mind: I

IMPRESS everybody who meets me in one of these three ways: either I IRRITATE them, INTEREST them, or leave them INDIFFERENT to me — Which?

It is impossible for you to meet anyone and talk with him without feeling toward him in one of these three ways. Asked to explain why you feel as you do or to specify what you like or dislike, you may not be able to do so.

We can explain only that which is clear to our conscious minds, and the reason for this impression is not always conscious. But you have a very definite SUBCONSCIOUS impression. The less you can explain it the more deep-rooted it is likely to be. Such a feeling started the well known little verse:

> "I do not like you, Doctor Fell,
> The reason why I cannot tell;
> I only know and know full well
> I do not like you, Doctor Fell."

On the other hand, you like certain people instantly. Others leave you with the feeling that you have been looking at a blank space on the wall.

Each impression is due to the personality of the individual himself.

To begin to understand your own, it will be well for you to ask yourself the following questions: Which of my traits do people like? Which do they dislike?

What in my manner, expression voice, personal appearance or attitude has been interfering with my success?

How can I make people ENJOY seeing me, doing business with me, visiting with me, listening to me, working with me?

Which do I have more of—friends or enemies?

Do I have more or fewer friends than most of the people I associate with?

How can I put my best foot forward in every instance, and keep it there? What should I do to make more people remember me kindly, speak to me constructively, think of me frequently and seek me happily?

Is it not possible that there may be something in my own personality that causes almost everybody to treat me in certain ways?

Have I any unpleasant mannerisms?

What do I do that "rubs people the wrong way"? What, within myself, is holding me back? What, within myself, sometimes causes people to impose on me, neglect me, criticise me?

Why do I not get more invitations from the people and to the places I would most enjoy?

Why have I lost friends in the past?

What, more than anything else about me, do most people seem to admire? Is this thing REAL or only an affectation?

There are many more such questions, but these will give you a fair idea of the kinds of things to look for in yourself. It is essential that you correct them if you want the great door of Opportunity to swing wide for you.

A man's personality, utterly regardless of his merits or faults, can induce us to long to promote him or to hold him back; long to help him or to see him fight it out alone; long to vote for him or to see him defeated; sacrifice ourselves for him or pass him by.

The same is true of your own.

Though you possess beauty, brains, money and position, yet have a repellent personality, you can live and die unloved and unsuccessful.

Though you have none of these, yet develop a winning personality, you may acquire by this alone almost anything you desire. Ugliness, poverty, obscurity—these are but pebbles in the pathway to those of a magnetic personality. Learn to do this by eliminating the negative, obviating the neutral and cultivating the affirmative traits of your own nature. The location of many of the great doors of opportunity can best be discovered by studying yourself. Often they will open for YOU when they would not for others, because you hold the key to them in your own innate capacities.

Key 4. HEALTH.

Safeguard your health. The average man is committing suicide by inches, digging his grave with his teeth and driving nails into his own coffin with stimulants, dissipation, lack of rest or other forms of bodily abuse.

That he does so ignorantly and innocently does not alter the facts nor minimize their results.

Every person should avail himself of science's latest discoveries about food, care of the body, longevity and vitality. Certain foods, especially meat, which have long composed much of our American dietary have been found to be useless and some actually harmful, while others which we have always neglected we now know are far more nutritious. If you wish to be equal to your big chances when they come, you must have a strong body, a steady nerve and plenty of physical energy. These are easy to acquire if you will live according to the laws of your body and not according to the dictates of your appetites. Overweight is dangerous and extreme underweight is also.

A certain amount of exercise, of the KIND YOU REALLY ENJOY, is necessary to bodily vigor.

Eight hours of sleep is necessary for the average man or woman. Stimulants, late parties, dissipation of your vital energies through harmful channels of any kind cut down the quantity of life and ruin its quality. Take care of your health even if it does prevent your going out socially once in a while. Trying to keep up with their neighbors or to outshine them has slammed Opportunity's door in the faces of many worthy men and women.

Without health all the wealth in the world would be useless to you.

Health cannot be bought, borrowed or stolen—but it CAN be conserved.

Key 5. THE CONSCIOUS MIND.

Guard your THINKING.

Destructive thought has killed more people than all the wars. Worry wrecks more homes and ruins more happiness than all other inimical forces combined.

Make it your business during the next year to watch your thinking and make it constructive ALL THE TIME, in accordance with what we have taught in the first lessons of this course and in our other course, "Practical Psychology."

The latter explains the conscious mind, its powers and possibilities, as the present course explains the subconscious.

Watch your visualizations. Always picture yourself in the position YOU WISH TO OCCUPY, never in your present one or in any position of unhappiness.

No matter what the bare facts may be at the time, no matter how discouraging the actual conditions, no matter how depressing your situation or environment—REFUSE TO THINK OF THESE THINGS. Turn your attention to other and better things, preferably to something you want. Every time it reverts to the unhappy present turn it gently but persistently in the direction of your desires.

Key 6. YOUR BRAIN.

Learn as much about the human brain as you can. Yours operates in accordance with certain very definite laws. Much information concerning the KIND of brain, IN GENERAL, that any man possesses can be seen from the GENERAL proportions of his head.

I am not referring to the old phrenology, but to the new science of Brainology which is based on brain anatomy, and upon the new discoveries about brain areas.

Much of phrenology was scientific.

It became discredited only when the unscientific attempted to exploit it.

Key 7. YOUR INDIVIDUALITY.

In addition to a study of your personality, which is best defined as "the sum total of what you express to the world," give earnest thought to your own INDIVIDUALITY—that is, the PARTICULAR qualities which, more than all others, seem to constitute the core and kernel of YOU.

Make up your mind to be YOURSELF, to fill the place YOU were born to fill, to think your own thoughts, live your own life to the fullest, highest and best of which you are capable.

Learn to BELIEVE IN YOURSELF, not conceitedly, egotistically nor vainly, but with the self-confidence born of the realization that you CAN do what you want to do.

It is what you ARE that counts in the end, and long before the end.

WORTH, ABILITY, CHARACTER and INDIVIDUALITY are so rare, so valuable and so much in demand that yours will be rewarded more fully and quickly than you can believe, once you develop them and give the world a chance to see them.

You are unique. No one quite like you ever lived before, and none exactly like you will ever live again.

Make the most of your DIFFERENTNESS.

Find the Open Doors

When you are misjudged, criticised, ridiculed or misunderstood just remember that every person who ever amounted to a hill of beans WAS criticised. But seldom by his betters. When a man tells an unkind story on another he is telling a worse one on himself.

So long as people talk about you, you are not dead. Also, people do not take the trouble to criticise those they consider their inferiors.

As a matter of fact, the highest compliment that can be paid to you by certain kinds of people is their criticism. That it is unintended only makes it that much more genuine.

Key 8. YOUR RIGHT VOCATION. If you want one of the very largest, widest doors of all to open to you and later on to open many others for you, study one more thing about yourself — what you would LOVE to do. To begin to get an accurate idea of the kind of vocation you were born to follow, if you do not already know this, think back and ask yourself WHAT KINDS OF THINGS YOU ENJOYED DOING IN YOUR TEENS.

In other words, what KINDS of ACTIVITIES did you engage in during that time, OF YOUR OWN FREE WILL, DURING LEISURE and VACATION TIME? Here is an amazing and fascinating fact recently discovered: EVERY PERSON WHO HAS SUCCEEDED SIGNALLY IN ANY VOCATION HAD SHOWN A DECIDED GRAVITATION TOWARD ITS ACTIVITIES BETWEEN HIS OR HER TWELFTH AND TWENTIETH YEARS. The great subconscious mind never sleeps, never rests and never forgets. If you will get into the work you love, it will find doors of opportunity for you that you cannot now even dream of.

What we love to do, the subconscious mind is ALWAYS CONCENTRATED UPON.

For this reason it forever seeks out newer and better ways of approaching perfection in anything we love. Every invention and every improvement of importance in any line has always been worked out in the subconscious mind of SOMEBODY WHO LOVED THAT KIND OF ACTIVITY and whose mind, therefore, worked on it AUTOMATICALLY, DAY AND NIGHT, ASLEEP or AWAKE. You will never do your highest or best outside of work you love. And no matter what your age may be you could soon outstrip competition if you would enter the vocation you have always loved.

This success will come to you for two big reasons, first, because your subconscious is full of ability along this very line and will give it to you immediately; second, because most of your competitors will have gone into it without enthusiasm, and THEIR subconscious minds therefore give them no such assistance.

Key 9. PERSONAL APPEARANCE.

Take pride in your dress, grooming, cleanliness, taste and general appearance.

Your personal appearance is a walking advertisement. If the business in which you are engaged is owned by another, your poor appearance discredits his business, and he resents it. If you take pains with your personal self you are a better reflection of him and his business and he appreciates it. I do not mean that you should dress expensively—quite the contrary. But you should dress neatly, and in clean linen; so quietly that no one is conscious of what you have on, but aware, subconsciously, that you look well.

Kathleen Norris says, "A woman is well dressed when she can bear the closest scrutiny of others, but when nobody turns to look."

Certain colors, styles and lines go best with your particular complexion, figure, age and height. Learn what these are and use them. You will find that confining yourself to the few colors and shades most becoming to you will enable you to dress far more becomingly yet more reasonably than you have been doing.

Key 10. THE FIVE TYPES.

People, like all other creatures of every species, fall into general classifications. The Five Biological Types are science's most recent grouping.

This classification is also more fundamental and simple than previous ones.

Certain people, by reason of their power or position, often command important doors through which you should pass if you are to make the greatest progress in the shortest period of time.

Your boss, chief clerk, the president of the concern, your neighbor, your employee, your friend or loved one—all of these affect your life. Any of them may hold a key to the very door which comes next in your onward march. They command the next step up, as it were, and their approval or disapproval, assistance or resistance may make or mar your chances at a critical moment.

After a study of your own nature and of general human psychology an understanding of EACH OF THE HUMAN TYPES will often help you in winning such a one. Also it will help you greatly in recognizing your own weak and strong points.

Human Analysis teaches you how to avoid what each type always resents, and how to approach and deal with each in the manner his type always prefers. For instance, certain things which always please a fat man always displease a thin one; certain methods which always win a florid, high-chested man irritate the pale, long faced one; treatment which appeals to the small man irritates the large one; and certain actions which leave other types unruffled arouse instant and fiery anger in another.

These and hundreds of other vital factors can be seen at a glance when you have familiarized yourself with the meaning of bodily size, shape and structure.

Remember that EVERY PERSON YOU MEET can in some degree help you onward or hold you back, and that he will do the one or the other largely as a result of your treatment of him PERSONALLY.

An understanding of the Five Types of human beings gives you a pass key to many doors.

LESSON VII

How to Make Your Desires Materialize

WE have now covered the first laps toward the land of Heart's Desire. Through Definiteness we decided on our destination. We took the first stride toward it through Affirmation. By Preparation we came a long way, and as we came nearer we recognized (in the last lesson) several entrance gates to the City of Our Dreams.

It now remains for us only to pay the toll and pass through. The beauties inside the Great City far over balance the fee, but it must always be paid before we can enter.

Each gate is a toll-gate but unlike a toll-gate in that ONCE YOU HAVE PAID THE FEE for that particular gate you need never pay again to enter it. Always thereafter this gate is open to you to leave or enter at will.

But if you wish to enter other sections of the Beautiful City you must go outside and enter from their front gates also, paying each ITS fee, after which THAT section is forever open to you to roam in as you choose.

For although each constitutes a part of the Wonderful City, each is separated from the others like the old Roman cities where each section could be entered only from the great outer walls.

Thus it is that any person may travel through any part or as many parts as he desires. If he prefers a restricted existence rather than pay the entrance fee, no one can make him go farther. But if he desires the widest knowledge, the richest experiences, the fullest success, he may, by paying the price for each, attain the right to roam at will through any and all that please him.

Look around you and you will see that the vast majority of people make the former choice.

They live and die in a few sections on the outskirts of life. They think in a few areas of their brains. They run the gamut of a few emotions over and over. They pay the price for a few of life's necessities and let it go at that.

The sad part of it is that they put forth as much effort to maintain themselves in these narrow existences as would be required to earn the toll-price into the larger ones. For although the fee itself is greater the farther you go, the easier and easier does it become to earn it. We face new problems and bigger ones but they are easier to solve than the first ones because we have developed.

It is this which makes it possible for the successful to be more successful with little effort; for the rich to make millions; for those who are already famous to win thousands of friends where the unloved and unknown make but one new friend a year, or none. Only those realize this who have tried it. The others remain behind because they assume that if it costs so much in hard work to get through the FIRST few gateways, going farther and doing more with one's life would require more strain and struggle than they are willing to make more than it is worth.

Each human being must decide this for himself.

But the greatest secret of the successful is that the GREATER THE NUMBER OF SUCCESS THE EASIER BECOMES THE GATHERING OF THE PRICE, AND THE RICHER THE JOYS BROUGHT BY EACH.

In other words, THE GREATER THE WORTH THE EASIER THE PRICE.

The distance we cover depends on the number of hurdles we are able to take and the speed with which we cover the distance between.

We may run along for quite a while on smooth ground, thinking "Everything's going to be smooth from here on," but pretty soon looming up ahead we descry an obstacle. It may be a low one which we scarcely notice. Or it may be a high one.

If we refuse to scale it, thinking it looks impossible, or if we are tired of running, we can stop right there and our progress ends. The Scorer marks us up on the Big Board as having gotten so far.

But if we draw upon our courage we will always find that this hurdle, high and forbidding though it appears, is nothing compared to some of the first ones, BECAUSE WE HAVE DEVELOPED STRENGTH from jumping those before—a strength we are not aware of till we put it to the test, but which never fails us if we take a good running jump and TRY FOR IT.

All along the track you will see splendid human souls who might have gone over the top and on under the wire as winners with the cheers and love of the multitude from Life's grandstand to gladden them.

But they didn't know it. They sank down beside the track and now watch the others pass them by. There come times in every human life when the game doesn't seem worth the candle. But it is. When the price looks bigger than the prize. But it never is.

The price is always less, when you come right down to paying it, than it looks to be—just as a piece of work looks impossible as long as you postpone it but is suddenly easy when you begin.

Life always lets you make your own decisions and she takes you at your word. Your words always express themselves in your secret attitudes.

To try to fool others is bad enough, but to fool yourself is fatal. You never can really fool your subconsciousness. It knows whether you really WANT a thing or not, and whether you are in earnest. If you are not it lets you alone. But if you are it will FIND A WAY. It will help you get what you really want MOST.

You may not believe it at first glance, but many poverty-stricken, sick, shiftless failures ALREADY HAVE WHAT THEY WANT MOST IN LIFE.

They won't admit it to you, but in their inmost souls they know it is true. They don't really want riches, health and success MOST. They only WISH they wanted these things most.

What they REALLY WANT MOST OF ALL is DOING WHAT THEY PLEASE WITH THEIR TIME, TAKING THINGS EASY, SLEEPING LATE, OVEREATING, BEING FREE OF RESPONSIBILITIES—and they are GETTING EVERY ONE OF THEM!

They delude themselves with the notion that they are getting them for nothing–that success, health and happiness would cost more. But the fact is that they are paying the HIGHEST PRICE for the worst articles when THE VERY BEST could be had at a bargain.

If you have ever seen a man trying to get out of work, you know that he worked twice as hard at it as those who pitched in and did something.

If you have ever seen one of those women who, as they constantly phrase it, "had to save herself," you have seen one who wore herself out at the job.

If you have ever seen a self-pampering invalid or a self-pitying person of any sort you have seen some one who worked. Like a Trojan twenty-four hours a day and got nothing for it but the disease he was looking for, the troubles he anticipated and the poverty he feared. Meanwhile he enjoyed the things he really wanted most-idleness, weakness, pretense—and HE KNOWS IT.

Your great subconscious will get for you THE THINGS YOU WANT MOST IN LIFE. It will do so more completely and more quickly than you can believe. It will do so with unerring accuracy and unfaltering, unswerving perfection.

If you want happiness, success, fame, it will show you how to get them. They must be paid for, but the price is not as high as you think, not even as great as that we pay for failure.

I often think of the world as a colossal department store. In it are all the things we want, displayed on the counters within reach of all, and to be had the moment we pay for them.

If we really want the things we SAY we want, we will do what we always do to get the things we want in the store—walk up and pay for them and TAKE them.

You see something you say you want. But if you are not willing to pay for it, Life knows you only wish for it.

Offer to pay her the price and you will hear her whisper, "This isn't really as expensive as marked. I will give you a reduction"—and she takes off a large percentage.

A friend in Denver once told me she "wanted a new spring suit more than anything." We were walking down Sixteenth Street a few days later and there in a front window she saw the VERY suit she was looking for—for $35. (In the olden days $35 actually bought a suit good enough for anybody, you remember!)

How lovely!" I exclaimed "and to think You have the $35 right in your purse. Let's go right in and get it before somebody else does!"

Would she? No. She had said she wanted that suit MORE than anything else in the world. But she didn't even want it as much as she wanted the $35.

She WISHED she had a new suit like this one, but what she really WANTED was the money. "But what about the person who hasn't the $35?" I hear you ask. And the answer you will find is the UTTER TRUTH. It is this: You can GET it, honestly, legitimately, quickly and SURELY, provided YOU WANT IT.

You can get it by giving up for it the leisure, false pride, or whatever it is that you have been PREFERING to that amount of money.

In other words, if you have not the $35 it is because you have taken something else IN PREFERENCE to it; because you chose, consciously or subconsciously. To forego this money you might have been making rather than part with the time, energy, sleep or good times which you took IN ITS PLACE.

Decide to restrict yourself because you "can't get the money for things you want" and the money you do get will come that much harder.

But make up your mind to MAKE DESIRES MATERIALIZE ALL THE MONEY YOU NEED for the things you want—and from the hour of reaching that decision you will make five dollars easier than you now make one.

The richer you become the easier it is to make money. The less you have the more difficult to get more. "To him that hath shall be given, and from him that hath not shall be taken away even that which he hath." It has often seemed that there was a deep injustice in this declaration of the

Scriptures. Also a threat. But it is more of a promise than a threat, and more than all—it is a LAW. It is not something the Creator is going to do to you or against you. It is something you do to yourself. Once you decide to pay the price things begin to come your way. More and bigger things gravitate to you and come with less effort than it took to get the first little ones.

It is almost as if we find a storehouse of riches almost for the taking when we have once managed to get a window or door open.

Often this is a surprise to us. All successful men and women who are frank will admit that many good things followed in the wake of that first big effort, and followed almost without further effort.

It is as if we looked through the front window of a store, saw something inside we wanted very much and having paid the price for it discovered that there was an endless supply of much more desirable and valuable things (which we hadn't seen from the outside at all) available at much lower prices.

"Nothing succeeds like success" is an old and true saying. Another not so old but equally true is that nothing fails like failure.

The world always helps you along whichever way you are going. If you are headed uphill it will help pull you up. If you are headed downhill it will give you a push.

We should not complain of this, but awaken to the fact that it IS a law, and instead of fighting it put it to work for us.

If you want to go uphill you must manifest this to the people around you. They are all driving along Life's Highway too, and they see you, think of you, and get an impression of you.

If you want to go down all you have to do is to let it be known and you will have plenty of kicks and company.

The world gets one of its deepest impressions of you FROM THE DIRECTION IN WHICH YOUR CAR IS MOVING. Everything about you tells what that is. Even children and those who catch a glimpse of you for only a moment sense this and act toward you accordingly.

You never deceive them very much or very long in any way. Bluffing and pretending do not deceive anyone. These only make you resemble a man who tells you he is traveling north when at every corner possible he turns south.

All of life is a journey along the great Highway. We are always coming to crossroads. We ALWAYS make our own choice. We turn or go straight ahead—as WE CHOOSE.

Make Your Desires Materialize

We come to scores of these corners everyday and the world notes the turns we make. It will give you plenty of time to get to your destination in the North, and many a lift besides, provided at the cross-roads you keep heading in that direction.

Another strange thing about it is that the higher up you get the MORE help the world gives you, and the lower down the harder it kicks.

You can see it for yourself. If you haven't a cent and ask the world for a quarter to keep you from starving, it will not give it to you very quickly or very graciously. It says it "can't encourage that kind of thing." It is afraid you "might not deserve it."

But if you are a millionaire. With more money than you know what to do with, people will gladly loan you millions, and if you happen to be a banker with greenbacks piled mountain high in vaults they will come to you and ask you to make room for their extra money also.

To the big dinners the hungry are not invited. The guests are those already overfed.

If a railway magnate drawing a salary of $200,000 a year takes a trip over another road he travels on a pass, with drawing rooms and special service. But if a tramp tries to steal a ride on a beam next to the wheels underneath, he is kicked off.

The man with a library so big he doesn't have a chance to read half his books is the one to whom we present rare volumes, while he who has none gets none.

The people who are surrounded by love, whom EVERYONE loves, are the ones we also love, while those without it are ostracized.

"This is all true," you say, "but how is one to get started in the right direction? Especially when, as you say, the whole world is busy helping us downgrade already?"

The answer is: Change the CAUSE and you also change the EFFECT.

Your present condition, as pointed out in the previous lesson, is the natural and inevitable outgrowth of the attitudes and feelings HARBORED in your subconscious mind.

Most people secretly cherish the delusion that this is not a law-ruled universe, and that somehow they will be able to get something for nothing. Look again at the word "harbored," for it reveals the crux of your situation.

All kinds of things come into your consciousness. You can't help seeing and hearing and even sometimes thinking these destructive things. But you CAN refuse to HARBOR them.

The things that get down into your subconscious mind come out in your life.

But remember, nothing can get into your subconscious mind save as you dwell upon it and encourage it.

"But how can I start forward NOW, from this very spot?" you ask. To begin to go uphill in life instead of down, to get the help of your own powers and those of other people in your uphill climb, it is only necessary for just now that you TURN AROUND.

Other things will come later, but for today this will be enough. It will not be necessary for you to make a great showing or scale a peak or two today. In fact I will ask you not even to think of the twists and turns and detours you may imagine lie ahead.

To get the price for anything you want, gently open your mind to the idea that you CAN get it, somewhere, somehow. Do not dwell upon the things which just now seem to stand in the way of your getting it.

In doing this it is not necessary to dump out by main force the old, weak outlooks you have been harboring up to now.

It is a law that two things cannot occupy the same place at the same time. So, turning your attention toward the good thought drives the bad one out.

Soon this becomes a habit, and then out of your subconscious will come the ideas of HOW to get the price of what you want.

There is an old saying, "You can't have your cake and eat it too." We are facing every hour of our waking lives the question, "Shall I eat this cake now and be without it in future, or shall I keep it and have it then?"

The vast majority of people make the mistake of greedily devouring all of life's cake in youth and early adulthood. They leave school for something pleasanter—and pay the price by being compelled to do the bitterly unpleasant things at small pay in their old age, or until they "back up" and pay the long-evaded price by the study which every grown person can follow for self-education. They follow their instincts instead of their ideals and wonder in later life why the good things, the great and beautiful things, have passed them by.

People look for a soft snap now—and in future years resent the soft snap which another (who has earned it) enjoys.

Elbert Hubbard told many things when he said, "Blessed is he who is not looking for a soft snap, for he is the only one who shall find it."

Walk up to Life's counter and PAY for what you want. You will find that many valuable premiums go with every cash purchase.

Refuse to pay, and she treats you as the store treats those who are "just looking around." Spend your time trying to jew Life down and she will treat you as the store treats the bargain-hunter. Try to take anything away for nothing and she treats you as a shoplifter. A pair of middle-aged twin brothers come to my mind vividly whenever I think of this law of Compensation. I recently dined at the home of the successful one. The other dropped in for a chat during the evening, after which we dropped him at home on the way to our hotel. I had gone to school with them and knew the life story of both. They had equal advantages, equal opportunities, equal training, equal heredity—an equal chance in every way. One was always looking for "the easiest way," and the other for the BEST way. I will call the former E. and the latter B.

E. considered himself much smarter than his brother and thought him a fool to go to so much trouble. His attitude was that by keeping one's eyes open and being shrewd one could somehow get the best in life when the gods were not looking. Instead of going after what he wanted in the straight way he was always on the look out for a little side-path that would be easier.

When they were boys at home E. induced B. to do part of his work around home—to carry in his share of the wood, to milk the cow on the nights when it was his turn, and all such things. For this he held himself in secret esteem, thinking how clever he was, and his brother in secret contempt for being "an easy mark."

He didn't realize of course that the more extra work we give ourselves in youth the stronger our backs become, and that every time B. did him a favor he indirectly did two for himself. When they went away to school they shared a room. E. took the best bed, the largest clothes closet, and waited for his brother to make the grate fire every morning. Knowing

B. would help him cram for examinations he neglected his studies and sat near enough to his brother to copy his answers on test days.

When he had spent his own share of their allowance he borrowed from B. and failed to pay it back. When he had neglected to send his laundry out he borrowed his brother's collars for parties.

B. didn't need them so often. He didn't go to so many parties—"a little slow" E. thought him.

But B. was not as slow as he looked. He too wanted to "cut" classes and "ditch" studies when the gang dropped in and invited him out for a lark. But he had imagination and ambition. Through the former he could see what such a course would do to his education, and through the latter he was spurred to look for bigger game.

Through his common sense and intelligence he was able to see that the jolly times of the present were not worth sacrificing his future for—the worthwhile future he always had in mind. He could see it was a small change in comparison, so paid it out day after day in the things he gave up. When they had graduated both were offered political positions at good salaries through the "pull" of their father, a prominent state senator.

E. accepted but B. declined. He too liked the excitement and "white lights" of the big capital city, but decided to go into the Northwest to work in a logging camp. The salary was less and he would be thirty miles from the nearest town, but he was thinking it would give him better opportunities for a future.

I need not give you more details, though the whole story is interesting beyond measure. The significant fact is that today B. is a millionaire lumberman of Seattle, famed for his big heart and level head—and E. is a clerk in his office.

As we drove home that evening E. made the usual excuses for himself and the usual criticism of the more successful brother. "I work eight hours every day," he complained. "My own brother puts in about four, closes his desk at two in the afternoon and goes out to play golf! I get a salary and he has millions. I live in a boarding house and he in a mansion. Life certainly has favored him!" Giving up the little things NOW pays big dividends in the TOMORROWS.

What are you giving up today—this very day and hour—in order that a year from today may be bigger and better? If nothing, you may be sure you are eating next year's bread today. Furthermore, a slice foregone today grows into many loaves by a year from today.

Successful men and women, whether you can realize it or not, are only "cashing in" on their past efforts, sacrifices and hardships. The failure has as surely chosen to live in the hour, letting tomorrow take care of itself.

When tomorrow must take care of itself it cannot in addition take care of you. Take care of yourself today and tomorrow will take care of you.

Another story from life comes to my mind, about two young women who grew up in the same small town and were chums through their public school days. The parents of both were poor but G.'s not quite so destitute as were L.'s.

When it came time to go to college each knew she would have to earn her way through if she got further education. G. could not bring herself to work for her board and room as L. did—her "pride," she declared, "couldn't permit her to." She married a cafe owner whom, she confided to L., she "didn't really love, but he made enough that she could 'take life easy.'" This she proceeded to do while L. was away at the university doing housework for her board and room, janitor work in one of the university buildings for her tuition, and library work for her clothes.

G. lived a pleasant life in their little home town, with a servant of her own, pretty clothes, a horse and buggy (this was in pre-auto days) and took life pleasantly in general.

"How can you give up four whole years?" she asked L., who was home for a few days at Christmas, "when you'll have nothing to show for it at the end of that time except a few ideas? You'll be that much older, less attractive, less eligible. I wouldn't change places with you for anything.

"Why, to think of your doing plain ordinary HOUSEWORK like my Hannah, and JANITORING like old Mrs. Whitby, the scrub woman—it's silly. Why don't you come home, marry some nice man while you're still young enough to get one—and act like the rest of us?"

But L. kept on, through the hardships which horrified G. were nothing compared to the heartaches nobody ever knew about. She didn't mind the work, but how she DID mind never having a DAY or an HOUR of her own! How her soul yearned when on Saturdays other young men and women went laughing past the house and took the street car for the football game! How she ate her heart out because not a single one of the young men EVER asked her to go anywhere!

Of course she could not have spared the time to go if he had, but it would have been such a consolation to be invited. She knew of course that it didn't help matters any for her to be seen at four o'clock every afternoon in brogans and denim skirt scrubbing down the old circular stairs as her fellow students filed out from late classes.

By the time L. had graduated G. was tiring of her cafe-owning husband, who wanted babies in the house, and was thinking of the divorce which she soon after secured. Her alimony was sufficient to keep her in pretty things and a fair living, so she came to the big city where L. was by now taking her postgraduate course.

L. with her seriousness, plainness and studiousness was more of a mystery than ever to G., who insisted that she "drop those mouldy old books and have some fun." G. soon married again—a bond salesman this time—but he died some years later, leaving her only $6,000 in life insurance.

This was soon spent on the clothes and travel which she considered necessary to catching a new mate, but by this time she was so much older and so overweight from self-indulgence that she was not successful.

Today she works in a St. Louis drug store for $21 a week and complains that "life has never treated her as well as it did her old friend L"

L., by the way, after thirty years of unrelenting mental and physical effort made a million. She is happily married to a brilliant, broad-minded man and they do together the work they both love.

"It simply isn't fair," wails G. "Some people get everything."

In his famous essay, "Compensation," Emerson says: "The law is eternal—nothing in nature is GIVEN. All things are SOLD."

And he might have added, "to the highest bidder."

For Nature is somewhat like an auctioneer. She has no favorites. He who is willing to pay most gets most, and he who pays least gets least. You cannot see the wheels go round, but they do.

Nature also keeps books—the most accurate set in the universe—and on them each of us can have a charge account, every so often payable. Then one day she comes in person to collect. No duns, no bills in advance, no notice—just THE PRICE, on demand.

When for any reason she gives you plenty of time, think not that she has forgotten. She will come upon you unawares, hand you her bill with compound interest, and you must meet it on the spot.

But if you pay cash for her wares you are on her favored list as a valued customer. You will always get the best she has—and gifts besides.

The really brainy people meet her obligations IN ADVANCE. They know that with real success it is pay-as you-enter. The price of success is never as high nor as hard to get as the failures have been frightened into thinking. In life, as in many other things, the cheapest is the best.

"Dreams fulfilled," said someone, "are things bought and paid for. It all depends on whether we are ready to pay the marked price or wait till bargain day."

Frank Crane says, "Every man's career is a struggle between the two natures in us, the angel and the brute.

"The first thing to do, therefore, is to recognize that all decent life must be in terms of conflict. Because you feel this unceasing war within you is no sign that you are 'bad' or selfish or meaner than other people. You are simply human. You might as well complain that you do not have three hands, or that you do not possess supernatural powers of vision or hearing, as to complain that your inclination does not always agree with your duty.

"Having recognized this fact, don't worry over it. Don't grow morbid. Don't call yourself names. Don't develop self-contempt. And above all don't get into the mire of self-pity.

"It's a fight. You have to make it. Go to it gaily, with high courage, and with gladness that you are disposed to fight and sure to win.

"You can always dodge the fight by yielding to your lower nature. But you know the nasty side of that. It means a weak, flabby, unclean mind, a spirit that must loathe itself.

"But you can be much more comfortable than the sensualist if you will make up your mind that you will do what is right every time, no matter how you feel. This will not give you the same kind of pleasure that the self-indulgent have, but a far better kind.

"For there are two sorts of enjoyment: one, that of yielding; the other, that of overcoming. And it is the overcomer who gets the crown of life.

"For instance, there is pleasure in lying in bed, in eating and drinking and gratifying the various animal cravings of the body, also in reading books that divert you but require no mental effort; in going to the theater, in being flattered, praised, complimented. In all these things your pleasure is passive.

"There is pleasure, on the other hand, in exercise, in going without food and drink that would harm you, in denying the body's demands so as to satisfy the wants of your intelligence, of pleasing your conscience by trampling on an appetite, of intellectual discipline, etc.

"All these are the soldier kind of joys. They are better than the soft kind, because they last longer, they strengthen your mind and body, they make your tastes finer, your whole enjoyment of life keener, your range of delights wider, and altogether you get a deal more fun out of living.

"The latter joys are just as 'selfish' as the former. But an INTELLIGENT selfishness is unselfish. HE THAT SAVES HIS LIFE SHALL LOSE IT.

"Scientifically speaking, all you have to do to go to hell is do nothing at all. The wind blows that way. Just do as you please, don't resist, gratify all desires, never mind conscience—and hell will be along pretty soon.

"Heaven is uphill all the way. But it's keen and bracing exercise. It means a healthier body, livelier mind, and happier spirit every day. And at the top, you always get the Morning Star!"

Crane goes on to say, "Life has been called all sorts of things. Life is a dream, a gambling game, an opportunity to get all the fun and the least pain possible, a probation preparatory to the next life, a value of tears, etc.

"Suppose we consider life as a business proposition. Look at it from a practical, profit-and-loss, shrewd and common-sense viewpoint.

"Very well. First, what can we get out of it? Only wages. There are no endowed and privileged ones. All are day laborers; for every one, when the work's over, must leave all he has gained and go back to that nothingness from which he came, as stark naked and poor as when he arrived.

"All the billionaire gets out of life is exactly what the brick-layer gets—his board and clothes and amusements.

"It's happiness we all strive for, of one kind or another, whether beer and cakes or turtled feasts, overalls or dress suits, pinochle on a cracker box or stock gambling on the market, social distinction, wealth display, political success, intellectual achievement—it's all happiness according to taste.

"How is happiness to be secured, how can one be sure to get his pay?

"BY FINDING OUT WHAT HE REALLY WANTS. This is not so easy. Most people work a lot for what they think other people THINK they want. How can one find that out? By ascertaining those forms of pleasure that are frauds and bring on misery. The conclusive argument against drunkenness, licentiousness and the like is that they are swindles, gold bricks; they promise joy and pay suffering.

"How can one tell what sorts of things pay and what sorts do not pay? BY THE COLLECTIVE EXPERIENCE OF MANKIND, and by accepting the guidance of reliable teachers.

"The cumulative experience of mankind shows that only those acts pay which are fundamentally just, fair, honest and KIND.

"What's the good of morality? Morals rest not upon authority, but are the MASSED WISDOM of the world. The person who is not moral is a fool. He is a sucker, a greenhorn, fully as much as the country-jake who thinks he can beat Wall Street experts. Immorality docks the happiness pay-envelope every day.

"If you are helpful, unselfish, courteous, patient, reverent, loyal, just and benevolent, you get a large daily bonus.

"If you imagine that crafty, unclean, cruel or conscienceless people are happy, get right well acquainted with one, and see.

"Why work? If it's happiness that is our wage, why not eat, drink and be merry; why not loaf and play? Because human beings are so constituted that they secure the MAXIMUM of satisfactory self-expression only by doing some part of the world's work. "Why study to improve the mind, or to develop one's spiritual capacities? Why not go in for all the fun we can get each day? Because, by increasing our mental and spiritual powers, we get the more permanent, the higher and rarer forms of happiness—we get gold and not copper.

"What we call goodness more than pays every day, it leaves something over, a DEPOSIT IN THE BANK OF HAPPINESS, which becomes a RESERVE FUND from which we draw DIVIDENDS."

When I was about eleven years old I belonged to a church in a little western mining camp. Of the many experiences it engraved on my mind none went deeper than one which occurred at a Wednesday night prayer meeting. A man who had usually been silent before arose and said, "Never ask God for anything unless you really want it and are willing to pay for it. As some of you know, I had been out of work for several months—against my will, as I told myself—when I finally prayed earnestly for something to open up.

"It wasn't a week till I had a good job offered me and then I realized I hadn't wanted it at all. I really preferred letting the rest of the family earn the living. But God took me at my word."

"That is the gospel truth," exclaimed a little woman whose sharp tongue had got her the nickname "Mrs. Pepper." "I asked God to make me more loving. Shortly afterwards I was thrown with a lot of people. It was mighty hard to love! But I knew God had taken me at my word—to teach me not to order things if I wasn't in earnest.

"I knew I didn't deserve any credit for loving pleasant, attractive, congenial people. I knew real love meant loving everybody—the un congenial, unpleasant and unattractive. Since that I do not bother God for anything unless I am willing to take the bother of paying for it."

The law of compensation is an impersonal, almost mathematical one, not the arbitrary thing it sometimes appears to be.

You will get a clearer understanding of this if you will think of your life as a crowded pantry shelf. To make room for anything else you would have to remove from that shelf something you wanted less.

So it is with your life. It is FULL, but what OF? Leisure? Pleasure? Ease? Self-indulgence?

"No," you will say, "only a little of these."

"Very well," says the Law of Compensation. "If you want something you haven't got, merely take off the shelf something you already have, and make room for the newer and better and more desired thing.

"Take off some of the idleness, and put Effort in its place; take off some of the mental laziness and put Study in its place; take off some of the indefiniteness and put Plan in its place; take off some of the frivolities and put things more worth while and sensible in their place—and soon you will have this thing you want.

"You have filled yourself of Life. No one but YOU can say what shall remain upon it and what, if anything, be removed.

"Take Your choice."

The Law of Materialization

We have now come to the last lap of our journey into the land of Heart's Desire. It remains only to enter into the City of Our Dreams. Through Affirmation, Preparation and Compensation we have come to Materialization. We have planted the seeds and are ready for the harvest which never fails.

We have remade our own spirits through the remaking of our moods; we have decided definitely just what we want; we have set the gages; we have taken every necessary step.

We have built the strong foundation of Preparation; we have learned how to find the many doors of opportunity and recognize them; we have learned that the price for passing through each and on into more and more beautiful things is not unobtainable but easy to get; that everything we want awaits us as soon as we have fulfilled the eternal laws which operate behind all materialization.

Thousands of men and women have written me the story of the successes which crowned their efforts as soon as they had stopped groping, side-stepping or drifting and applied the simple but eternal laws which I have explained to you in these lessons.

I wish I might reprint every one, for truth IS stranger than fiction—and also more interesting. But I will select typical ones that we have space for. I will let each tell you his story in his own words:

How I Overcame Wrong Attitudes and Attained Happiness

By Marla Kirkwood, New Orleans

I grew up in a family that tried to live on its "traditions." Both of my parents had been reared in the luxury of slave-owning surroundings before the Civil War and could not adjust themselves to newer ones. "The good old days" and the hopelessness of the new were favorite topics of conversation. Myself and sister, who made up the rest of the family, were trained in the old fashioned ways and taught that instead of looking for "careers" we should find some nice men and marry.

But the nice men did not arrive on the scene, at least not the ones we wanted, and the family finances dwindled year after year till it became necessary for me to go to work. I was then past thirty, with no training whatever, but with the family idea of personal superiority strong within me. I looked weeks before I found anything to do and then the pay was so small I would not have considered it had I not needed it so badly. The work was not difficult and I did it efficiently and without much effort.

I therefore wondered why my pay was not raised as promised when the month of probation was over. But my employer would make no explanations. Instead I was told my services were no longer needed.

I got other positions but lost each one in turn apparently for some mysterious reason which no one would mention to me. In spite of my admittedly good work I could not hold a place long enough to be promoted or secure even an average wage. As soon as I would become familiar with my work and begin to congratulate myself on how well I was doing, out I would have to go.

It may help others if I explain here that I had been taught to be efficient, that I preferred to do things well, that I took pride in my personal appearance, tried to make myself as useful as possible to my employers, and in every way lived up to all the "rules" which are supposed to lead to success.

One night at the request of the head of my department, who had heard her in Denver many years before, I attended Mrs. Benedict's lecture. I was not interested in psychology, human analysis, personality or similar subjects. I considered them fads, too far-fetched and impractical to apply to everyday life.

Almost her first words were, "Your predominant mental attitudes make your life." It sounded impossible, stated baldly like that, and I inwardly resisted it with some arguments of my own for a few minutes. She went on to explain HOW and WHY this was so, piling illustration upon illustration, proof upon proof, until when she walked off the platform an hour and a half later I could not believe I had been in that auditorium more than ten minutes.

I was too proud to admit to my friend that any of her talk struck me, but I knew it did. As we walked to the corner my friend said, "Maria, I wanted you especially to come with me tonight, for I like you and I don't want us to lose track of each other even if you do leave the office."

I was thunderstruck and asked her what she meant. "I mean," she said, "that the manager told me today he was going to let you go on the first, and I felt I ought to tell you, so you could do something about it. You could if you only would, and I know how much you'd like to stay."

I asked her to explain and she said, "Maria, you are a very dependable worker. You are quick and keen and have initiative, and Mr. J. admits it, but he said he knew you felt superior to the rest of the girls AT HEART and they all know it too. He said he had Miss D.'s position in mind for you when she leaves next month, but she is in charge of four girls and none of them wants to work under you."

I asked her permission to go to the manager for another chance, and did so the next morning. Meanwhile I spent most of the night taking stock of myself. I knew this secret attitude of superiority had always dominated my inmost mind and had gotten me a deal of satisfaction. But I could readily see what it had done to my life.

I had then been working for seven years and was getting a much smaller salary than others of similar experience. I recalled how just this thing had happened every time in spite of the high quality of my work. I had never expressed this attitude in words but I realized of course that it had always talked as plainly as any words could.

I fought it out with myself that night and went straight to the manager next morning, confessing the truth frankly and promising to overcome it if he would give me another chance. He acquiesced and I went at it in earnest.

I determined to eliminate the effect by uprooting the cause, as Mrs. Benedict suggested, not merely pretend. I did not miss one of her lessons. She showed me the way so simply, sanely and scientifically that it was really easy.

That was four years ago. I am now the manager myself in that firm and far happier than I ever expected to be. I am writing this in the hope that it will give others the realization the lack of which stood in my way so many years.

How I Succeeded in Salesmanship

By John C. MacDonald, Chicago

Two years ago I heard you lecture in Milwaukee. At that time I was employed in the shipping department of one of the leading stores. I had tried selling but without success. I had a fairly pleasant personality, at least my friends said I had, and I was determined.

I liked salesmanship more than any other kind of work and was never happy at anything else. But every time I tried it I failed completely. Once I sold books, another time period furniture and at another automobiles. All I had ever accomplished was the spending of the money I had saved each time for my venture—then back I'd have to go to a clerkship.

Of all the things in the lessons the newest and most unbelievable to me was what you said, Mrs. Benedict, about the power of affirmation. I was thirty-one at this time, more or less of a skeptic, and the idea that talking to one's self could be anything but the sign of a "cracked" mind was rather a joke.

I remember laughing at it on the way home that night with another man of the class. He finally said, "I'd have said the same thing at your age, but I'm older now, and one of the things my experience has taught me is the power which thinking or saying anything over in one's mind has on his conduct." I thought about it while getting ready for bed, and almost constantly the next day. By the time I reached the auditorium for the next night's lesson I had a gleam. I recognized that the reason for my failures was not the talk I gave my prospects but that which I gave myself.

I had had a whole set of affirmations and didn't know it! Only they were the wrong kind. I never approached a customer without thinking to myself, "Now I'll bet he doesn't want my stuff. He's going to resist me, sure as SHOOTING. To overcome his opposition what shall I say? It probably won't do a bit of good, but I'll tell him this."

It was only the truth that I told them, and it would have sold them frequently, I now know, if I hadn't been so unsold on myself. The more I thought of it the more I understood that my big obstacle was not selling the goods—I could do that, I knew—but selling myself TO MYSELF. And you had said this was the biggest thing affirmation could do for us. I began to come to, and to see how completely my negative affirmations had hurt me. I decided to get myself out of reverse. I won't trouble you with more details except to say that today I am in Chicago, where competition is far keener than it was in Milwaukee, and that for the past year I have averaged just eight times as much as I ever got before. I have waited to write you about it so you could see it was no sudden thing, but the kind that lasts.

For your own information and those placed as I was, I might add that I used several kinds of affirmations before I decided on the one that suited me. I finally settled on this, and I never approached a customer or prospect without saying it, thinking it, FEELING it, looking it from my eyes and ACTING it:

"I have something useful to this man. It is worth all I am asking for it, and I am HELPING him by bringing it to his attention, whether he buys from ME or not."

Instead of wondering whether or not he was going to buy I concentrated on making it so clear to him that he couldn't HELP seeing it.

I said further, "He will sense my sincerity and that will help me make the sale. I won't think about the WORDS. I'll simply express my honest enthusiasm over my product in whatever words come to me at the time."

I studied my line from A to Z. I was so full of it that I had more proofs than I ever needed. I was a success from the first week.

How I Mastered an Overmastering Sorrow
By Mrs. A. C. Downs, San Francisco

My only son went to war and was killed in the Argonne Forest in 1918. When I received the news all the goodness and gladness went out of life for me. My husband and three daughters were almost as heart broken as I, but I could think of nothing and nobody except myself and my poor boy.

Our home became a place of gloom and I am a bitter, stricken, resentful woman. I stopped attending church. What right had God, I cried, to send me a wonderful boy and just as he reached his glorious blooming take him away? I had my name removed from the organizations to which I belonged—even the Red Cross. I accepted no invitations, encouraged no one to come to our house, and went nowhere whatever.

I was fast becoming a self-pitying recluse when one of your little books, "The Fallacy of Grief," fell into my hands from the daughter who had heard some of your lectures. I read it at first only with contempt for one who, doubtless without having had any such experience herself, dared to condone the wrong that had been done me. Later when my daughter explained that this little hook had been minted out of Mrs. Benedict's own great sorrow I relented and read it again and then again. By the time I got around to wanting to hear her she had left the city, but I had this one little book. It made of me a different woman. When she returned two years later I had regained my faith and understanding, and resumed once more my place as the mother of the three lovely young girls whom I had been neglecting, had once more become helpful wife, was "doing my bit" an giving my mite for civic betterment.

How I Got What I Wanted

By George F. Walac., Seattle

Early one evening in June, 1920, I was passing the Masonic Temple in Seattle. A billboard in the foyer attracted my attention. It announced Mrs. Benedict's lectures for that week. Groups of people were going in and I followed the crowd.

I have always been sorry I did not note the day of the month, for it marked the great turning point in my life.

"You can get anything in this world you really want," said Mrs. Benedict during the course of the lecture. Of course I didn't swallow that preposterosity! She asked us to decide, between then and the next evening, just what we wanted more than anything else in the world, and get that much of a start before the class opened.

I didn't need to decide. I had known for twenty-eight years exactly what I wanted and why I wanted it and what I would do with it if ever got it. But of course I didn't expect it.

The idea, however, that you could actually get ANYTHING you wanted was so ridiculous that I went back the next evening and joined the class just to see how she was going to extricate herself from the tangle.

Naturally, I listened to everything she said in the light of my own long cherished ambition. This was to own a large stock-raising business and breed high-grade horses and cattle. I had worked at various things and been trusted and respected, but I had never been able to save enough to start at what I wanted to do.

Through those lessons I found what had been holding me back. It came to me in a story she told from life—about the man who was so sure his business was going to fail that he went to the bank to borrow some money. This was in a small city and his bankers were well acquainted with him personally.

Knowing him to be CONVINCED that his business was going to the wall, they refused to lend him the money. He offered it for sale to two young men and the bank LOANED THEM THE MONEY INSTANTLY. For the young men were POSITIVE they could make a big success of the business, and the bankers knew that with this spirit they were sure to win. The story jolted me out of a rut and waked me up. Next morning I went to several men who had known me in and around Seattle for twenty years and told them what I wanted to do. They knew my experience and seeing my enthusiasm and determination were induced to back me for a start.

I am now out of debt and the OWNER of my dream!

How I Attained My Ambition

By Helen V. Thurston, New York City

I have long felt that I owed it to other aspiring women to write the little story of how I realized my own ambitions. I have hesitated because it is almost impossible to talk about one's own affairs without appearing conceited. However, those who wish to will have to call me that. I am writing this just as it happened, for the sake of the others who need the same things that helped me. I won't bore you with the "story of my life," but to see how much New York meant to me and why I felt it was the center of the universe I will explain that I grew up in a little Minnesota town near Minneapolis. I was ambitious to become a commercial artist—to illustrate books and advertisements and all such things. Like every child I took to a pencil like a duck to water and early in life my fond parents knew I was going to be one of the world's geniuses. But I was an only child and they could not think of my leaving home.

As I grew older they talked me out of planning on New York, the one place of course where I wanted to go and where I knew I must go to succeed in this work. Everyone agreed that since more than 99 percent of all American books and national magazines were published there I could never be a real success anywhere else.

But they also regaled me with the competition I would meet, the loneliness I would have to combat, and the failure that almost surely awaited me. At last, when I was twenty-four and had about decided I never could have done it anyway, Mrs. Benedict gave a few lectures in the City Auditorium of Minneapolis, and I attended. I stopped thinking about the powers that would compete with me and oppose me in New York and began to do what she advised—think of MY OWN POWERS.

I decided to go. When my parents knew I was in earnest they were glad, for they admitted they had been a little disappointed in my not having gone on with my ambition.

I announced my intention to my friends—" burning my bridges behind me," as Mrs. Benedict advised, and the following spring arrived in New York. It was one of those dampish, drizzly, chilly late afternoons in April when I landed, and I pretty nearly lost hope.

But I dug Mrs. Benedict's book out of my suitcase and spent the evening reading it in my little white cotted room at the Hotel Martha Washington. By the time I was ready for sleep I KNEW nothing could down me.

I read that book till I had to have it rebound. Every time I'd see a telling sentence in it I could fairly SEE Mrs. Benedict standing there as she had on the platform in Minneapolis, saying, "I BELIEVE in you. Go ahead, make your plans and preparations—and you'll win."

I didn't find things easy, as you may know. The field was crowded to bursting and I was as green as grass. But I grew and I ripened and I STUCK.

For almost two years now I have been making a splendid salary as designer in a big cloak-manufacturing house. My parents live here now, so we are not separated after all, and the world looks wonderful.

LESSON VIII

Your Secret, Subconscious Self

Do you recall the slightly baffled sensation you experienced when a physician to whom you had gone in time of need handed you a prescription?

You took the "scrap of paper" because there was nothing else to do, and on your way to the drug store scanned it interestedly trying to decipher its meaning and especially to figure out what bearing those mysterious hieroglyphics could have on your very real and very personal problem.

But you decided, about the time you found the prescription clerk, 't were a vain ambition for a mere average man to aspire to understand the cryptic scientific code, bandied so nonchalantly between these wise technicians. You confessed it quite over your head, paid the bill and tried to forget it.

Could you have stepped behind the counter and heard the drug clerk translating your prescription to himself it would have amused you to see to what agony scientist No. 1 had gone to put into Latin for scientist No. 2 the simple directions for concocting for you a simple remedy which in plain United States was merely peppermint or castor oil.

The scientists in this case are going on the ancient theory that they would lose your respect and incidentally your money if they came down off their Minerva-like pedestals and told you the everyday contents of this bottle. Moreover, you might be able to make your own medicine next time, apply your own remedy—and THEN where would they be!

Medical science has contributed much to the health and happiness of man, but it could have helped much more and many more had it been placed within the reach of the everyday man as it might easily have been!

Now comes a new human science called Psychoanalysis—a science destined to do for mankind far greater things than medical science has ever done; to cure not only the mind, which the physician overlooks, but physical ailments the physician has never been able to reach.

It is not an intricate science. It deals, as do all sciences, with the simple though stupendous facts of everyday life. It can be used by every individual who once secures an understanding of it, and help him in the solution of his most pressing, personal problems.

But practically everything that has been given out to date has been, like the prescription, couched in mysterious phraseology, and written by scientists to other scientists OVER THE HEADS of the everyday man whose sufferings they purport to relieve.

Musicians will play the ultra-classical, though it put the audience to snoring in eight minutes, and scorn the simple things everybody longs for; because they play not for the people but for their critical contemporaries.

Singers sing to their fellow artists, learned men talk to the learned, scientific writers write for other scientific writers—all out of fear.

Between and around these few are the unlearned, the unmusical, the unscientific—that backbone of the nation, Mr. and Mrs. Everyday American and their children.

They are in trouble. Worry, fear, poverty, grief, sorrow, disappointments and disillusionments overwhelm them.

When the struggle becomes acute the most intelligent go to books for help. Among other things, they read reams on this new and wonderful psychoanalysis.

It is about as understandable as the prescription. The reader, like the patient, seeks, struggles, pays the bill and tries to forget.

But he can't forget because the problem is still unsolved, not because psychoanalysis could not have solved it, but because he found nothing understandable to apply to his own troubles.

Here is a course, putting into plain, simple American terms the scientific truths recently discovered about the subconscious mind, with definite, specific explanations of exactly what it is, how it works, where it comes from, where and how it so vitally affects your life; plus definite specific instructions for applying this knowledge to your own personal affairs—in short, a prescription in English.

It is so plain you can make your own medicine next time, and after a while perhaps avoid the necessity for remedies altogether.

There is nothing in this course a child can fail to understand, yet every word is scientifically accurate and deals with the greatest problems of human life.

After all, nothing in the world need be made mysterious. Nature is performing miracles all the time, but she speaks a simple language. All the greatest facts of life can be stated in clear, helpful terms and made to do something worth while.

Here are a few of the hundreds questions about ourselves which are answered in this pleasurable, practical course:

Why are we so different in so different in our dreams from the person we are in real life?

How does unhappiness produce disease and why do joy and success cure it?

Why do the rich, the powerful, the beloved and beautiful commit suicide?

Why do criminals always go back to the scene of the crime?

Why does falling in love improve your mental, physical and spiritual health?

Why do we sometimes hate the one we most love?

Why does a wife call her husband "just a big boy" when he also thinks of her as "a mere child"?

What is the true explanation of love at first sight?

Why do we get over our wildest love affairs while tamer ones last through the years?

Why do lovers often feel sure they have met and mated in a previous existence?

Why do we take instantaneous and intense dislikes to people?

Why do boys fall in love with older women and girls have violent loves for mature men?

And how does this reconcile itself to the fact that women dislike to marry men younger than themselves while the older the man the younger he wants his wife to be?

Why do you change certain details when relating a dream?

Why are we afraid of certain things and why do we avoid certain others without knowing why?

Why do we often become angry, morose, elated or excited over trifles?

Why do we forget the names of people we know perfectly well, misspeak ourselves and say things we don't mean before we realize it?

Why are we poor when we want money so badly?

What is the secret of every person's supreme subconscious wish?

From the deck of a steamer you see an iceberg. Always afterward you think of it as consisting of just what you saw—no more and no less. You describe its outlines to your friends and explain its size and shape as being what was visible to your eye.

Yet you saw but one-tenth of that iceberg. The other nine-tenths were floating beneath the surface, entirely out of sight.

If you have never seen a big iceberg, drop a miniature one into your glass next time you are at table, and the same thing on a smaller scale will happen.

Your mind is like that iceberg. It has its upper and nether parts—the conscious and subconscious. The conscious may be likened to the tenth of the iceberg which is discernible above the surface, for its operations and processes are always apparent to you.

It consists of the thoughts you think from moment to moment in your waking hours, but lose when you fall asleep.

This conscious mind is busy handling the experiences which arise in your environment—the "awareness" of your surroundings, sensations of what you are doing, seeing, tasting, touching, smelling. All plans, visualizations and imaginings which catch and hold your attention are also a part of this surface mind.

You express this conscious mind more or less externally and can readily detect its operations. You can open the door on it any instant and catch it at work. Right now, for instance, you can watch your mind thinking of this page and what you are reading. You can look on while it reasons, judges and decides about what is printed here.

In short, this conscious element of your mind is the mind we are all familiar with, the mind we have always known we possessed, the mind dealt with in academic psychology, the mind that does our CONSCIOUS THINKING.

But recent discoveries have shown that this surface mind, which we had supposed comprised all our mental processes, is less than one-tenth of the total human consciousness.

These discoveries reveal that underneath this conscious mind, part and parcel of it, bound up and wound around it, powerfully influencing it but OUT OF SIGHT are the "submerged nine-tenths" called the subconscious.

This subconscious is the warehouse, in which you have been unconsciously and involuntarily storing away all the impressions, memories, feelings, accumulated force and "aftermaths" of EVERYTHING THAT HAS EVER HAPPENED TO YOU.

This means not only all the things you are conscious of having experienced but millions of sensations you were unaware of at the time. All have stowed themselves away down there in the pigeonhole of that submerged nine-tenths of your consciousness, TO BE HEARD FROM LATER IN LIFE.

Many of the mysteries about yourself which have baffled, discouraged or inspired you are solved by the new science of Mental Analysis, which explains this secret self that lies deeply buried but ALWAYS ACTIVE within each of us.

The conscious mind may be called the "retailer mind." It is compelled to deal with non-essentials, the externals of your hourly experiences, the thousands of details that arise in your immediate environment.

But your subconscious mind knows nothing of these. All its power is directed toward the attainment of your deepest desires. It is a wholesaler and does things only in the by-and-large.

It is not so much concerned with what you are doing, saying or experiencing at this moment, as with the MASSED RESULT of the experiences through which you have already passed, plus the probable effect upon you of those you are now facing.

Your subconscious mind does not so much think as FEEL. It does not believe or reason, as does your conscious mind. It KNOWS.

Nothing you see, hear, say, think, do, feel, or experience is ever lost. Each is preserved forever in the deeps of your subconsciousness.

It is as though you lived in a houseboat on a great ocean, into whose depths something dropped every time you had a thought, a feeling or any kind of experience whatever.

Some of these are of such a nature as to throw overboard the seeds from which would grow beautiful water lilies, ferns and lacey mosses. Some would bring forth weeds, others poison ivy, while others would fringe the shore with great trees whose strength would delight you and whose shade would comfort and bless all who came that way.

Some of your deeds and desires would fling into this ocean only trash—chunks of pig iron, bits of wood, baubles, toys, debris—trappings and trimmings of idle moments, dark thoughts, primitive instincts—all would lie there at the bottom of the sea. Divers could find every one—some distorted, some washed cleaner than when they went in, but each and every one affected in some way by being there.

Many of the thoughts and things we had supposed lifeless would turn out to be fertile seeds. They would have sprouted all manner of strange, exotic, ugly and beautiful plants, each bearing fruit according to its nature and sending up to the ocean's surface the results natural to itself.

We do and say many things which are the result of the things we previously submerged in this subconscious sea.

A man does things that are "foreign" to him—not what he intended. They seem to do themselves.

He means to say a certain thing, to express a certain thought and instead says something entirely different. He forgets the names of people he knows perfectly well, answers "No" when he means "Yes," and in a hundred ways entangles himself against his will.

He says "that was accidental," "I said that unconsciously,"or "I wasn't myself." But none of these is really true. The fact of the matter is that all of them were done by his subconscious. They are not accidental but in accordance with the definite law that we tend constantly to express to the outer world whatever is in the back of our minds.

We also tend to forget whatever is displeasing to the ego and to remember whatever is pleasing to it.

One of the well-known actors in America told us this:

"I am often asked to dinners and other social affairs with people in whom I have no interest whatever—people with whom I have nothing in common and with whom I would rather not be bothered.

"I found that almost invariably I jotted down these engagements on my calendar for the day FOLLOWING the actual date, and was always being called up afterward and reminded of my absence.

"After a while it dawned on me that my subconscious wish not to go caused me habitually but innocently to put down the wrong date and always to make the mistake for the day after so that it would be safely over before I could be reminded.

"I arrived at these conclusions because of another strange experience I was always having of putting down engagements with personal friends for the date PREVIOUS to that in the invitation, evidently because I was subconsciously anxious to go.

"More than once I arrived at these houses a day or even two days prior to the party—as unconscious of this mistake as I was of the opposite one."

These experiences happen to all of us—as when we find it so easy to be early at any affair we wish to attend, but late to those we dislike.

This matter of our secret desires is illustrated by the kinds of things we dream about.

How Our Dreams Reveal Us

Secret lies back of every dream and everything that happens in a dream. Though science has but recently discovered that secret this discovery is so far-reaching and fundamental that already it has cleared up some of the deepest mysteries of human personality, aided in the curing of all manner of physical diseases, mental disorders and heretofore inexplicable ailments.

The new insight it has given into the psychology of every human being and especially into his deepest desires, has revolutionized the procedure of physicians, psychiatrists, psychologists and all whose work it is to help humanity straighten out its tangles.

This startling but strikingly scientific secret of the origin and meaning of dreams is that EVERY DREAM is THE FULFILMENT OF

ONE OR MORE WISHES THAT HAVE BEEN THWARTED IN OUR WAKING LIFE.

In other words, everything you have or do or say or experience in a dream is the expression of some desire, longing, craving, yearning or wish which has been cheated of expression or repressed during the daytime.

One look into your own dreams will prove to you that this is true. You will recall how many times you have been doing in your dreams what actuality prevented your doing; how your dreams contain so many more of the desired elements than does real life, and how much more intense are your dream experiences than those of reality.

The poor who go to bed hungry or those who are dieting against their will, dream of feasts and banquets where there are quantities of just the food they like best. The man who retires thirsty dreams of cool springs, babbling brooks, steins of beer, goblets of wine, pitchers of ice water, or whatever kind of beverage he prefers.

A young woman friend who homesteaded a "dry farm" in Montana, told us that over and over again when she was most longing for it she dreamed of finding a beautiful deep spring on her land.

An intense repressed desire of any kind ultimately expresses itself in some form in our dreams. We dream of doing things we do not countenance in our waking thoughts but we dream them because, subconsciously, we desire to do the thing or the thing it symbolizes.

In many instances the conscious mind is not aware of this desire at all or, if it is, pushes it into the background for moral, ethical or other reasons.

No one should be blamed or criticised for the evil or "immoral" things he does in dreams. The fact that he dreams of doing them proves that he does NOT do them in his waking life.

Any desire that is fully gratified during the daytime is satisfied. It "gets out of the system." It is only those we are prevented from "getting off our chests" in the day that we dream of at night.

You live two lives—outer and inner. The outer one consists of what you SAY and DO, the inner of what you THINK and WISH.

The world witnesses much of your surface life and decides from it that you are a certain kind of person. But you know, with poignant sadness, how little any one knows of the REAL YOU.

You have a thousand thoughts, desires, ambitions and longings no one has ever dreamed you possessed. You have some faults, too, that they would be rather surprised to see. But you have beautiful ideals, sympathies for the sufferings of others, many generous impulses and big hopes of helping humanity which no one suspects and which you feel no one would understand, regardless of how hard you tried to explain them.

One of these lives is your SURFACE life, the other your SUBMERGED life. Each has its own consciousness, its own experiences and operates in its own way.

"All the world's a stage," said Shakespeare, and all of us are actors and play many rôles. The tenth part of your mind which controls and handles your surface life is, as stated, the conscious mind. It is at the helm during your waking hours. It directs the rôle you play in the many-act drama in which you appear day by day on the stage of your hourly existence.

The part you play out here on the stage of this everyday conscious life is a part that has to conform to "appearances." You say certain lines, you do certain things, you act a certain way because the exigencies of life, the amenities and the world in general demand it.

These compel you to do a great many things you do not like to do under any conditions—in your social relationships, in your work, in your business, in your duties as a citizen, parent, friend, and as a member of society.

The Surface You, accompanied by the conscious tenth of your mind, is forced to go through these parts all the time you are awake.

When you "lose consciousness," out comes the other nine-tenths of your mind—the Submerged You—and takes charge of the stage.

In a flash he clears away the trappings of that sordid, humdrum play called "everyday," and instantly up goes the curtain on the perfect, the ideal, the longed-for dreams of "What I Want." This is the dream and the "stuff" of which it is made.

In it all is as you desire. You are the star of the cast, the envied, the influential, the handsome, the powerful, the all-important personage around which everything else revolves. Your real self, halted, hampered and hurt during the hours of consciousness is now strong and free and favored in these hours when only subconsciousness reigns.

In your dreams you are always different from the person you are during the day. Instead of being at the mercy of reality, as you are in your waking hours, you begin to play some rôle you WANT to play, to act a part you WANT to act, to be some person you want to be, regardless of how fantastical these desires may be.

In the dream there are no laws, no rules, no regulations, no inhibitions. The dreamer harks back a million years, before any of these restraints came to repress and civilize the intense, instinctive self of man, to that ancient stage of human development when every creature was free to do as he pleased in just the degree that he was able to VANQUISH HIS ENEMIES.

This fact explains why we fight so hard in our dreams for what we desire and why the action is so much more crude than during our waking life.

The conventional self which dominates us during the day gives way, at night, to the primitive self which brooks no opposition, knows no defeat, has no scruples, no morals, no conventionalities—nothing but desires and their doings.

Because the dream takes us back to the ancient stages when the keenest sense man possessed was the visual one, our dreams are mostly purely VISUAL experiences.

The senses of hearing, touching, tasting and smelling, all of which figure prominently in our conscious life, are relegated to the rear in dreams because these were less acutely developed than sight in primitive man.

Only those of the keenest auditory sense or gifted in music ever hear sounds in dreams. Only those whose gustatory senses are most highly developed ever taste things in dreams. Only those with the keenest of noses ever smell anything in a dream. Next in acuteness to the sense of sight is that of touch, and this figures frequently in dreams.

But for the most part we dream in MENTAL PICTURES. The average dream is but a series of visual images—a moving picture in which we play the leading rôle which exists around and through and for our personal selves.

In dreams the mind places obstacles in our pathway for the joy the ego experiences in demolishing them, and this is especially true of the dreams of Americans who, more than any other people, measure a man's success by the difficulties he has overcome.

This conclusion is based in our analysis of hundreds of individuals from almost every civilized country.

In California we recently conversed on this subject of the ego in dreams with an operatic star whose name is famous the world over—so famous that she was at that time traveling incognito to avoid the homage of the multitude and have a few days of rest and quiet.

She told us a dream she had had the night before. Here it is in her own words:

"I was always intensely desirous of fame. Even as a child I knew I must be a great singer or life would not be worth living. I constantly pictured myself as a famous opera star—a silly performance for an unattractive little girl whose parents were as poverty-stricken as mine.

"As the eldest of a large family of children I was responsible for little brothers and sisters who were constantly getting into the kinds of troubles that demanded my attention.

"This often irritated me beyond endurance and made me more incensed than anything in the world except one. Our parents owned a small chicken farm, and when I was not having to leave my day-dreams, fairy books and personal pursuits to care for babies I was being compelled to look after the chickens—see that they were let out occasionally but kept away from the garden.

"I hated herding those chickens with all the blind hate of childhood. I felt humiliated every time I had to look after them. Was that any business for a future star to be in? I used to think to myself.

"That was twenty-five years ago.

"Last week I came to this little Inn and registered under another name without letting anyone know who I was. No one suspected. The result was that I, who have been accustomed to homage and special attentions everywhere, was treated like the Miss Average American I was supposed to be—no favors of any kind. In fact quite the opposite.

"They gave me a North room when I had specified a Southern exposure; the girl at the newsstand was flippant, a bell hop was insolent, and all around I suffered from inferior service—the kind most everybody gets these days but which I have be spared for several years because wherever I went they knew who I was.

"I suppose—in fact I admit—that all this irritated me. It humiliated and exasperated me. I could not get it off my mind. Had it not been for my intense desire to have a week of complete seclusion, I would have told them who I was at once. As it was decided I would do so as I was leaving, just in time to get even with everybody.

"I went to sleep in that humiliated frame of mind and this is what I dreamed:

"The flippant news stand girl, accompanied by the bell boy who had been insolent, came to my door and told me to come down to the back yard. They rather ordered than invited me to come. I resented it but felt I must be as dignified as possible.

"When we reached the back yard it looked exactly like that back yard we had at home twenty-five years ago.

"There was the one scrubby tree, the weeds and stones and general sordidness I remember so well as characterizing that rear lot of ours.

"These two pointed out to me a large flock of chickens running loose, and told me that though it was their task to keep them out of the garden, they were going to a concert that afternoon and I must do it in their place.

"I bitterly resented this, especially their thinking I was such a nonentity as that. But the final insult came just as they were leaving.

" 'Here are the twins,' they said, handing me over two soiled, squalling squirming babies. I did not seem able to resist nor put into words my unutterable fury at this procedure, and before I could do anything they were gone.

"I had a very interesting book and sat down to read, only to be incessantly interrupted by the babies getting into a nearby ditch and the chickens picking at the lettuce.

"For a while I tried to carry out my orders, then decided I would show them. When they returned the chickens had eaten up all the garden and the babies were wallowing in the water, completely covered with mud—their dresses hopelessly ruined.

"They rushed in exclaiming that the concert was a great disappointment. The star had not appeared.

"Then they spied the babies and the chickens and began to scold me. I let them say just enough to get themselves in deep.

"Then I pointed to the Western sky which had by then darkened and in which the evening star was just visible.

"There they saw—blazing across the firmament and illuminating the whole world—my name in letters of flame, MILLIONS OF MILES HIGH!

"They gasped and exclaimed: 'Why, that's the name of the star who didn't appear this afternoon.' Whereupon I explained very modestly, 'Even a star can't be in two places simultaneously, and I was here you see.'

"'Then as the horror of the thing they had done came over them and they began to apologize, I haughtily lifted my skirts away from them and their muddy babies and sailed off, leaving them utterly crushed and bitterly bewailing the fact that they had missed this chance with the world-famous star they adored!"

This dream is so obvious it scarcely requires explanation. Nevertheless it is interesting to note how true to form it runs and how it illustrates almost every phase and element of dreams.

To begin with, the opera star's dream has the clarity, vividness and intensity which characterizes most of the dreams of successful people.

Any individual who is getting from everyday life so much satisfaction, fame and fortune as this illustrious woman, does not think in the double symbols which are forced upon the unsuccessful or disappointed.

Things as they are being highly gratifying to her, this woman thinks in terms of things as they are, with little subterfuge, pretense, or symbolization.

The star's ego had been wounded by the news stand girl and the bell hop, and she reasoned thus to herself, "They would treat me very differently and deferentially if they dreamed who I was." So in her dreams these two unappreciative people (whom she supposes know of and adore the person she really is and would give anything to associate with her personally) are reduced to utter humiliation, and she triumphs gloriously.

All the ignominy she permits herself to suffer tending the chickens and the twins is endured for the sole purpose of thoroughly humiliating those two people who snubbed her during the day. (You note how she didn't really tend the garden nor the babies very long, but got her revenge even before the parents returned, by letting the babies ruin their dresses and the chickens ruin the garden.)

In her dream she achieved complete revenge—even to the sailing off with her skirts held away from them as she would like to do in the hotel lobby.

The babies and chicken-tending were old images stored away in her subconscious from childhood and used in this dream as symbolizing the extreme humiliation which she felt when ignored and insulted by the girl and the bell hop.

Her name, lighting up the entire sky in letters of fire, is the one mental image which above all others would symbolize fame in the mind of one who had had always been ambitious. The evening star was a very obvious symbol of herself, "the star," closely connected with the famous and shining name, blazing there in the firmament for all the world to see.

This dream differs from the average dream in that it was exceedingly long, and at the same time coherent and integrated from beginning to end.

There were no missing links, no disjointed parts. The entire experience was vivid, co-ordinated, with every part fitting into place like a mosaic into a pattern.

"I often remember snatches of dreams," she said, "and fleeting dream-experiences that do not appear to belong anywhere, but this one was as definite and dramatic as a play, with nothing extraneous, nothing isolated. It was more clear, in fact, than almost any actual experience I ever had."

This latter fact is often true of our dreams and for two excellent reasons:

The first is that the dream is the product of the subconscious which constitutes nine-tenths of the mind and is nine times more powerful.

The second is that in dreams our attention is not diverted by irrelevant or marginal things such as distract us during waking hours, but is concentrated exclusively on the dream. You will recall how in dreams you are never interrupted by other people's taking the stage, and are never aware of any time, place or condition other than those of your dream.

"My dreams seem to be nothing but left-overs from the day's experiences" says many a one, and this at first glance seems to be the only tangible significance of most of our dreams.

But that there is a far deeper meaning you may see for yourself by noting that though many a dream BEGINS with some event of the day, it never STICKS TO THE FACTS of the original occurrence but branches off into other directions, injecting all manner of new details which are in themselves irrelevant.

In every instance you will note that the dream is built around a recent event which was in some way a DISAPPOINTMENT TO YOU. In the dream you go back and make changes to suit your subconscious self.

You live over certain elements of the experience, or live it over up to a certain point. From that point onward, instead of adhering to what actually happened the dream carries out what you WISH had happened.

And now we come to one of the most interesting things about dreams— their symbolism.

As you have read this lesson, perhaps you have been thinking, "But how can my dreams come from my desires? Why, I have often had dreams in which I did things I didn't like and experienced all manner of things I didn't desire."

This apparently paradoxical condition delayed for many centuries science's unraveling of the real meaning of our dreams.

Then a few years ago there was discovered the most significant fact of all—that we dream not only in pictures, but that those pictures are full of symbols.

In other words, the subconscious, which is in control of our dreams, is full of symbols, each of which represents, in the mind of the individual, something very definite. This symbol stands for this definite something because of its having been connected with some experience of the individual's life (usually in his childhood) in such a way as to fasten it into his subconscious mind.

There are several reasons for this, the chief one being that the subconscious is not a reasoning but a feeling, knowing mind. It simplifies all things, reduces them to their lowest common denominator.

So when the individual passes through some especially vivid experience it is filed away in the memory—not as a detailed, minutely recorded thing like a page of statistics, but as a highly colored picture.

In every case the picture will relate to whichever element was experienced at the moment of the highest pitch of emotion. This emotional element is what makes any experience vivid in memory.

More will be explained concerning these pictures and their far-reaching effect upon the individual's life, in the next lesson, but for the present it is sufficient to know that your mind has automatically been filing away these symbols ever since you were born and that very early in life you acquired one for almost every kind of thought, feeling or group of thoughts and sensations you experienced.

Dreams, being almost exclusively in pictures staged by the subconscious, deal in wholesale fashion with these old mental pictures of ours.

The best illustration of how the subconscious mind utilizes old symbols in the making of new dreams is seen every day in the office of big city newspapers.

Every newspaper has filed away, numbered and indexed, every picture it has printed in previous issues. This department is known fittingly, though uncannily, as "the morgue."

These pictures correspond to the pictures you unconsciously filed away in your subconscious as symbolizing your previous experiences. That your subconscious, like the newspaper office, files these away AT THE TIME and then forgets them till they are needed again, makes the analogy a perfect one.

There are thousands of these old pictures, photos, illustrations, cartoons and diagrams stowed away in the newspaper's "morgue."

The keeper of the morgue remembers only the merest fraction of them. But when a striking thing happens—when something "breaks," as the newspaper world says—the morgue is called upon for any pictures which can be utilized to illustrate the story in that day's issue.

This accounts for the fact that you sometimes see ancient photos, with hats, coiffures and clothes that have been out of style for twenty years, used in connection with new stories.

The editor used these only for lack of newer ones. New pictures of private individuals are not easily secured by newspapers, just as new symbols are not easily acquired by your subconscious mind and, as the newspaper is compelled to use pictures (symbols) representing an individual as he appeared at some function or affair twenty or thirty years ago, so the subconscious digs up and uses in our dreams old, old symbols which stand for experiences, thoughts and emotions which we experienced many years ago.

Your conscious mind may be likened to the city editor who keeps in momentary touch with everything happening around him. Your subconscious acts and reacts precisely as does the keeper of the newspaper's picture gallery. It takes no more notice of what is passing in your immediate surroundings moment by moment than the morgue keeper takes of the news happening in the great city.

That isn't his job. But when anything exciting or interesting, and especially when something highly dramatic or sensational, happens in your everyday life, either as a desire or an actual experience, the city editor of your conscious mind reports it to the keeper of your old subconscious picture gallery and he furnishes the illustrations for the picturesque edition that floats before your mind in the form of dreams that night.

Every dream gets its original impulse from some recent personal experience or desire which hinges on something that has just previously happened or been hoped for, as does every story or article printed in the daily paper. By ten o'clock in the morning the dreams of the night before are as out of date and forgotten as is the newspaper of the day before.

The conscious mind is busy, just as is the city editor, with the problems of the present—getting ready to print a new edition.

What the dream edition prints in your mind's eye that night will depend on which of the day's experiences have most intimately and emotionally affected the ego or your subconscious wishes.

This accounts for the fact that we dream many dreams during each night, some related and some unrelated to each other. Though many people do not recall their dreams the next day no one has yet been found who, when suddenly awakened, was not in the midst of some sort of dream.

He may forget it an instant afterward, but he will have at least some slight realization on the instant of waking that he was having some kind of dream-sensation.

When you dream of having things or doing things you dislike or are indifferent to—that is, whenever the desire is not apparent in a dream, think back through your experiences and see if you can not recall what the dream-pictures symbolize in the back of your mind. For the following law operates in every dream:

When a dream contains elements which are, so far as we know, underlined by the conscious mind these elements are symbolic of something which is deeply desired either by the conscious or subconscious mind, and usually by both.

Nightmares are merely dreams containing desires whose symbols are not pleasant ones, and in which the action, which is also symbolic, becomes so intense it awakens the conscious mind from sleep.

A case illustrating the use of symbols in staging subconscious wishes in dreams came under our notice several years ago.

A nurse of high standing in the city of San Francisco wishes to have analyzed the following dream which had recurred until it had become an obsession:

She said, "The hospital has an insufficient staff of nurses so I am busy all day and part of the night. This has continued for many months and I am getting so worn out physically that unless I am able to free myself of the distracting dream which often awakens me with its horror I shall have to resign.

"Every time I fall asleep, if only for a moment, I have this dream:

"I am standing at the foot of a bed in the ward, where of course I have witnessed many deaths. The white screen which we always place around a cot in the last moments looms up in this dream as clearly as it does in my waking hours.

"But instead of a stranger it is one of the former hospital doctors who lies there dying. I see his agony and the death struggle, his appeal to me to save him.

"But just as I try to do something the dream ends—soon to begin all over again."

The full understanding of her dream so clarified the subconscious of this young woman that in four days it ceased to recur—a recovery much more rapid than is possible in most cases.

Her frankness, sincerity and previous scientific training, added to the fact that the dream was easily analyzed according to symbols, made the cure a simple one.

The death-bed had become, unconsciously, a very significant symbol in the nurse's mind—the symbol of something she deeply desired.

She had, despite valiant efforts to the contrary, and despite the fact that she would not admit it to herself, fallen in love with one of the hospital physicians who was already married.

Some months prior to her coming to us this physician had resigned from the hospital board and had moved to another city. The last time she had seen him was when they officiated jointly at a death-bed scene in the ward.

She had lived this last moment with him over so vividly, had recalled the emotions with which she had been torn at the time (knowing, as she did, that he was leaving) that it became fixed in the subconscious as a symbol of his presence.

Subconsciously she had longed to have the wife's place, to minister to him, endear herself to him and be able to do something very great for him—something that would make him care.

To save man's life is the surest, quickest route into his gratitude and affection, so the subconscious devised this little drama.

When she met her situation frankly and when she realized that the dream came from her own mind and was not, as she had feared, a premonition of the impending death of the doctor, the condition cleared immediately.

A dream composed entirely of symbols recurred to a woman on an average of two or three nights a week for over twenty-five years. She said:

"In this dream I am laboriously climbing over huge bowlders, deep ravines and tremendous crags in my efforts to reach the top of a high mountain whose sides are almost perpendicular.

"Far down below—straight down below in the bottom of the canyon—there dashes over the rocks a mad, rushing, foaming river. I am constantly on the lookout to prevent myself from falling for I know I would be mangled to death long before I reached the bottom if I should lose my footing.

"Now the strange part of this is that I am never really frightened by this great height nor actually in danger of falling, for I am wearing thick-soled, heavy mountain shoes which enable me to secure a sure and solid footing. Though I can never climb as rapidly as I desire I am always making good progress.

"Another strange thing in this dream is that I always have one boon companion—William Jennings Bryan. He walks by my side, though he never takes hold of my hand nor offers to help me. But he is extremely courteous and we chat pleasantly and in the most simple friendly way as we climb upward.

"A great many people are in our party, but Mr. Bryan and I seem to be finding the path by which they are to climb. Every little while we lean over the precipice and call down to them. They make headway and some of them climb very fast. These seem happy and exceedingly grateful to us for showing them the way and blazing the trail.

"In this dream Mr. Bryan and I are very simply clothed—he in an old fashioned suit and I in a durable brown serge. Mr. Bryan carries in his right hand exactly sixteen different kinds of flowers—columbines, brown-eyed susans and other wild flowers—while my arms seem to be loaded with those dark red blooms called 'Bleeding Hearts.' "

This dream, so symbolical from beginning to end, is crystal-clear when the woman's supreme subconscious wish, plus her childhood experiences, are made known.

She had grown up in the wildest part of the Rocky Mountains, and mountains became to her the symbols of "the heights" to which her ambition pointed. This ambition was to be a great orator—an orator like Bryan, whom she had first heard of when he ran for President in 1896. Mr. Bryan became to her the symbol of her oratorical ambition.

Having lived all her life in the fastnesses of the mountains this young woman's symbols all bore the marks of her early environment. This accounted for the fact that though she was a woman of middle age when she told her dream and had for many years lived exclusively in great cities, the symbols in the dream had never changed.

Neither did the dream-elements alter so much as a hair's breadth, and the reason for this too is obvious.

Her ambition, her supreme subconscious wish, had never changed. From her youth she had desired one thing above all others—to be a great speaker. And though she desired it so much that she became a well-known lecturer, she still dreamed the dream because she had never reached the complete fulfilment of her ambition.

She came, in years, to have audiences which filled the largest auditoriums, but she had other ambitions than speaking to great crowds, though this element was naturally always present in her desires.

That Mr. Bryan carried sixteen kinds of flowers to one was amusingly symbolical of Bryan's first slogan, "Sixteen to One."

The most significant symbol in this dream is that of the "Bleeding Heart" flowers that "loaded down her arms."

She grew up in poverty, and her youth was black with those hardships known only to pioneer and especially mountain pioneer regions.

At an early age she came to sympathize with all the poor and struggling because of her own struggles and poverty—and to think of their broken hearts in the terms of the "Bleeding Heart" flowers that grew on the mountains near her home.

She longed to help these others who were poor and ambitious up the heights along with herself, and wanted to do it through oratory—the simple sincere kind Bryan used. In all her dreams, even after she came to realize this ambition in great measure, she dreamed the same thing over and over because she was still struggling, still climbing, still trying to go higher and take more people.

Sometimes their burdens seemed to "load her down," as did the flowers they symbolized, but always "they made progress" and always she was confident she would not fall into the canyon symbolizing Failure because she wore mountain shoes and planted her feet solidly on the ground.

They were symbolic also of her certainty that she "stood on solid, scientific ground," that she had grounded herself in what she was teaching; that she had a good foundation for what she was doing.

Her plain brown serge symbolized the simplicity which the woman had always held as an ideal.

This dream is more pleasant than otherwise—containing just enough of the struggle element to stimulate the courage and test the ambition—so she has never tried to be rid of it, and indeed is better for having the greatest ambitions and ideals run off in this dream-movie to keep her reminded that the top has not yet been reached.

The subconscious has been called "the treasure vault of memory." In it is preserved the record of every thing we have ever heard, seen, read, learned.

It never forgets. Everything you ever knew you know still—whether your memory is able to dive down and bring it from the bottom of your consciousness at this moment or not.

One reason why all persons are not able to do this now is that we have, until the last few years, been ignorant of the fact that the mind did remember, and have taken it for granted that things passed entirely out of our mental grasp—that we had "forgotten."

A clearer understanding of the subconscious enables even the beginner to revive in consciousness many things he had imagined completely erased from memory.

The subconscious is always on the alert. We now know with complete certainty that it never sleeps—in fact, that it is more active when the conscious mind sleeps than during our waking hours.

We have seen proof of this many times in our own lives—as, for instance, when we can awaken without an alarm clock to catch a 4 a. m. train if we really want to take the journey.

Nurses in hospital wards full of patients sleep soundly through all manner of outcries but awaken at the whispered request of their own patients. A mother sleeps through many disturbances but rouses at the merest movement of her sick child.

The country man upon coming to the city is unable to sleep the first few nights but his subconscious soon adapts itself and he sleeps as soundly through those same noises a week later as he did out on the farm.

"Does the mind have a body or does the body have a mind?" is a question over which the philosophers have wrangled for centuries. Today we know that both are true and that the subconscious mind, of which these ancient arguers were unaware, is the bridge between the body and the mind.

The conscious mind functions through the brain but the subconscious functions throughout the entire body—the cerebrum, the muscles, the solar plexus, the nerves—apparently through every cell in both body and brain.

That this is no far-fetched theory is shown in the fact that its first American exponent was that greatest living material scientist, Thomas A. Edison. He says, "Every cell in us thinks," and has proven to his own satisfaction that nothing is dead matter but all is living energy expressing itself in various forms.

There have always been those who realized the influence of these submerged selves of ours and there is not a thinking human but who realizes that many things in his life, however much they may mystify others, are but the outward expression of something in his inner life.

But it requires an unusually high grade of intelligence and an unusually frank heart to acknowledge what Mental Analysis shows us so clearly today—that:

Your money,
Your possessions,
Your good luck and bad luck,
Your ill health or perfect health,
Your environment,
Your life as a whole—

are the harvests from seeds you planted in the soil of your subconscious in days gone by.

But whether you realize it or not, these things are true. You are reaping what you have sown. The results are in accordance with laws—laws that are inexorable, unchanging, and absolutely impersonal.

Your life today is the net result of your yesterdays. Your tomorrows will be the net result of those yesterdays plus the seeds you are planting today, this hour and this instant.

The only way to make the tomorrows what you wish them to be is to learn what you have already planted, how to uproot the weak and cultivate the strong things that are growing in your personality, and how to plant from this hour onward ONLY THE SEEDS whose fruit you desire to reap in your coming years.

This course, by showing you these things, can enable you to remake your life, as it has already done for thousands of our former students.

All great souls have recognized and declared that they were strangely aided by something within themselves but which they did not "reason out."

Every famous composer has said, "No, I can't tell you how I thought out the music because I did not do so. It came to me. I put down what came."

Every great poet has said, "I can not tell you how I wrote this poem because I do not know. It said itself in my mind, and I wrote it down."

Every famous orator has said, "The right thoughts never come when I am trying to write out a speech. My audience is the other half of me. The best ideas come only when I am face to face with the crowd."

Every illustrious minister has declared, "The best parts of my sermons are never written in my study but come into my mind as I stand before my congregation."

The "flash of inspiration" which comes to the lawyer at the crucial moment in his trial of a case, comes not from his conscious but from his subconscious mind, as he will tell you himself.

The reason so few people achieve greatness is not that there are but few with the spark of genius in them, but the source of greatness—the subconscious mind—is clogged in all but the few. The mental machinery of most people is full of monkey wrenches and junk, the brakes are all on and the cylinders are skipping.

The average mind is as disorganized as a rag bag.

Almost every individual leads a Dr. Jekyll and Mr. Hyde life, with part of his mind pulling one way and another pulling the opposite. Then he wonders why this split personality makes no more progress.

There is no mystery about it. Such a man is never able to present a solid front to the world.

A unified personality is the first requisite for success or happiness under any condition whatever.

The energies, mentality and interests of the average individual are disorganized, disrupted, chaotic, jumbled in a mixed-up heap. Few people see the ruinous effect of this splitting of the personality, and some even consider it an achievement.

A man calls himself clever when he is able to live one life outwardly and another inwardly. He is able to appear at a social affair disliking the whole thing—the guests, the interruption to his business, even the hostess—and all the while talk and act as though charmed, flattered, delighted and happy.

"Good gracious, what an insufferable bore!" he exclaims to his wife the instant they are out of earshot.

"Society compels me to lead this double life," he will say, "My business requires it, social amenities demand it."

And to an extent these are true. But we are coming to realize that insincerity of any kind, reacts back on the personality with fatal consequences.

First among these consequences is the disintegrating of the consciousness and no man can succeed whose two minds are not working in harmony.

It is not easy to lead double lives, even though they be comparatively innocent ones. Concealed facts are always popping out into open sight. Slips of the tongue, glances and postures—a hundred things betray the man who would keep out of sight his real and actual self.

The subconscious is like a vast irrigation system with every muscle a tiny headgate in the great network. A man may learn to watch one or two or even a dozen of these headgates in eyes, mouth, voice and manner—but they are so numerous he can not watch them all, and from whence he least expects it there will break out the tell-tale overflow.

This latest of the human sciences shows us what we have been doing to ourselves, our lives, our chances in life, our loves, hopes and aspirations; how we have been unconsciously poisoning our own wells at their source; how we have administered mental narcotics to ourselves when we most needed mental stimulation; how we have built up the present from our own individual, racial and biological past into a structure in which we now live and through which our personalities function, express themselves and meet the world.

It shows how we may easily and immediately reverse the process and begin to get the things we want out of life.

The laws which rule us and our lives are divine, unalterable. He who obeys them, whether he do so consciously or unconsciously, reaps the rewards that other people call "good luck." He who consciously or unconsciously violates them pays the penalties he calls his "bad luck."

The supremest effort of life, therefore, should be to learn what the laws are which rule human happiness and how they operate, that we may consciously and constantly plant the seeds for the harvests we want.

This course in Mental Analysis has made these laws so clear, concise, graphic and understandable that any one can put them to use in the solving of his everyday problems. They bring results from the first moment of applying them, in happiness, health and success.

Some may say, "These things sound impossible." It is inevitable that some would say this. Every step in human progress has been opposed at first and forced to fight its way to recognition against skepticism and criticism.

Thinking men and women know that the human race is in the infant stage of its development; that a few hundred years from now human beings will be doing things as beyond our present achievements as ours are beyond those of prehistoric man.

And those who have given the subject thought realize that this progress is coming, as it has already begun to come, through the one thing that has given man sovereignty over the globe—further understanding and development of his consciousness.

LESSON IX

Your Emotions

MAN is superior to animals in proportion as his mind is superior to theirs, and to the extent that his intellect, not his emotions, rules his actions. One man is superior to another and achieves results superior to the other's in exact proportion as his mind is in better working order, more under his control and better understood by him.

"If I bring my own sufferings and successes why have I not been taught this before?" others will ask.

There is but one answer. We are never taught the things most vital to human happiness.

Fathers and mothers are so busy getting food for their children's stomachs and clothes for their backs, they have no time or energy to investigate or explain either to themselves or to their children how the human mind controls human happiness.

The result is that parents who would not think of feeding their children's intestines canned food, feed their intellects with canned ideas—ideas so outworn, so stale and putrid that the child is forever handicapped in the race of life.

Teachers and preachers—the other two forces which train the young mind—are so harassed by the overpowering problem of making small salaries suffice for necessities that they have neither heart nor head for remoter human ones.

Thus we grow up, knowing "a lot of things that ain't so"—things that are easy to teach, pretty to preach, but impossible to live up to.

We are told that "virtue is its own reward"—and see the most virtuous people all around us rewarded with kicks and poverty.

We are told that "genius is the art of taking infinite pains"—only to discover that the most painstaking people are in bookkeeping cages getting $20 a week, while every genius is notoriously incapable of taking pains with anything save what he loves—even his shoe laces!

We are taught that "success comes from hard work"—but note how the day laborer gets four dollars for working his hands eight hours, while the banker makes a fortune by working his head four hours a day and playing golf the rest of the time.

The secret of success is not hard work, painstaking effort, nor even virtue—though each of these is essential to supreme happiness.

The secret of success for every human being lies in the harmonious working of his conscious and subconscious powers.

Those who have succeeded have, in every instance, consciously or unconsciously, used their minds as they were intended to be used; those who failed unconsciously violated the laws of the mind and reaped the inevitable result.

This submerged nine-tenths of the consciousness is of the utmost significance in every human life. It has unlimited capacity for good or evil, according as it is used or misused. Each individual's life is made or marred by this vast subterranean sea of urges and impulses.

This great self is infinitely strong, infinitely courageous, infinitely powerful. It exists for one purpose, and one only—to externalize you, to bring you self-expression, to secure for you an untrammelled personality, to attain for you your supreme subconscious aim.

From birth to death it strives to set you free, to enable you to be yourself, your truest, real-ist self.

The greatest psychological discovery of recent ages shows us that the entire personality of every human being is built around some one deep, consuming desire—some supreme subconscious wish.

In one individual this supreme desire is for one thing, in another for something else, depending on the type and temperament of each, but no human being lives who does not have some deep desire at the core of his heart.

That every man builds his life around this supreme wish is the explanation of many of our otherwise incredible inconsistencies, strange reactions, and of the remarkable accomplishments of apparently mediocre men and women.

Many persons know what their supreme life wish is. The most successful always know, and their success is due more to this knowledge than to any other one thing.

When we say "that man knows his own mind," we are saying much more than we realize. For there are many who do not know and these many are the failures in life.

Those who only guess are the half-failures.

In utilizing your subconsciousness, strenuous effort is neither necessary nor desirable.

This mind is already organized and ready to work out for you whatever you desire. It does not need urging. It is the real you. It contains all your aspirations and impulses already. It does not require encouragement any more than a river needs to be encouraged to flow to the sea.

All it needs is direction. It is keyed for action, and has been every day since you were born. It is like a race horse that has been trained for the track. Take the reins in your hand and let it work for you.

You have never tested the powers within your own personality because society, schools, teachers, preachers and parents are organized against every kind of spontaneous expression of the individual.

That is why it is in danger of committing suicide—this society of ours. That is why some of its members are constantly turning against it and doing damage in the form of murder and war.

We must live understandingly before we can live uprightly.

Do not waste time and energy trying to "get out of yourself." The man who tries to get out of himself before he has cleaned house is working in the wrong direction.

The person who feels impelled to get out of himself has something wrong inside which he can not bear to look at. So he goes to the theatre, drinks, gambles, speeds, scolds, spends money and time foolishly.

But it does no good. He can not get away from himself. The moment the excitement is over back he slumps to the old self which is worse than it was before, because it knows and he knows the wasting of time, energy, money and thought in the attempt to drown his troubles has harmed him, entangled him more deeply and pushed him farther back than ever.

The teaching, "forget yourself for the world" is a beautiful deal—one we must more and more live up to if we hope to be truly happy. It is necessary to the progress of the world for us to lose ourselves in self-forgetful service.

Your subconscious is either backing your work or "bucking it." It will back you in anything that is in accordance with your supreme wish. You will do the amazing tasks with amazing ease once you start.

But anything which is in opposition to it will go slowly, sadly, heavily, and inefficiently.

Whatever aids and abets your supreme subconscious aim you will labor over for long hours absolutely without fatigue, but whatever takes you in the opposite direction leaves you actually physically exhausted at the end of ten minutes.

How gladly and gaily we do a task today when it furthers some particular project! How glumly and grumpily we do the very same thing tomorrow if it no longer furthers that project.

With what vim a young girl who has always disliked housework helps mother with dinner and the dishes when her young man is there to see!

How easy it is to forget bills we owe—but how that same memory of ours does work when the other fellow owes us!

How simple to remember the addresses, the initials, and even the telephone numbers of new people we are interested in, and how difficult to remember even the names of those we are indifferent to! The only difference in all these cases is the difference in the way in which a subconscious wish is affected.

"If it is possible for my subconscious to get for me anything I wish why have I never gotten the things I most desired?" is a reasonable and inevitable question. because you have violated the laws whereby the subconscious operates.

You, like everything else in the universe, are a part of, not apart from natural law. Your being is responsive to and built in accordance with certain divine rules, regulations and edicts. When you disobey those you suffer, when you obey them you succeed.

You must free your subconscious of the shackles with which you have all your life crippled it; you must take off the throttles with which you have been choking it; you must give the strong self of you a chance to work for you; you must take your hands off the bridle of this swift racer that champs at the bit, and let him go.

Every great, successful, big or famous person has differed from the failures wholly and solely in proportion as he learned there was a deep voice within him, listened to that voice, and let it out for all the world to hear!

First of all get rid of the notion that people and things and life in general are "against you." Nothing can harm you but yourself and the only way you can permanently hurt yourself is by the misuse of your mentality.

Luck is not against you. Luck is what you make it. Conditions and circumstances may be adverse to you at this moment, but if so, they are the ones you have made by your previous thinking. Stop that kind of thinking or you will go on piling up more adverse conditions for tomorrow.

Your subconscious may be compared to a great ocean liner. As we gaze at her across the blue ocean what do we see?

We say we see the steamer. But what we see is her upper decks, masts and fluttering flags; the waving, smiling passengers—the life and action of her.

But there is far more to that steamer than this. There is her great body—the lower regions, the steerage, the hundreds of workmen, tons of cargo, massive machinery and powerful dynamos.

The upper decks look important, but the thing that determines how far and how fast she travels, what she carries, and whether or not she ever reaches port, depend on the way the unseen forces work down in her hull.

The outside of you that men see are your upper decks. People, and perhaps you yourself, imagine these are all there is to you.

But it is only a fraction. The direction in which you go, what you do with your life, how far you travel and the port at which you arrive, all depend on the workings of the subconscious mind down there in your hull.

That subconscious is not only nine-tenths of your mind but nine-tenths of you. It is far stronger than anything and everything else within you, utterly fearless and unafraid.

It possesses powers beyond your wildest dreams. When you put yourself in harmony with it, it will carry you surely and safely to your desired destination. It will get for you anything you really want.

Why You Give Up Things

You want many things, but you always give up those you want less for those you want most. Thus, in the by-and-large of your life you do what you want to do; you get the things you really want.

If you are unsuccessful it is because there was one or many things you wanted more than you wanted success.

Look back over your life and you will say that in your life as a whole you have been doing those things which, in general, appealed to you more than the kinds of things you refused to do.

Perhaps you want money and yet are poor.

But no one ever had a supreme subconscious wish for money. The subconscious, as has been stated, knows nothing of things, details, or the concrete. It knows only certain fundamentals—those big, basic urges of your personality.

It knows many of these but takes it upon itself to fulfill in your life the one which, above all others, you want most. It has never heard of money and never can, for money, as money, is nothing but worthless chunks of metal and useless pieces of paper. Even your conscious mind, which does know and deals with money, does not want money but only the self-expression which money would bring.

Since the subconscious gets for you whatever you want most, if the thing you want most is of such a nature that you have got to have money to get it, your subconscious will find a way for you to make money.

It can find the means to any end you supremely, subconsciously demand. It will do so by keeping your eyes open for opportunities furthering this end.

It deals only with ultimates. Money, which has less intrinsic and ultimate value than almost anything with which we come in contact, is never in any man's supreme subconscious wish as such. It is not even in the supreme wish of the miser, but is desired and obtained by him wholly and solely as a means to protection. (The miser is always the result of a fixed fear—the fear of poverty—the product of a poverty-stricken childhood.)

But because the fear-attitude prevents great results in any direction, the miser, with all his skimping, never makes a great deal of money.

No self-made millionaire in the world ever cared for money as money. He had some kind of supreme subconscious wish requiring money for its full expression. It is precisely this which, every rich person will tell you, drove him to make money.

Once it is made very few very rich people care for money. They conserve it only in so far as its conservation serves that same original wish.

Fame Through Fortune

Here is a man whose supremest subconscious wish is for fame. His subconscious, which knows and remembers everything about him, contains the necessary elements and brings them to the surface as they are needed.

He has certain gifts, talents, abilities. He lacks certain others. The quickest and surest route to the materialization of his supreme wish is through these talents. His subconscious suggests these routes.

If these talents are superior he will rise to fame through them. The greater these talents the greater the urge to express them and the greater his ability to serve, entertain, amuse, or enlighten the world. In return, the world applauds him, gives him fame, pays him well—and his supreme wish is gratified.

People are always glad to pay for what they like. The public is always generous to the able man. Whether or not he cares very much about money he is glad to have the public's money purely as a proof that he has succeeded—that his ego has satisfied itself, proven to itself that it can do this thing.

Ambitious Americans

In America success is all too often measured by money. Since money is the great American standard, and since every ambitious individual desires to live up to the standards of his environment, the ambitious American is compelled to seek money.

Let a man with a message attempt to carry that message to the American public. Though it be the greatest message in the world, that public will not ask "How much good does this man do?" It will not even ask "What is his message about?"

This public will ask but one question. That question will consist of six words: "how much money does he make?"

Though you produce the greatest thing that has yet been produced, the American public will have none of it nor you if you can not make it pay financially.

In self-defence, therefore, any person who has a great message to give to America is compelled to make that message pay. He must have the confidence of the public, as does any man who aspires to help the world.

It is inconceivable to the average American that you could have anything worth while unless you are making a financial success of your life.

Instead of railing at the one who makes a great deal of money, use that energy to re-educate the public if you are really in earnest.

If You Want Money

If you want money you must do what every person did who ever made money: produce something the world wants and knows it wants. The world is always willing and glad to pay for what it really wants.

But it is determined not to pay for what it does not want, just because you want or need the money. And you can't blame it, can you?

Remember, you can only get money via the world. For it you must give value received. To do that easiest and quickest, you must make your supreme subconscious wish into a real desire to produce something the world needs. Once you have done this, the same forces which have always and will forever bring your supreme wish to pass in your life will point the way.

Your Successful Subconscious

Let us repeat: Your supreme subconscious wish dictates your life. It permits nothing seriously to interfere with its materialization. It is autocratic, implacable. What you want most of all, as a condition in your life, it will get for you.

In the getting you are often compelled to forego many or hundreds of things you want, but want less.

Your subconscious causes you to sacrifice these many things, and all things, if necessary, to the accomplishment of this supremest desire.

You must relinquish this, sacrifice that, forego the other. You feel all this in the depths of you. You do not like giving up the eating of your cake but—if you want the cake more than you want the pleasure of eating it, you will not eat it. Your subconscious and supreme wish will not permit you to. You made this choice yourself. Your subconscious takes you at your word, and not only relieves you of most of the labor by performing it itself, but refuses to permit you to greatly interfere with its activities.

Your conscious mind may falter and fail, but your subconscious, once saturated with your supremest desire, is always successful.

Subconscious of the Successful

The most successful men and women, once they have decided on their supreme aim, automatically adapt themselves to this great law.

Every successful person that ever lived gave up many things for the sake of his big ambition. At first he did so consciously. He had many backslidings. But as time went on his conscious and subconscious minds worked in such unison that his subconscious sentinel learned at last habitually to turn away from the door of his mind the things that would interfere with the big desire, without his ever being conscious of making a decision.

This is the secret of the great concentration, the "one-pointed" mind, the keen thought-capacity of every successful person.

His mind is not necessarily superior to that of the average man, but he does what the average man fails to do—keeps the decks clear and ready for business. He keeps out of his mind, automatically, habitually, consciously and unconsciously the thieves that would steal his mental energy.

After a time his subconscious becomes so expert that it short-circuits most of the wasteful, inimical things that are headed for his mental house, thus conserving his mentality for the constructive, the worth while, the big thing in that man's life.

The subconscious performs, in addition to all its other services, the function of an expert private secretary guarding the front office of the mind. He permits no visitor to interrupt the president in his private office when he is at work.

Thus is the president (his conscious mind) enabled to think out the plans, the ways, means and methods for making him a success.

Your Wish Is a Want

The reason your subconscious attains for you your supremest wish is that this deepest desire of your life is not a mere wish at all, but a goading, driving, overwhelming want.

It is necessary, up to this point, because of the inadequacy of language, to call this a wish. But from this moment onward we shall call it what it is—the supreme subconscious want. There is a world of difference between wishing and wanting.

When you wish for a thing you get it—sometimes. When you want a thing you always get it. For a want is not a mere surface feeling, but a deep, desperate craving that demands not things nor people, nor trifling details, but great general outlets of self-expression. You must satisfy the greatest one or die.

This supreme want is far more important than life itself to many human beings.

These are the supreme successes. They had rather die than miss their goal. The man who wants a thing more than he wants life is filled with an enthusiasm so irresistible that it literally burns away all obstacles from his pathway.

What and Why Is the Suicide?

The psychology of the suicide has been till now a mystery.

"No clue to the motive," say a man's friends when they can find no cause for his desire to die. How seldom does the world ever guess the real reason for those sufferings which so rack a human soul that it relinquishes life rather than bear them! How seldom indeed does the man himself know the subconscious source of this urge, beside which life itself seems trivial.

Yet today we know that every person who commits suicide does so only after he be comes overpowered with the conviction that he can never achieve his supreme subconscious want.

The Woman Suicide

The woman who commits suicide because her lover has deserted her does so because she is convinced that she has lost the only person through whom her demand for a particular kind of self-expression can be met.

She does not think this out. All she knows is that she wants this particular kind of mate, or the particular life that he can give her. Her subconscious want is so strong that it has risen to the surface of her conscious mind and is there recognized by her for what it is—the one thing which makes life worth while.

Her error lies in the delusion that this individual is the only individual through whom she can attain this particular kind of self-expression, this particular response.

Many a woman who has attempted suicide and been saved by resuscitation, or because the bullet went wild of its mark, has lived to realize that this man was, to her subconscious self, only the means to an end; that her fixation upon him resulted from this subconscious certainty of his exclusive ability to furnish her with an avenue for self-expression.

She learns later that the world contains others who will serve this purpose as well, many of whom are far superior to the man she once thought indispensable to her existence.

The "Money" Suicide

"Women commit suicide because of love troubles; men because of money troubles," say the statistics. Here again we see the working of the supreme want.

The supreme subconscious want of woman is more often bound up with love than that of men and, of necessity, must be. She is the mother of the race, the propagation of which depends largely on her love-life. But the support of the home, the securing of life's necessities, is more often man's mission than woman's, and its full expression depends indirectly upon money and the success which money implies.

When a man commits suicide because of money-troubles it is never because he feels he can not live with out the money, but because he feels he can not live and face the disgrace, humiliation or shame the money loss would mean.

In every such case his supreme subconscious want is for something which only money, directly or indirectly, can provide.

We choose the lesser evil always; or rather, we choose the evil which to us appears to be the lesser. The standard is the supreme subconscious want. Everything is measured by its capacity to further that want. We make our own choices. Each individual who is not feeble-minded determines the course of his own life, and does so as much by the things he unconsciously leaves undone as by the things he consciously, volitionally chooses to do.

Honeymooners, tourists, and passers-by may see Niagara Falls as only a great spectacle. But to the engineer, the scientist and the man who stops to think, it is a great spectacle, plus.

He sees its mighty avalanche in the terms of power—the power that furnishes light and heat and driving energy for cities hundreds of miles in every direction—a torrent, swift, swirling and stupendous. Dashing over the precipice its gigantic force instantly annihilates everything before it, but with its energy harnessed in electricity by the mind of man it becomes a powerful constructive current.

Within every individual there is a seething current of feelings, impulses, instincts—his emotional Niagara.

It is primal, elemental, overwhelming. If uncontrolled it will handicap, cripple or completely destroy him—according to the type and temperament of the individual.

In some types the emotions are for the most part like a wide Mississippi. Such are the unruffled people. In other and very methodical types the current is apparently measured out with the precision of an irrigation system, while in others it is a rapid mountain brook with its current never still and never put to any constructive use.

If we waste our emotional energy on non-essentials we are like the brook that babbles and bubbles without doing anything for itself and evaporates, till at the end of its life journey it is nothing but a trickle, financially and otherwise.

If, for any reason, we have little emotional energy and open the headgates only enough to do this little thing and that, in methodical routine, our conserving will do but little good.

You have seen men and women who took the same street car at the same corner at the same moment every morning for years. This is the conserving type—and it conserves everything, from food to feelings.

Such a man is never late at the office. He never misses a day, he never leaves five minutes early. But he never goes to the top. He lacks emotional energy—that great power which in men corresponds to horsepower, and should be called human power.

His human power is always under control, chiefly because there is so little of it. He measures it out as a New England grocer measures out sugar—two grains at a time!

These people run their lives like train schedules and are about as impersonal.

At the next desk there is a man not half so faithful, not a tenth so careful. He is late occasionally, has a day off now and then and instead of doing his work like a machine, slows down some days and races like mad others. But he is the one who gets invited to the social affairs at the boss's house and when a promotion is being passed around he is the man who gets it! He is full of human power. Half organized, he can go farther and faster and accomplish more for the heads of that business than the emotionless man.

But if the emotional man forgets to control his torrent; if the powerhouse of reason is closed up so often that the force of the Niagra is not transmuted into electricity for running the main plant—his life—he can and will wind up a failure.

The most desirable human possession in the world is emotion. Without it, man is colorless, bloodless, lifeless. He can neither experience a great enthusiasm nor kindle it in others.

But it must be controlled by his mind, and its power turned into constructive channels if he would be happy and successful.

Emotional energy may be likened to an electrical current in other ways. It is sometimes decreased, as when we are asleep.

For the most part we are not made conscious of it because it is expended as fast as generated—used up in the activities of every day.

But there are other times when we are conscious of intense feeling—when something pleasant or unpleasant has happened which generated, sometimes instantaneously, an excess of this current.

Whenever this happens you do one of two things. You can not turn the current back to nothingness. It is there. It is intensely alive. You either express it or repress it.

If you express it you are immediately relieved. This explains why the types that have the most fiery tempers forgive quickest. They get it "out of their systems."

It also explains why those that say nothing when angry nurse their grudges. The people who tell you what they think when offended are never pernicious. Those who hide their feelings usually seek revenge later, sometimes long after you have forgotten the incident. They have "saved up," stored away their emotion, awaiting an opportunity.

Keep the cork out of a bottle (which is what the outspoken type is doing) and there is little danger; put the cork in and it ferments. Keep the lid off the kettle and the boiling will do no harm. But keep it on tight and there will be an explosion in some direction.

If the emotion you feel is one which can not be expressed freely and fully in the way it craves; if for any reason you are compelled to push this violent feeling into the background, you may imagine you have short circuited it, but Mental Analysis proves that such is not the case. You have only stored the current.

A switching of the current to something else, through which it can be fully and freely expended, is the only solution in this case.

Every emotion is the combustion that ensues when something has happened which set fire to instinct.

Each of your instincts is a pile of tinder, laid ready for lighting, and handed down to you from remote ancestors. These bundles of tinder "catch fire" easily. They are always ready to blaze up.

Some of them flame out early in life. The instinct of assimilation burns in the new born babe. It is hungry. There is no thought behind its cry for food—nothing but blind instinct.

Other instinctive fires are lighted later on—the sex instinct at adolescence and higher ones as we proceed through life. We become more reasonable as we grow older because reason is given more and more ascendancy as the fires of instinct die down.

But all emotions are the temporary flaring up of the instinct fires. The expression "he got into a heated argument," is not an accidental phrase.

Neither is it accidental that we say "he is a cold nature." Such people are never as emotional as the ones we call "warm natures."

If you can imagine for a moment that though you are a human being, you are full of little banked fires called instincts which are fanned into flame by certain things, you will never again wonder why it is that you become heated literally as well as figuratively when gripped by emotion.

Emotions are of two kinds—pleasurable and painful.

When something occurs to arouse an instinct you do one of two things, as referred to above—repress or express. If you gratify the instinct, the accompanying emotion will be pleasurable. If you thwart it the accompanying emotion will be painful.

Thus, when you become hungry your instinct of assimilation is active. If, when thoroughly aroused, you can sit down to a delicious meal, the emotion is a pleasant one. But if prevented from eating the emotion generated will be a painful one.

Society, as we all know, is organized against the free and full expression of certain instincts.

Laws, rules and social customs exist for the purpose of regulating the expression of certain primitive ones which have come down to us from such remote ages that they are habitually and easily aroused; and for the rewarding of certain other and higher instincts which are so recent in us that they must needs be constantly encouraged and upheld to be kept growing.

Thus we see society praising generosity—an expression of the recent instinct of altruism—and punishing profiteering which is an expression of the remote and primitive instinct of greed.

It rewards the courageous and ostracizes the coward because his cowardice is the expression of the ancient instinct, Fear.

It teaches the young to emulate the example of the ambitious, the idealistic, the fastidious, though ambition, idealism, and fastidiousness are instincts, too. But they are high instincts and make for the good of society as a whole.

Society knows this and safeguards itself so far as it is able. By exacting penalties of various kinds (according to the destructiveness of the instinct involved in each case), it compels more repression of the lower and additional expression of the higher.

This is necessary and right, and will eventually lead to the elimination of the worst and a development of the best in man.

But meanwhile this does not alter the fact that present-day man, possessed as he is of powerful primitive instincts, finds it very difficult to adapt himself to civilization's code.

Something is always occurring to strike the match to an instinct and unless it happens to be one which society favors he either expresses it (in which case he risks society's penalty), or he suppresses it (in which case he pays a personal penalty in some form, depending upon his own type and the intensity of the urge).

Neither of these is desirable. Therefore, it is imperative that the fire of every emotion be permitted to burn out, but that instead of being allowed to destroy should be put to constructive use.

Suppose there is a bonfire in your back yard. If you throw water on it, it may smoulder and break out later. If you allow it to go unchecked it will endanger not only your own house but the homes of your neighbors and perhaps the entire community in which you live.

There is but one thing to do. You must control that fire and give it something constructive to use its force upon.

In your house there are a number of things you have planned to cook. Bring them out, put them over the blaze and let it be doing something worth while with its heat-energy. Then when it has burned itself out you have done something constructive instead of destructive; you have hurt no one, accomplished something for the betterment of your own affairs and perhaps in the doing prepared extra food for the hungry. This would be sublimation.

Some types find it very difficult to sublimate and others do it almost automatically all their lives. Extremely bony people, extreme brunets and those with extremely incurving profiles find sublimation most difficult, but are the very ones who need it most, for they are people of intense feelings. When their feelings are destructive they either wreck things in their expression or repress them so deeply they sometimes wreck the individual himself.

These people are the extremists who either bury an emotion completely or defy the universe.

You will recall that the individuals with these characteristics either stay entirely away from a thing or go into it with a faithfulness that is unending.

The keynote of a man's nature which we sometimes speak of as his individuality is largely determined by his predominant instincts.

These instincts are outlined in the externals of that individual. Every general kind of inner impulse which is common to the human race has outer gateways through which it travels to reach the world and which are indicative of the amount and intensity of that particular urge in the individual's makeup.

Every individual becomes emotional most quickly and most intensely over the things which concern his predominant instincts.

Thus it is that the thing which arouses one man to furious anger leaves another unstirred and still another mildly resentful.

Each is reacting according to the amount and intensity of his pugnacity instinct, a characteristic which shows plainly in his jaw.

Look about amongst your acquaintances and you will see that the references made herein are corroborated in every one of them.

Whether man or woman, the one who is constantly quarreling, "having it out" with people, is an individual with a longer, wider or more protruding jaw than the average. The most noted American example of this was Theodore Roosevelt.

The person who does not become angry until something important or constantly repeated arises, has a jaw that is not extreme in any direction, while the one who lets everybody step on him and never shows anger has either a very receding jaw, a very incurving mouth or fat features.

The immediate effect of completely expressing an emotion is a feeling of satisfaction. This is true regardless of whether the instinct is destructive or constructive, recent or remote and also regardless of the type of the individual.

But if the instinct is a destructive one and the individual a man predominately of high instincts—that is, if he is highly evolved, idealistic or thoroughly civilized—this feeling of satisfaction will soon give way to one of regret, self-criticism or, in extreme cases, remorse.

If he is low-grade evolutionally—if he is a man most of whose instincts are primitive and remote—this feeling of satisfaction will last for a long period and the action, no matter how unsocial, may never be regretted.

If you are one of those who are constantly making certain kinds of mistakes and constantly being torn with regret for having made them, remember this: you are dominated too often by some primitive instinct; but the great majority of your instincts are high grade or you would not have the regrets.

Such a man can always learn. He can adapt himself, improve himself, and if you half try you can overcome your weaknesses. But the remorse you have had, the twinges of conscience you have suffered are certain proof that you have high-grade ore in you to a greater extent than the average person.

Let this fact sink in, then make up your mind not to spend any more time blaming, criticising, despising or loathing yourself, for these mental attitudes are fatal to work and happiness.

You have done enough of that for a hundred lifetimes. Hereafter use all your energy self-confidently, apply it to constructive things. From this time on never waste another moment in remorse no matter what you have done.

When you make mistakes the next time don't become depressed. You can indulge in a little healthy disgust if you must, but never discouragement. Remind yourself that every person in the world who ever made anything worth while, made many grave errors and committed many sins.

The difference between great minds and the rest of mankind was not that the great ones did not make mistakes but that they refused to be crushed by them, got up, shook the dust off their minds and proceeded to make up for it by doing something constructive.

You must do the same, or the future will find you more and more unhappy. Unhappiness leads to more sin, wrong and crime than anything else in the world, but happiness is a powerful aid to goodness.

A man came under our observation several years ago whose health had become undermined. Metabolism tests proved that no specific thing was organically wrong but showed almost every organ functioning sub-normally.

He had once been a man of means, with a good business, but had lost it several years before. Since that time he had gradually gone down financially, physically and mentally, till his friends could scarcely recognize in him the person they had once known.

Yet he had no bad habits, his system was organically strong and mechanically perfect. So far as could be determined there was nothing to account for his disintegration.

His home life had been ideal and his wife was devotion itself. He loved her dearly and took pleasure in the achievements of their two girls who were talented musicians.

He could shed no light on the matter, either for his physicians or for us. He ate well and slept well. But he had lost all interest in living and refrained from committing suicide only out of consideration for his family.

An analysis showed that the trouble had started during a period when he began to despise himself for having done what was, to his high sense of honor, a contemptible thing. Thousands of others would have had no more than a momentary regret, if any, but this self-loathing ate its way into his mind till it consumed him.

He had been sent as a delegate from his district to a convention, but owing to the illness of one of their daughters his wife could not accompany him.

On the train he met a very charming woman whom he had known very slightly in his youth, and who had become so successful a business woman herself that she also was a delegate to the convention.

It happened that they stopped at the same hotel and, entirely without prearrangement, ran into each other constantly during the convention. As each was there alone they ate most of their meals together and, by the time the convention neared its close, he had become decidedly though not deeply attached to her.

He was not a talkative man, but during their last day on the train and in response to an inexplicable impulse in the midst of a champagne supper on the diner, he told her the details of a highly dramatic but regrettable episode in the girlhood of his wife.

Her sin had never been found out, and she had atoned for it by a life of goodness and gentleness. She had confessed it to him fully and he had not only forgiven her but forgotten it now these many years.

An hour after his arrival home he would have given ten thousand dollars to have the story back. At first he lived in the fear that the woman might relate the story, but when her death a month afterward precluded this his regret at having told her was not lessened.

In his own estimation, his conduct had been all the more unpardonable and unforgettable because he was by nature a man of extreme reticence and unusual refinement. His regret became remorse. He could not look at his wife nor hear her voice on the telephone without being reminded of what he had done.

The incident repeated itself in his mind all day and in his dreams all night. He considered himself beneath contempt. He grew to despise himself. He secretly called himself "rotten to the core" and, as he expressed it, "a man without character, devoid of all manhood."

This so wore on him that nothing seemed of any importance in comparison. He had always prided himself on his character and now felt he had none. The result was inevitable to one of his sensitive temperament.

He soon began to lose his grip on business. This made it increasingly difficult for him to give his wife and daughters the things they desired and this in turn increased the self-contempt which was causing the trouble.

Being a business man and a rather ultra-practical one at that, he had never conceived of the idea that his mental condition was in any way responsible for his physical and financial ones. But he at last sought advice.

When told that the strange situation could have had none other than a mental foundation he recalled the sufferings just related.

Upon being shown that his remorse, which had become a prolonged, painful emotion, was not only the cause of his disintegration but the proof that he was by nature a man of the highest impulses, he began to get well, and is today a bigger, better business man than he was before.

To be forced to do things calling for extreme development of some instinct which in that individual is underdeveloped, causes almost as much emotional stress as the thwarting of overdeveloped instincts.

A case clearly illustrating this came to our notice in a Western city some years ago.

An ambitious young woman had risen to a very responsible position for one of her youth—private secretary to the president of a large importing house. But she became so ill-tempered that her employer finally told her she could have a month in which to redeem herself, at the end of which time she must leave unless her disposition had improved.

She was especially chagrined at this for she had only a few months before been promoted to the position after years of keeping her eye on it as her goal.

She adapted herself easily to all the duties save one: The president insisted that the new secretary take his dictation herself.

She had done little stenography in her previous position, but was in practice and got out the letters in expert fashion. But after each dictation period she was so emotional that the merest trifles caused her to cry or scold or laugh hilariously.

When she came to us she was on the verge of a nervous breakdown, due to the suppression of one instinct, and to the demand for another which in her was but little developed.

The overdeveloped instinct was that of approbation. She demanded constant praise, and had always received much of it from previous employers. The president was not given to compliments and no matter how excellent her work, never told her it was so nor seemed to be aware that she was a remarkably competent secretary.

She was also very pretty and this was the first employer who had not, in some nice, indirect way, taken notice of this fact.

In addition to this, he dictated much more rapidly than she had been accustomed to and though she got every word and punctuated correctly, it was at the cost of intense effort, because she had very little of the instinct of manipulation upon which easy hand work depends.

You are well acquainted with the fat man who never loses his temper save when his meals are interfered with.

His emotions are painful or pleasurable in accordance with the degree in which his stomach is satisfied. Such a man becomes as enthusiastic over good food as other types do over good music, good books, good ball games or good business deals. In this man the instinct of assimilation is paramount.

An intellectual and charming woman of thirty-five, who had taught in Columbia for several years, decided to put her knowledge to a wider use and one which would bring her better financial returns.

She entered into a partnership with another college woman and they were very successful.

The other woman was full of common sense and practicality as well as learning. She was, moreover, a bundle of energy. She loved the work and never tired of it—retiring at one in the morning and arising at six more refreshed than the other who usually retired several hours earlier.

Though their work was but a few hours in duration it began at eight o'clock each morning. The first woman was always late.

She could not bring herself to get out of bed, and must take a warm bath in which she lay relaxed for twenty minutes before bringing herself to dress, and became very angry if warned to hasten.

She finally returned to the teaching where her working hours were in the middle of the day.

When relating the experience after studying Mental Analysis she said, "I used to become so furious with my partner when she urged me to get up early, hasten through my bath or sit up after ten o'clock that I was ill afterward. I had never been compelled to hurry or rise earlier than eight, and my half hour of relaxation in the bath was as much a part of my day's schedule as meals, and much more necessary to my peace of mind.

"I blamed myself for losing my temper, especially as she was right and our success depended upon my being prompt, but that didn't help matters. I know why now. The instinct of inertia is overdeveloped in me. I can work long and hard once I am up and out, but I demand frequent periods of complete relaxation, lots of sleep and to begin the day with that feeling of utter comfort which nothing but a warm bath gives."

A wife found that she was losing her husband because of her frequent emotional explosions. She made all manner of sacrifices for him—loved him devotedly, and permitted him to impose on her in numberless ways. But when he dropped cigar-ash on the carpet, left his newspapers strewn over things, threw his towels in a wad on the bathroom floor, or failed to hang up his clothes, she flew into a rage. She could not explain it.

That the emotion was out of all proportion to the importance of the thing itself, she well knew. What she did not know was that the homekeeping instinct which man shares with all birds, beavers and nest-building creatures was overdeveloped in her.

Her one desire in life was to keep her home nest in apple-pie order. She had married a man who had so little of this instinct that her ill temper on these occasions seemed to him nothing short of insanity. She gradually learned to use that emotional current to tidy up the house that much sooner, instead of expending it on her husband.

"What shall I do about my boy?" a mother said. "I try so hard to please him. I cook only the food he likes; I wait upon him and adapt myself and the household to his wishes. But he seems to hate me."

The boy admitted all this and his shame at the treatment he gave his mother, but said she unknowingly did one thing which so irritated him that he was actually growing to hate her.

"She is always afraid—afraid of the future for me and for herself. She is afraid we may get ill; afraid she is getting a cold; afraid that it is going to storm; afraid that something will happen to one or both of us.

"Now I am afraid too, but I am trying to keep my fear to myself, to forget it and outgrow it. But she waves it in front of me all the time and I can't forget. I am not naturally self-confident. I suppose I get this fear-attitude from her. I am sorry she suffers from it, for I suffer too. But her insistence on holding every kind of catastrophe before my imagination enrages me more and more."

The mother, when told what ailed her son was completely taken back. She had "only done it for his good,"—to warn him and induce him to be prepared for the exigencies of life. A little lesson on how to cure worry changed her and the son and the household in a month's time.

But not all emotions are inimical ones. Those of love, patriotism and religion show how an emotion can stimulate and purify the personality.

Sympathy, forgiveness, generosity and all forms of humanitarianism are good emotions which lift us far out of our small selves, and give us the joy of being all human for hours or days at a time.

Every kind word, every courageous deed, every act of voluntary self-sacrifice, is full of emotion. Every pioneer, every trail blazer in any line of endeavor goes on and on in the face of difficulties which seem overwhelming to other men, because he is sustained by an emotion they do not feel.

The mother gives of herself, her love, service, toil and life itself, all for the emotion of mother love. The father works long hours at uncongenial tasks, not actually for the boss but for the wife and babies at home.

The first step in conquering destructive emotions and encouraging constructive ones is to study yourself.

Begin to think of yourself as you are and as you know you are, without whimpers or pretences. But don't let anything in your nature cause you to give up. Look it square in the eye and half the trouble is over.

We handicap ourselves by putting on the blinders of self-evasion. We refuse to be frank with ourselves. We subconsciously know we are full of faults but we exaggerate some and ignore others.

Some of the emotions you possess could, if capitalized, make you a real success in life. But you have not thought of emotion as having any such power. The world has not recognized it until very recently. History and biography dwell on the less significant elements of its great men and women, forgetting or leaving to the poets the emotional qualities which are at the foundation of every famous name.

The opposite extreme are those who imagine emotionalism alone is something to be proud of. Such people pride themselves on their sensitiveness, their "high strung" natures—forgetting that only as we direct our emotions into worthwhile channels for accomplishment, for the good of ourselves and our fellows, can strong emotions become an asset.

Every organism, to live, must be sensitive to the stimuli in its environment. But if it is too sensitive it will forever be in the business of dressing its wounds and have time for little else.

Supersensitive people are like the little flowers called "sensitive plants" which curl up at the merest touch. They are always looking at their feelings with a microscope. Others are just as emotional but spend their feelings outward and upward like a sunflower that is so enthusiastic about the sun it turns its face from East to West each day to keep looking at it.

Your character is the result of your conduct. Your conduct is the outward expression of your inner emotions. If you desire a strong and beautiful character you must learn to use your emotions toward building the things you want to come true in your life.

Though it is not an easy thing to believe, it is nevertheless true that we can apply our emotions to good ends. We can turn their current into positive channels where it will, like the torrent of Niagara, furnish power for doing many big things we can not do by reason alone.

Whenever you have a destructive emotion don't swallow it and try to forget it. Don't hate or love a thing, desire to do or crave not to do a thing, and sit still. Get up while the mood is on and do something you have been neglecting.

One of the ablest men I have ever known told me he had mastered three languages by carrying a little grammar in his pocket and studying it while waiting for his wife in the hall, on the street corner or wherever he had an engagement to meet her.

"The first five years after we were married, I, who am a naturally prompt person myself, was so incensed at her unvarying tardiness it threatened to wreck our marriage. She could never understand my ravings. Each time she felt she had been unavoidably detained. I was ill sometimes for days after one of these explosions.

"When I realized I could neve change her I hit upon this idea of improving the time. This was my wife's one serious fault. We have been ideally happy for thirty years since—in which time I have not only learned these new languages but read and digested much of the world's best literature."

This is but one of thousands of possible ways in which an emotion and a period of precious time, which would otherwise be used to tear down, can be made to build up.

Just as surely as you can use your emotions after they are aroused you can prevent the wrong ones being aroused most of the time, by learning, as you will in the last lesson of this course, how to gain conscious control of the attitudes which bring forth your habitual emotions.

It is these habitual explosions that endanger our happiness. They can be made constructive instead of destructive by changing our predominant mental attitudes from negative to positive—an accomplishment perfectly possible to any person of average intelligence.

LESSON X

Mental Miracles

IN the back of his mind, each individual has a mass of fixed preferences and prejudices.

The FUNDAMENTAL predilections of his nature are due to his type and are held in common with all others of that type. Their origin is biological, as has been fully treated in our course, "The Five Human Types."

But in addition to these, and alongside of them, there are myriads of little attitudes peculiar and personal to each and every individual and which come from his training, his education, his environment and his experience.

To realize the difference between the biological foundations of your nature—the things that make you in the by-and-large—and the hundreds of inclinations and indispositions which are privately and personally "your own make," you might visualize a half bushel basket full of apples. These are your type traits. They make up your fundamentals.

But after the basket is as full of apples as it will hold you can pour into the chinks a very large amount of navy beans. These are akin to the personal peculiarities which "fill in" the main outline called You.

In every individual over five years of age there are literally thousands of these miniature but mighty eccentricities which help or hinder us. They vary as widely and exist as universally as the human beings who possess them—which helps to account for the fact that no two people in the world are exactly alike.

The average man, though he possesses—and is only too often possessed BY—these automatic attitudes, seldom realizes their existence in his subconscious, much less conceives of their causes. He often imagines he makes his decisions volitionally, when his friends have long since learned that under certain circumstances he is sure to react a certain way.

He always gives reasons and he is perfectly sincere in imagining these reasons are the real foundation of his decisions.

But a mass of complicated machinery run by very definite psychological and physiological forces, of which he is entirely unconscious, really works out the reaction he gives to almost every situation.

He knows little or nothing about psychology and so neither sees his mental wheels go round nor even dreams of the vast plant in which they operate.

As before explained, we get the main fundamentals of our natures—the outlines—from our biological type. But the dents, fancies, faiths and fears are impressed on us by environment.

There are three kinds of fixed feelings—fixed fears, fixed faiths and fixed fancies.

EVERY FIXED FEAR COMES FROM AN EXPERIENCE WHICH PRODUCED SO PAINFUL AN EMOTION THAT THE MEMORY SANK DEEP INTO THE SUBCONSCIOUS MIND.

The reason we are so often unconscious of the origin of these fixed feelings is, as stated earlier, that the conscious mind deals in thoughts but the subconscious in feelings; and because they usually arise from experiences which occurred in childhood before the conscious mind was developed. But the subconscious, being thoroughly alive even in babyhood, remembers the emotion while the conscious one FORGETS THE CAUSE.

The more intense any feeling (emotion) the more does the conscious mind tend to forget it. This is true for two very interesting reasons.

The first is, that since we can not think deeply and feel deeply at the same moment, any intense emotion (feeling) temporarily dethrones the conscious thinking mind and thus prevents its having a very clear conscious memory of what happens.

(You will note how little you can recall of the things you did or said during excitement or any intense emotion.)

The subconscious (which never forgets anything and especially never forgets an emotion) is deeply concerned with every emotional experience. Every intensely emotional experience makes an impression so deep that its permanent mark is left on the subconscious. Secondly, to be reminded of any deep emotion so interferes with the work of the conscious mind that it is automatically on the defensive.

When an emotion is extremely painful a scar is left which is easily irritated ever after by anything which reminds the subconscious of the original pain.

We so often have revulsions of feeling against people and things without in the least knowing why. Whenever this happens it is because the person or thing which you automatically dislike—while doubtless innocent in itself—BEARS A RESEMBLANCE TO THE SYMBOL by which the old painful experience was recorded in the subconscious.

The subconscious, as you will recall, does not deal in thoughts nor details but reduces everything to simple symbols which ever afterward stand for the original.

When, for instance, you take an instantaneous dislike to an individual, even before you have spoken to him, it is because he brings up the symbol of some past painful emotional experience.

The way he combs his hair, or the tilt of his ear, may bring up the old ugly picture subconsciously. You may never have noticed that the person you disliked combed his hair that way and you may not be consciously aware now that the present man does, but the subconscious noted it in the first man and is reminded of it by the second.

Foolish as all this seems to practical everyday souls, it is invariably the real reason. The conscious mind is not so impressionable but remember, the conscious mind REASONS whereas the subconscious FEELS—and that, blindly.

This illustration holds good only concerning people whom you dislike INSTANTANEOUSLY.

The following little rules will clarify the reasons for your likes and dislikes of people.

When you dislike a stranger INSTANTANEOUSLY and BEFORE HE HAS SPOKEN, it is because something about him reminds you of the SYMBOL of a painful experience.

When you dislike a stranger AFTER THE FIRST FIVE MINUTES OF CONVERSATION with him it is because of HIS PERSONALITY.

When you dislike him after LONG ACQUAINTANCE it is because HIS TYPE CONFLICTS WITH YOURS.

Faith is the opposite of fear. It operates in exactly the opposite manner on the mind, body and spirit of man. Faith is a stimulant, fear a deadly narcotic. Faith is food, fear is poison. Faith develops, fear destroys.

Recalling again that the subconscious does not THINK but FEELS and that faith is a feeling, you will see why faith has been necessary to the uplift of mankind.

Thoughts are cold things compared with feelings and "the faith that moves mountains" is always a matter of heart more than head.

EVERY FIXED FAITH COMES FROM ONE OR MANY EXPERIENCES WHICH PRODUCED EMOTIONS SO PLEASING AND UPLIFTING THAT THE MEMORY OF THEM SANK DEEP INTO THE SUBCONSCIOUS MIND.

This accounts for the fact that cold logic never swerved any man from any religious faith which had fully satisfied him in times of need.

Conversely, no man was ever completely won to any religious faith till his emotions had been appealed to, no matter how logical the evangelist.

No public speaker ever became famous on his reasoning. His "heart as well as his head" had to talk. We are creatures of feeling much more than thinking; but our success in life depends upon directing our feelings by thinking.

All of us are swayed in favor of certain people purely upon our feelings. We see men and women whom we instantaneously like or even love, without being able to tell why.

They may have none of the qualities we have always supposed necessary to the winning of our love, just as the other person we disliked may have had them all—but we love them—that's all.

This illuminating new science of Mental Analysis shows us it is no accident that we instantaneously like or love another person. Whenever this happens it is because that person reminds the subconscious of a symbol which stands for SOME HIGHLY PLEASURABLE EMOTION or group of pleasurable emotions in our past experience.

A man of our acquaintance who owned a grocery store told us that for thirty years he had made it a point to wait on every woman who came into his store wearing a fur hat.

No matter what he was doing he let a clerk take his customer and gave his attention to the fur-hatted woman.

He had just one other fixed feeling and it was of an opposite nature. Whenever a man came in wearing an oil coat he waited on him only if there was no one else to do it and hustled him out as quickly as possible.

He had no idea of the origin of these fixed attitudes till the above explanation was made. Next day he recalled vividly two experiences which he had not remembered for many years and which had given rise to the fixations.

As a boy he had lived in Canada where the winters were long and severe. His mother, whom he adored and who died when he was seven, always wore a fur hat in the winter months (a fact which he did not consciously remember, but which was corroborated by her photographs and by his uncle, the mother's brother, with whom he lived).

Into his childish and sensitive subconscious had gone the memory of those happy emotions which his mother had given him, and all of which were symbolized by a woman in a fur hat.

The explanation of his repugnance to men in oil coats was equally easy to analyze, once he was given a clew to his subconscious.

His father, though a predominantly kind man, was a very austere one and as a boy he had been very much afraid of him. His father often threatened to punish him but he could remember only one time when he did so and that was one time when he did not deserve it.

The father accused him of taking an ax to the woods and losing it when, as a matter of fact, he had not touched the ax and had seen his father take it away himself that morning. The father denied this and gave the boy a severe whipping.

When he did so he had just come in from looking everywhere for the ax and still wore his heavy oil coat. "I never smell an oil coat without experiencing the same sufferings I had during the few moments my father was lashing me."

In this case the oil coat had become, in an emotional moment, the symbol of injustice, unhappiness, punishment and disgrace.

Superstition against "Friday the Thirteenth," refusal to walk under ladders, hatred of having one's path crossed by a black cat, fear of raising an umbrella indoors, the superstition against going back home to get something without sitting down to count ten, and the certainty that breaking a mirror means "seven years of bad luck" are a few of the most widespread and popular fixed fears.

Almost every man and woman has one or more of these ancient superstitions so deeply planted in his mind that he would just a little rather avoid them.

The only thing that can be said about them is that they belong to the Dark Ages.

But all our fixed feelings are not of an intensely happy or unhappy nature. Many of them are tinged only with sufficient pleasurable feeling to make us know we have a definite preference, not necessarily a faith.

On the other hand, we may have just enough prejudice against a person or thing to experience a vague unrest or the merest opposition, without its being sufficiently poignant to be called a fear. But always an instantaneous opposition, however slight, is the result of some previous painful emotion.

A woman was obsessed by a fear of everything with a cutting edge. She could not work at her kitchen table so long as the butcher knife was in sight. Whenever she had to use it for cutting bread or cake she put it away as soon as possible.

If her scissors fell into her lap while sewing she could not take another stitch until she had removed them.

Whenever her husband or sons left their razors on the wash-basin in the bathroom she was ill half the morning.

If she saw a penknife on the desk when writing a letter she could not go on until she had put it in a drawer, and then was usually too upset to finish.

This condition had persisted since before she could remember, and was getting worse. The husband, after ten years of trying to cure her of it by telling her to "forget it," had finally accepted her strange fear and was careful to put all such things out of sight.

But her four sons were now grown and all living at home. They could never remember Mother's freakish terror and left their razors and knives about where she was constantly coming in contact with them.

She was told by the Mental Analyst that this obsession was nothing more nor less than a fear fixed in her subconscious by some past painful experience in which a sharp-edged instrument had figured and which had ever since been a symbol of that painful emotion.

She was asked to let the matter lie fallow in her mind for a few days; to make no special effort to remember but to leave her memory free to recall anything connected with such an experience which might account for it. We saw her every day for a week but she could remember no incident of the kind.

Her disturbance at not having been able to recall anything proved that she had been straining her conscious mind—the very opposite of the proper method.

We told her to loosen her mental grip and let her mind drift for a few days or even weeks—until the memory came of its own accord.

In a few days she returned. She had dug up from her subconscious the recollection which fully explained the obsession.

In her childhood her parents had been very poor. When she was three they lived in a tumbledown house where the windows had no catches and, to be kept open, had to be held up with sticks or other things.

One Summer day, for lack of anything else, the mother had propped up a window in the kitchen with a long butcher knife. A few minutes later she had seen her baby sister, whom she loved dearly, push the knife over, and in doing so permitted the window to fall upon the knife whose blade laid the baby's palm wide open.

But the subconscious does not always choose such obvious elements as symbols and frequently chooses less significant ones instead of the outstanding things we might expect.

This is aptly illustrated in the case of a woman who had two terrors, neither of which seemed to bear any relation to the other or to anything she could recall.

She was forced to the conclusion that she needed an analysis when she discovered she could not enjoy her new home—a beautiful frame house in a Middle-Western town—because of her long-standing dislike of the smell of new lumber.

They had moved into the house before it was finished and the odor of the pine boards became unbearable. Her husband suggested that she take a trip, that she was nervous and overwrought, but it was impossible for her to leave just as the new furniture and hanging were to be installed.

One other thing had greatly disturbed her—the fire siren.

This was one of those small towns where a steam whistle is used for a fire-alarm. The new home was within a block of the factory whose siren was used for this purpose. Its screech was deafening, and left her nervous for hours afterward.

When told that these fears were from something which had happened in her past and doubtless in her childhood, she could recall nothing at the moment. But next day she related this story which was afterward corroborated by her sister.

Its details came out as vividly as though it had happened the day before, which was not as surprising as it sounds. Though her subconscious had kept the memory below the threshold of her conscious mind, this secret hiding of it had caused it to be etched in with even greater vividness than it would otherwise have been.

This woman had grown up in a lumber camp. When about four years of age she had witnessed an accident at the sawmill. One of the men, in handling the logs, had slipped, lost his balance and had his foot carried with the log into the saw.

She had seen him fall, and almost died of fright as the great jagged saw-teeth sliced his foot from the ankle. She saw it fall off into the sawdust. Ever after the smell of lumber and the sight of sawdust were subconscious symbols of that experience.

Her aversion to sirens and other screeching noises was as obvious as the other elements, when we recall that this peculiarly shrill scream of the saw accompanies every cut into a log.

She was so much more taken up with the awful sight that she was not conscious of having heard the screech of the saw at the moment of the accident, but the subconscious recorded it as part of the symbol.

When this memory was allowed to air itself fully the obsession began to fade and in a few months had entirely disappeared.

A Minneapolis man caused much comment among his friends a few years ago. He was handsome, had more than average means, was much sought after by women, equally popular among men, and a success in business.

He was fastidious in his dress and person to the point of eccentricity. Any one of a dozen wealthy and beautiful society girls would gladly have accepted him in marriage. But he seemed to have no serious affair of the heart, though he paid homage to many women.

At thirty-six he met a young professional woman, a law student, who wore her hair cropped short like a man's and who dressed in extremely mannish fashion. They were married two weeks afterward.

The man was as much mystified as his friends at his strange attraction, and the only explanation he could give was this:

"I have always had a fixed fear of long human hair. Since I was a small boy I have never seen a long, loose hair lying on anything without its disgusting me. Occasionally when a stray one came home inside my shirt with my laundry it made me actually ill.

"I have never known why I had this strange aversion and all my friends laugh at me for it. I laugh at myself, but that doesn't help matters.

"In my youth when women wore their hair fluffy and flying about the face, I was terrified whenever I was with a young woman, for fear one of those long, silky hairs would attach itself to me. I liked several girls tremendously, but the fear of ever touching that long hair prevented my ever falling really in love.

"The young law student was a girl of brains, personality and native good looks. We had the same taste and ideas. She was no more interesting in many ways than some of the young society girls I had met, but I loved her short hair.

"I have been ideally happy in my marriage. My wife, now that she has given up law, and since she knows her short hair is a handicap to me as well as herself, wants to let it grow. She has discarded the mannish clothes and naturally the short hair is incongruous. But I can not bear the notion, nor explain why."

He was told the law of fixed fear and in about a week recalled an incident of his childhood which he had not consciously remembered for many years but which fully explained the complex and in the end cleared it up to the place where he was willing for his wife to have long hair.

When he was a small boy—somewhere between five and seven—he and his younger sister were playing one day in the woodshed where the laundress was doing the family washing.

This was in the days of the washboard and old-fashioned tubs to which were attached the big rollers for wringing clothes. The baby sister, who had very long hair, dropped her ball into the tub, ran and leaned over to rescue it, just as the laundress was ready to put a handful of clothes through the wringer.

The baby's curls were carried into it and she was lifted off the floor by her hair and suspended there for what was a terrified moment before the boy could make the laundress thoroughly understand what was wrong.

But every individual has, in addition to these painful ones, hundreds of pleasurable fixations which give him enjoyment.

You have preferences of many kinds which are as intense as they are inexplicable.

One woman of our acquaintance loves a certain strain of Dvorak's "Humoresque" so much that she is filled with ecstasy every time she hears it and keeps it on her Victrola to play whenever she is depressed or unhappy about anything.

The first time she heard it was one night in the dining room of the Biltmore just after the theater. The young man whom she loved and is now married to, had taken her there to supper. He proposed to her as the orchestra was playing this selection.

A noted business man of Kansas City who prides himself on his hard-headedness keeps twenty clean handkerchiefs in the right-hand drawer of his private desk because he finds he can talk big deals over with much more confidence if, at the moment of opening the discussion, he can also open up a crisp, creased, perfectly fresh handkerchief.

But handkerchiefs are not mere handkerchiefs to him. Indeed, they are a very great deal more.

He declares they have a personality all their own. The only kind he will use are those of the severest plainness but of pure linen. Whenever he is presented with one bearing an initial, a fancy border or a touch of color—different in any way from the kind he prefers—he not only does not use it but is upset till he has disposed of it.

The fact that this man can not remember what caused all this does not alter the law. Somewhere in his past he had a very pleasant emotional experience in which there figured a crisp, clean linen handkerchief.

An interesting illustration of how something which has been a symbol of a painful emotion can later become symbolic of a pleasant one is seen in the following.

In Denver in 1909, lived a splendid and sensible young woman who had one little fixation. Owing to an unpleasant experience with a cuckoo clock years before, she could not bear the ticking of watches or clocks.

She held an important position in which she needed a watch but instead of wearing it, hung it up on the wall as far away from her desk as she could see its hands.

She would not own a clock and at night put the watch under her sofa pillows at the far end of her room. This condition had persisted for fifteen years.

Then the young man who is now her husband and whom she was deeply in love with at the time, went to California and wanted some one to keep his valuable cuckoo clock for him while away. The young woman not only put it up in her room, but loved its ticking, cuckooing and everything else.

When teased about the sudden change she declared its noises were entirely different from those of all other clocks, and that it seemed to say, "Julius, Julius, Julius" (the young man's name), with every swing of the pendulum. It had been so long associated with him that to her, in his absence, it became a living symbol of her lover. The memory of the old unpleasant emotion was erased and has not returned.

In the lesson "Love, Courtship and Marriage" the effect of symbols on our loves will be taken up more fully. The aim here is to give a few illustrations of the power of all kinds of symbols in our lives.

A Chicago banker of fifty, conservative, conventional to a degree, and so austere as to be almost formidable, has one fixed preference.

He loves heliotrope and, though consciously despising the use of perfume, especially by men, must have a drop or two applied to his tie every morning before he can go to the bank. If he forgets it he makes his chauffeur turn around and take him home to get it.

He has had a standing order with his florist for twenty years, and every day before noon a small sprig of heliotrope is delivered, put into an exquisite little vase and placed by his secretary at a certain spot on his desk.

One day last year this secretary met with a sudden accident and was sent home from the office before he had arranged the flowers. In the excitement the little package containing the flowers was put into the taxi with him and carried away.

The banker told us himself that though some of the biggest bank heads in Chicago were in his office at that moment for a discussion concerning a loan of two million, and every moment important to them all, he could not begin the conference until a new bouquet had been obtained and placed in its vase at exactly the proper angle in front of him.

"I am fully aware and always have been of the origin of this fixation, though I have never told any one before. As you know, I am unmarried but, as you probably do not know, shall always remain unmarried. I have loved but one woman.

"She loved me in return. I was not a young, impressionable boy but a man past thirty when I met and cared for her.

"She always used heliotrope perfume and the first time I ever saw her a sprig of these little flowers was pinned to her muff. She died.

"To me she lives whenever I breathe this exquisite odor. I would not wish to live myself if I could not have it near me. I have felt this way for twenty years."

There are many people who have freakish fixations which they can not explain and which, unless they cause trouble, need not be traced to their source. They should, however, be cleared up if they become obsessions.

One such case is that of a man who never steps on a crack in the sidewalk. He can not carry on a coherent conversation when walking with you down the street because he is so concentrated on avoiding the cracks in the cement or boards.

A certain Boston woman can not overcome the notion that germs are in everything and lives in terror lest she will be infected.

She washes her hands fifty times a day, will not wear anything coming from a store without first having it laundered, and will eat no food save what is cooked under her own supervision in her own kitchen by a woman she has trained.

She is well acquainted with the fact that only lowered bodily resistance makes us susceptible to germs and that though they are everywhere we are safe from them if we keep in good physical condition.

But that does not eliminate the strange fixation. She is the bony type that can not bring itself to believe in "these new-fangled sciences," so is spending her life in trench warfare with bacteria.

A Philadelphia minister says that for twenty years he has not been able to pass a gate post, a hitching post or a fence post without wanting to kick it.

"Last Winter," he said, "the Bishop was in the city for a few days and we were entertaining him at our home. I hoped I might be able to avoid going near any posts while with him and engaged a car to take us wherever he wanted to go.

"But the last day of his stay was sunny. He wanted to go for a walk, and insisted on its being down an avenue of fine old residences in front of many of which still stand the hitching posts of the pre-automobile era.

"For the first block I managed to keep from kicking these things, but half way down the second one I had to step over and touch one with my foot.

"The impulse was overwhelming. I said something about knocking some snow off my shoe and managed, by turning into another street at the next corner, to get along without doing it again. But I had to do it that once, regardless."

Many people can not walk past a pin on the floor; others can not resist the temptation to look at every scrap of paper they see on the sidewalk. Others can not walk or drive without continuously counting the change in their pockets. Others must count the steps on every staircase they climb and know the number in every stairway of every home they frequent.

We know a man in Washington, D.C., who can tell you the number of steps leading into every government building in that city, and also the exact number of every stairway in the U.S. Senate.

A woman in Seattle said she never listened to a lecturer without counting the number of steps he took, from the moment he appeared till he left the platform.

A man in Indianapolis said he had counted every gesture made by a certain lecturer during a six weeks' engagement and had filled a notebook describing them.

This was not due to any special interest in the lecturer. He had done the same for every speaker he had listened to for many years.

Every person with a strange fixation such as these just described has acquired these strange avenues of expression because he was denied more normal outlets.

For instance, the woman who was so afraid of germs is a spinster of the most strait-laced type. She has held the same position for twenty-three years, is faithfulness itself and conventional to excess. She has not only not married but never had a love affair.

Many of the normal instincts have had to be repressed. Since she is of this severe type she had expelled them so completely from the conscious mind that the feeling which should have been given to them has broken out, as do all repressed urges, via the subconscious.

Her subconscious has merely produced a substitute upon which to expend her energy.

The minister who kicks posts lived for several years in China as a missionary and as it was difficult for him to learn the language, was denied almost all companionship. He acquired this habit there.

The man who counts the steps in Washington was disappointed in love years ago and in the preoccupation which submerged him at the time unconsciously acquired this habit.

Every person who, for any reason, is driven in upon himself breaks out again through channels which are slightly or extremely abnormal—depending on the type of individual and the severity of his suffering.

Every lonely person after a while takes on strange habits. All who are compelled to live much alone, and most of those who are forced to repress the mating instinct, ultimately become eccentric, and some unbalanced.

If your fixed feelings are fixed FAITHS—that is, if they reassure you, uplift you, sustain you, and help you to live a better, happier life, do not let anything or anybody take them away from you.

If they are fixed fancies of a pleasing sort, such as the preference for heliotrope which the banker has, by all means keep them.

Life is all too drab and difficult not to brighten it by these innocent and purifying means whenever possible.

A woman of our acquaintance who took her own part with great gusto in everything else permitted people to impose on her in just one way.

She allowed them to push past her into street cars, subways and all manner of other places. She gave up her place with no resistance whatever, seeming almost pleased to do so.

When asked for the cause of the strange inconsistency she said:

"Four times my life has been saved because I lost a place in line. Twice it caused me to miss a train—once because the man in front of me at the Pullman window dropped his change and tickets and kept me waiting while he gathered them up; and once because the baggage man did not get my trunk checked in time.

"Both these trains were wrecked.

"At another time I was refused admittance to a packed elevator. I was in a hurry and insisted on getting in. The fact that a large woman who was standing behind me was permitted to enter it did not lessen my anger.

"The operator lost control of his car which was overcrowded, and it dropped eight stories, killing instantly every person in it.

"The day of the historic Iroquois Theater fire in Chicago I was standing in line for a ticket when I discovered I had lost my purse and stepped out of line to find it. By doing so I lost the chance to see the play.

"If I had not lost my place I would doubtless have been among the hundreds burned alive in that awful disaster.

"Now whenever I lose a place in line I believe it is for some good purpose."

Bonaparte's firm faith that "the bullet had not been cast nor the shell tempered that could kill Napoleon" not only filled the minds of his enemies with fear of even attempting it, but carried him to many victories.

But if you have fixed fears of any nature you must master them or run the risk of their mastering you.

Nothing in nature remains stationary. The moment you are not getting stronger you are getting weaker. The man who stops climbing has begun to slide back.

To live a healthful, happy, honorable life you must be master of your moods. To be master of your moods, the first thing to do is: face the fact and begin to be honest and sensible.

Mental Analysis, this most searching and profound of all human sciences, has proved that most of our worst mental and physical ailments, disappointments and failures come from our refusal to be frank and straightforward with ourselves.

Whether the thing you are afraid of is big or little, real or imaginary, you can be free from it if you try.

You are one of God's creatures and God never meant any creature to be sad, dejected or frightened. We make ourselves so by violating His divine laws.

If your obsessions are those of regret for past sins of commission or omission, try to think of this subconscious of yours as a pool that you are going to drain by being perfectly honest with yourself.

And you CAN be because nothing you have ever done, thought, said or been guilty of was so very bad.

The force that rules the universe is big, beautiful, and above all, benign. A benign force, whether personal or impersonal, forgives or ignores our faults. Put yourself in harmony with the divine by forgiving yourself right now for anything that has been causing you regret or remorse.

No matter what you have done or failed to do, just remember this: you did the best your nature was capable of at that time, under those conditions, and with those particular temptations.

The worse it was the more is it necessary that you do that much better in the future.

You can not do anything big or fine with fear gripping and crippling you.

Whatever negative thing is in your mind and however long it may have been there, it can be eliminated by doing two things:

First, be honest with yourself. Admit to yourself that you have been a weak, silly fool or anything else that you have been. But don't let it discourage you.

Confession is good for the soul. It clears the air. It blows the cobwebs out of your mind. It is a mental vacuum cleaner.

Second, realize that whatever you desire to come true in your life can be brought to pass if you really WANT it.

It can be brought to pass by the same power that has brought most of the things you have in your life—your own subconscious mind.

It will not do so in a day. The subconscious does not respond to a thought until many times repeated. The only thing it reacts to instantly is FEELING. But through a law which is fully explained in the last lesson of this course, any desired impulse can be planted in the subconscious.

Once there, it will operate with the same unresting force as these other urges of ours which have been shot into it by emotion.

You can plant in your subconscious soil the seeds of anything you truly desire. It will bring forth its harvest according to its nature.

You must stop filling this great battery with negative energy.

By right thinking you can make all its energy positive, and that positive force will bring to pass whatever you deeply desire.

Man is a unit. Each human being is an organized community of living cells, of which there are over twenty-six trillions in the commonwealth of the brain and body.

This intricate and intimate relationship between all the cells of the human organism is effected through two channels—the nervous system and the circulatory system.

The living cables of the nervous system run from the brain through the spinal cord and solar plexus; and branch and rebranch until practically every cell in the body has its own tiny nerve.

By means of this sensitive system any part of the brain or body instantly influences—for health or disease, happiness or distress—every other part of the organism.

To illustrate to yourself how quickly and keenly the outside world, without tangible contact, affects the body through this delicate nervous system, recall what happened to you when you smelled something extremely disagreeable.

The impression was carried to the brain which instantly sent over its nerve-wires a mental telegram to your stomach. If it was very unpleasant you became nauseated.

If the revulsion was severe there resulted those violent convulsions of the stomach which cause vomiting.

Yet you had neither touched nor tasted the unpleasant thing—merely heard of it through your nerves.

The next day you are passing a bakery. You smell the delicious odor of bread. The brain dispatches a pleasing telegram to your stomach telling it to secrete the gastric juices preparatory to digesting some of that bread.

You instantly become hungry. If you can not stop and get a loaf to take home or eat it then and there—if you keep on going and ignore it—an interesting thing happens.

The juices which ran into your stomach on that hurry call have no food to work on. Since their energy (like that of everything else) must expend itself, they agitate your empty stomach—an abnormal process, which in turn makes you slightly physically and then mentally upset.

When that point is reached the circle is completed; you are back to the mind from whence the message first came.

Your body and mind always operate in this circle. Whatever affects one affects the other.

A mental disturbance not only harms the body, but because the body also affects the mind, comes back like a boomerang when it completes the circle.

A physical disturbance not only upsets the mental processes, but returns, via their influence, back to the body in that same vicious circle.

This little hunger for the bread is only the most elemental illustration. Every normal human being has hundreds and thousands of hungers.

The particular kind most frequent and intense with each individual comes, as a bread-hunger would ultimately have come, from your own inner nature. This inner nature will show in his externals and determine his type.

But life is forever tempting, reminding, awakening these sleeping tendencies, just as the accidental passing by the bakery awakened your hunger for bread.

Now if you had been excessively hungry-that is, had a deep INNER URGE for food–before you came to the bakery it would have been much more difficult for you to keep going.

And so it is with our type-hungers. They come from our inner biological systems, and are quick to flare up when anything occurs in our environment which appeals to them.

But whether the hunger comes from the over-development of an inner system or is aroused by outer stimuli, any hunger which is repressed and ignored expends its pent-up energy, as did the gastric juices, on something else. Thus we have discovered the Law of Repression.

EVERY INTENSE IMPULSE OR AMBITION WHICH IS REFUSED EXPRESSION THROUGH NORMAL, NATURAL OUTLETS, FINDS LESS NORMAL AND SOMETIMES ABNORMAL OUTLETS FOR ITSELF.

Today science shows that most of our unhappiness and failure and practically all our ill health, half health and disease are but the distorted expressions of deep desires long repressed.

Your mental and physical energy is like a river. It must flow onward and outward to stay pure and natural.

A pool becomes stagnant only when denied an outlet. The most foul water purifies itself in a few miles of rapid flowing.

Society in general, and conditions or relations in which we place ourselves restrain us and choke back this natural expression as a dam holds back a river.

Such a dam holds the water back temporarily, and nothing happens.

But if the pressure becomes greater and greater, after a while one of two things WILL happen: the dam will break or the stream will burst over in another direction.

Disease and wrongdoings are often the breaking out of the subconscious stream. Reversions are the result of the breaking of the dam itself.

Criminologists declare that crime is the result of the repression of the true personality and that criminals differ from the average man and woman chiefly in that a much larger proportion of the personality is thwarted.

These and hundreds of corroborative facts prove how closely the body, mind and spirit of man are intertwined, and how everything which affects one affects the other.

It is not necessary to dwell on these impulses in our minds nor to act them out in our lives.

Civilization has cost too much on the part of brave souls and is too great a boon to mankind for any individual to revert to the primitive where all this is lost on him.

He owes it to himself, first of all, and second to the world, to straighten his spine and live the life of a man.

We have been told this before. But we have not been told HOW to make a working compromise between these inner impulses which, for any reason, could not be expressed naturally, and the ideals we so much desired to live up to.

No one was to blame for this state of affairs. No one knew, until very recently, that choking an intense impulse DID NOT KILL IT.

No one suspected, for instance, the real reason for the chronic ailments, soured dispositions and "eccentric streaks" of old maids of both sexes; nor why people who live alone, people who are unloved or unsuccessful, develop certain kinds of maladies, mental and physical.

Today we know that the admonition to "forget it" merely crowds the unspent energy down into the lower reaches of the organism, from whence it emerges sooner or later in some less natural form.

The big lesson taught by Mental Analysis is that whenever you have any intense impulse which can not or should not be expressed, you are to look it straight in the face, realize that it is no different from the impulses of millions who have gone before you; that it is not perverted, disgraceful nor anything to be ashamed of AS AN IMPULSE.

The thing to be ashamed of would be the secret loathing of yourself for having it or permitting it to act itself out in harmful, dishonorable or destructive deeds.

After you have looked at it; after you have recognized it for the out of date or out of place impulse it is, say to this thing: "Yes, you were alright in your day, a million years ago before we learned that human progress depended on the development of the higher instincts. You are the natural descendant of the primitive in me, and as such are not to blame for being here.

"But if you think I am going to live down to your level just because you ARE here, you are very much mistaken!

"Now, you have a lot of energy. Stop whining in the dark there. Come out into the light and I'll put that energy to work. I am a twentieth century human being with a brain and I am going to live the life of one, not that of a man of dead ages.

"I have nothing against you. All you need is to expend that energy of yours. I'll find something right out here in the daylight for you to do. Get at it!"

As a result of our wrong systems of training the most sensitive and high-minded are often obsessed with a sense of shame and disgrace which cripples all their efforts, while the "tough-minded," as James called them, express more of their inner urges, accomplish more, keep their health and get the good things out of life.

They do not do this necessarily by expressing destructive urges in the original form, but often by an automatic sublimation natural to the biological type.

Other and finer types—taught by parents, teachers, preachers and society that certain things are vile—believe it and grow to despise themselves.

No human being can stay well or do good work who secretly loathes himself.

It is small wonder that some of our orthodox churches are empty. Renunciation and repression are stunting, saddening, sickening doctrines. They weaken, disintegrate and destroy.

The sense of "original sin," of an inner filth that can never be quite eliminated, is fatal to health and happiness. Of its own force, it is ultimately fatal to any sect that teaches it.

God never intended any living thing to be cowed or shamed. Everything in nature grows UP, not down. It grows with its head toward the heavens.

When human beings listen less to men and more to the sermons in every sun-seeking flower, they will begin to be good, happy, healthy and successful.

The average individual tries not to think or feel certain things. He crowds them out of his mind and thinks they are gone.

Today we know that whatever is pushed out of consciousness recedes into subconsciousness.

If these throttled thoughts concern deep desires they come back again and again. If rejected over and over they finally return behind the "false face" of some unaccountable attitude which we do not recognize as connected with anything we have previously felt. We now know these are merely old urges in disguise.

Most of our physical ills, emotional explosions, outbursts of temper and faults are these repressed impulses on masquerade.

As children we were taught that the way to dispose of Satan was to say, "Get thee behind me." We were told that when we did this Satan vanished.

Today the science of Mental Analysis shows what we have always suspected—that Satan stayed right there and has been talking over our shoulders ever since!

It shows us that we have got to do something besides put Satan behind our backs unless we wish to be pushed into the very things we fear.

Fortunately, it shows us that the things we must do to turn his power into constructive channels is much easier than the things we have been doing in our blind and ignorant efforts to get rid of him.

Every human fault, like every disease, is the result of dammed-up energy.

Everything in the world moves, and does so because it is full of energy. Nothing is ever still, even for an instant, no matter how much it may appear so.

Everything—from the particles in the wooden chair on which you sit to the constellations in the sky—are moving, moving, moving.

Motion is the law of the universe. Motion creates energy and energy must expend itself.

If you do not permit it to expend itself in natural, normal ways it expends itself in abnormal, unnatural ways—depending always on the type of individual and the weakest point in his physical or mental makeup.

When you see no evil effects for a time you imagine you have obliterated this impulse.

But you have only bottled it, and the longer you keep the cork in the more it ferments. Some day it will explode.

Any work, situation or condition which compels you to keep on doing a thing you do not like to do causes the gradual building up within you of a mass of aversions and repulsions which eventually break forth.

They may not break out in open rebellion against THE THING ITSELF. In fact we have discovered that the greater the dislike of a thing on the part of certain types of people the less likely are they to voice their resentment or to show open resistance to that specific thing.

These are the people to whom comes the greatest harm. Whenever you express open opposition to a thing you "let off steam" and relieve the pressure just that much.

The types that "speak out" have far fewer subconscious complexes than the silent, timid ones, though they often have the very ones they and their friends would least expect to find in them.

A young boy was left alone while his mother went to the corner grocery. A box of papers he was playing with caught fire from the open grate. He was too young to know how to put out the fire and afraid to run away from it. So he ran to the back stairs, threw the blazing box into the basement and slammed the door.

He had a few moments of apparent safety.

But the house burned down.

It used to be supposed that some men had an aim and others had not; that some knew what they wanted and others had no preferences; that some men were blessed with ambitions and others didn't care.

Today we know that every individual has many subconscious wishes and ONE OVERWHELMING SUBCONSCIOUS LONGING toward whose attainment every act of his life is consciously or unconsciously directed.

EVERYTHING WHICH TENDS TOWARD THE FULFILMENT OF THIS SUBCONSCIOUS WISH REACTS CONSTRUCTIVELY, HAPPILY, HEALTHILY BACK UPON HIS BODY, MIND, WORK, AND LIFE IN ITS ENTIRETY.

EVERYTHING WHICH HINDERS IT REACTS DESTRUCTIVELY UPON EVERY ELEMENT OF HIS PERSONALITY—PHYSICAL, MENTAL, MORAL, AND SPIRITUAL—AND TAKES ITS TOLL IN SOME FORM OF DEPRESSION, DISINTEGRATION OR DISEASE.

"An interesting illustration of how the thwarting of a subconscious wish can cause physical troubles and how quickly the removal of the barrier can cure came to my notice in 1910," said a physician recently.

"It also shows the lesser power of conscious wishes as compared to the great force of subconscious ones.

"I was sent for at 4:30 one afternoon to come to an office in the State Capitol in Denver where a young woman was ill.

"She was suffering with intense pain and had a temperature of 103.

"It developed at five o'clock, when the rest of the office force left, that she had been very anxious to see 'The Merry Widow' which was playing at the Broadway Theater that week, and was to have gone with the rest of the girls that evening to see it.

"She was much disappointed that her illness necessitated their giving the ticket to some one else.

"While we waited for the taxi which was to take her home she told me how sorry she was not to see 'The Merry Widow' but glad she didn't have to see the minstrels which were also in town. She very much disliked minstrels, she said.

"A moment later the telephone rang and she was asked for. I told the young man at the other end of the wire that she was too ill to answer. But before I could prevent it she took up the receiver.

"Two minutes later she walked out of that room free of her headache and fever—perfectly well.

"The illness, she told me as we walked down the hall, had come from a week's worry over not having heard from the young man, whom she loved devotedly. She feared she had lost him.

"When he phoned and asked her to go that evening to the minstrel show (having already seen 'The Merry Widow' himself) she found she would love the minstrels after all; that she didn't mind missing 'The Merry Widow' and was well enough to go."

The illness in this case was real. The desire to see "The Merry Widow" and not to see the minstrels was genuine, but existed only in her conscious mind, whereas the desire to be with the young man was part of a deep subconscious wish and, as such, able to make her not only glad to see the minstrels, but to become well instantly.

Fear causes more maladies, physicians say, than all other things combined. The man who is afraid is never a well man.

Strange as it may seem, it is the fears we repress more than the fears we express, which do us severe harm—another illustration of how things shoved back into subconsciousness wreak their force upon us under assumed appearances.

It is a historical and well-known fact that every war is followed by epidemics.

We have assumed that congestion of masses of men, poor sanitation and exposure were the inevitable causes, and certain it is that these have had much to do with it.

But hundreds of the leading physicians of the world have declared that the Spanish Influenza epidemic of 1918 was caused largely by fear in many cases and that at its height many people had every outward symptom of this disease without the slightest fever or any actually diseased condition.

They have gone a step farther and declared that patients died under the impression that they were afflicted with this malady when, as a matter of fact, they were killed by fear.

It was shown in a previous lesson that fixed fears always come from very painful emotional experiences of one's past.

The insidious and far-reaching effect of a single fixed fear was explained.

Imagine then the effect upon the individual of an integrated, organized GROUP of fixed fears—a "set" of them—surrounding some long drawn out or vital experience in his life.

Mental science distinguishes these groups of fixed fears by the name of complexes. They differ from others chiefly in the fact that instead of one element they have many.

Single fixed fears arise from momentary or even instantaneous experiences, such as the little girl suffered in the fraction of a second when she witnessed the saw cutting off the man's foot. Her fixed fear of screeching noises and the smell of lumber were born in that instant of intense emotion.

What can rightly be called a complex is the result of an experience of much longer duration—sometimes of years—which contained many characteristics. Several of these are symbolized in the subconscious mind with such vividness that being reminded of one brings the "total experience" forth from memory's vault.

A Cleveland broker who had a reputation for cool-headedness and self-control developed a violent complex against women's white kid gloves, plumes, French-heeled shoes and baby-Irish lace.

Whether displayed in shops or being worn by their fair owners, whenever and wherever he saw any of these things his composure instantly left him and he grew angry, disgusted and resentful.

Though he succeeded in concealing his agitation from his friends and employees, he declared it was hours, sometimes days, before he fully recovered.

These things upset him, he said, because they brought back to him with terrific force memories of a bitter period in his life.

Many years before he had been married to a charming and unusually beautiful woman whom he idolized—the only woman moreover that ever interested him.

She flirted with other men, gave him ten years of heart-breaking disillusionment and finally eloped with a clerk of his office.

She was a woman of extreme fashionable and fastidious tastes. She specialized in French-heeled shoes, white kid gloves, and the willow plumes and baby-Irish lace which were the mode at that time.

Whenever he saw any of these things the tragedy of the whole ten years engulfed him—the "total experience" lived itself over in his feelings, condensed and intensified.

LESSON XI

Love, Courtship and Marriage

You have often wondered why two people of the same family (therefore of the same heredity) and of the same environment (living in the same house under exactly identical conditions) would react in diametrically OPPOSITE ways to the SAME experience.

For instance, twin sisters lose their mother through death.

One is completely overwhelmed by grief, loses weight, becomes ill and is unconsolable, while the other grows rosier and plumper every day and

goes on just as before.

Why does one girl develop a complex and the other not?

Chiefly because of difference in type.

Certain types react to certain kinds of experiences destructively and others constructively, and do so habitually and automatically.

On the other hand, the girl who reacts with automatic constructiveness to her mother's death may develop complexes from different kinds of experiences which would not affect the other girl at all.

Whenever the mind is working destructively—when, for instance, you are full of fear—it throws the switch and sidetracks the body, preventing its running properly or safely.

When our emotions become tangled up with wrong ideas, destructive attitudes or opposition, they are at cross purposes with the body.

This always has its damaging results. These results may show themselves in the form of nervousness, ill temper, ill health, melancholia, neurosis, insanity, crime or suicide—always depending on the type of individual.

Or, they may merely cause him to wonder what is wrong between himself and the world; to form incomprehensible aversions to people and things in his environment; or to be vaguely restless, upset or unhappy, without knowing why.

Thousands of facts go to show that the dreamer weaves his own dream out of the raw materials in his own conscious experience and subconscious desires—that each dream is the dreamer's own psychic production.

This fact is of the utmost significance. It has shown the underlying causes for neuroses and other illnesses which, until the discovery of Mental Analysis, were inexplicable to physicians and supposedly incurable.

The psychologist is today curing many people of many maladies which the physician, dealing only with the body, failed to help.

"Within ten years," says a prominent surgeon, "every physician who undertakes to help a patient suffering from any functional disorder will make his first step the analysis of the patient's dreams."

Today we know that numberless operations, most organic and all functional ailments are the result of unhappiness, fear, repression or other negative mental conditions.

We know that nervous breakdowns, for instance, are due not so much to over-work as over-worry.

One of the most significant discoveries of recent times is that in every human being there is a SUBCONSCIOUS TENDENCY TO ESCAPE FROM THE FACTS OF LIFE WHENEVER THEY BECOME TOO PAINFUL.

In scientific circles there is a new but already well-known phrase describing this: "the flight from reality."

This profound and universal fact is revolutionizing the therapeutics of the civilized world.

It is explaining all manner of mental, moral and physical maladies and curing them because it deals with the real source of the trouble.

The particular way taken to achieve the "flight from reality" will depend, in each case, upon the type, temperament and training of the individual and the intensity of his sufferings.

The most repressive, sensitive types suffer most because they bury their griefs and disappointments deeper than others.

Those who express their feelings suffer least from the repressive ailments, as was proven during the World War.

Thousands of soldiers suffered from a baffling ailment. It robbed them of various phases of consciousness; it vented itself in all manner of mental derangements, with no two cases quite alike.

For the lack of a better name it was called "shell-shock," though these men had not been hurt by shells, and other men, under precisely the same conditions, had come through safely and sanely.

In many instances sight and hearing were lost, in spite of the fact that tests showed their eyes and ears to be in perfect condition.

Thousands of such cases were cured upon being removed from the scene of battle and thousands more became well in an hour after the signing of the Armistice.

What was the reason? The strange malady left as mysteriously as it came WHEN THE DANGER DISAPPEARED. In these cases fear and fear alone was responsible, say the greatest authorities now.

It was not an open, expressed, conscious fear. Any openly expressed feeling drains off through consciousness. These shell-shocked men were of the highest human grade. They had been taught that fear is dishonorable, especially upon the field of battle.

But self-preservation is the first law of nature. Each man's subconscious mind is concerned, not with patriotism nor any other modern innovation, but with the sole business of SELF-EXPRESSION for that individual.

These men refused to run or to be consciously afraid. But the subconscious WAS afraid and reacted with fear to that danger exactly as the hair of a cat rises when a dog comes near, and as a bird's heart beats when the cat approaches.

The greatest conflict came in the consciousness of these soldiers who had the traits of conscious courage and self-preservation most highly developed. These were precisely the men who suffered most from the shell-shock.

Their conscious minds refused to harbor cowardice, but the subconscious, always ready to take us out of a reality that is too terrible to be borne, developed a disease that REMOVED THE MEN FROM REALITY, from danger and even from a realization of the horrors around them.

It is a matter of history now that when the steamers carrying shell-shocked men were torpedoed and the patients flung into the water, almost every man recovered his sight, hearing, reason or whatever it was he had lost—all through the subconscious powers which gave him the diseases in the first place.

"The subconscious minds of these men," said a leading New York physician, "recognized in the torpedoing of the boat a new danger from which shell-shock could not save them—a danger, in fact, wherein every fiber of that organism must fight for its life. So the lost senses returned.

"The subconscious mind is the miracle mind of man!"

Dreams are the most frequent and the least harmful of these "flights from reality." Invalidism, hypochondria, drunkenness, drug-taking, all forms of neuroses and suicide itself, are but the different roads which different types and temperaments under differing conditions, take to get away from life-as-it-is.

In all these the conscious mind relaxes, forgets the troubles of the day, the disappointments, the hurts, the wounds—and reverts to temporary peace.

With the drugging or putting to sleep of the conscious mind the individual ceases to think. He reverts to that much more ancient and pleasurable thing—feeling.

His modern, civilized brain, which is yet so new it finds the struggle difficult, "goes off shift" and the subconscious mind—primitive, powerful, pleasing and pacifying—takes charge.

He ceases to deal with abstract thoughts or ideas.

He revels in the mental pictures supplied by the subconscious from its endless "morgue" of symbols.

The real reason for the popularity of the modern motion picture is the fact that it appeals to an age-old instinct, an ancient psychological habit of the human race—the habit of dreaming IN PICTURES.

Every person subconsciously recognizes in the motion picture the same kind of activity he has engaged in every time he dreamed a dream. Your dreams are your personal, private movie shows.

An even deeper significance of the popularity of the moving picture lies in the fact that it furnishes in the lives of the disappointed, the depressed, the discouraged, the worried and the ailing, exactly the same relief from REALITY as do the dreams in our sleep—but in a lesser degree.

People unconsciously prove this by measuring every moving picture according to its ability to grip and interest them; in other words, to make them FORGET REALITY.

When one says he did not enjoy a certain moving picture he is unconsciously saying that, for some reason, it did not take him out of reality.

The fact that there are different types of people, each requiring something different to take him out of the troubles of everyday, accounts for the fact that what one calls "a great picture" is called "absolutely no good" by someone else.

We unconsciously make every moving picture fill the pleasure requirement of the dream in another vital respect—by automatically visualizing ourselves in the rôle of the hero or heroine. We then live the whole story vicariously, with the action revolving around ourselves.

The surest way to attain health is to renovate the mind. One way to know whether yours is building for health and happiness or for distress and disease, is to watch your own mental movies—in your day-dreams and the dreams of your sleep—measuring and estimating their meaning according to the standards laid down in this lesson.

If destructive emotions pervade your sleep-dreams these same emotions are disturbing your waking life and in turn your health.

If you are constantly trying to escape reality you are in danger, mentally and physically. Instead of attempting to sneak out the back door, walk out through the front, into the facts of your life.

Loving and being loved is the supremest human experience. Under its magic influence we become changed beings—happier, stronger, sweeter, better. Without it we wither, weaken and disintegrate.

Its effect on health and achievement is immeasurable. Many have attained mediocre success without visible lovers, but none ever achieved greatness without a great love. It might almost be said that none save great lovers have scaled the heights.

This does not mean that the great love of a life must necessarily be for or from one of the other sex, though these are the most powerful and productive loves possible to man.

Nor does it assume that the loved one must be a flesh-and-blood creature.

The ideal whom many adore in secret and whose prototype is never found in real life, often serves greater purposes than any living lover.

Very idealistic, very sensitive, very repressive types seldom find mates as beautiful, refined, sympathetic or understanding as they demand, and this accounts for the fact that these are the very types which most often remain unmated, while their opposites marry early and often.

"No one lives who is not in love, all the time, with a person, either real or ideal," says Wilfrid Lay. "In many men and women this ideal personality is the only one loved, but often loved subconsciously, while for others there is also a consciously loved or admired real person.

"How to unite the conscious and unconscious love, so frequently at variance in the same soul, and center it upon one person of the opposite sex, becomes therefore a great problem of life today."

In civilized human beings the love-urge is second to the ego-urge many. In many it appears to take precedence of the direct ego-urge, though it must not be forgotten that love for an individual is always, and to a far greater extent than the lover realizes, an indirect expression of the ego.

To be loved is gratifying to the ego of every individual, regardless of whether he has ever seen or ever will see the one who loves him.

To love is to know a new power, to sense unplumbed depths in one's own soul, to realize his own strength, to express his spirit.

So powerful is the effect of love that, though loving and being loved by one of the other sex is life's profoundest experience, to love and be loved by a friend, a parent, a follower, a child or even a dumb animal, is uplifting, strengthening, consoling.

This has been proven in countless cases, such as have come within the range of your own observation.

You wonder why certain men and women become so deeply attached to a dog, a bird, a cat or other pet. But to the student of Mental Analysis there is nothing strange in this phenomenon.

Every individual craves personal love from someone, and to give out his own.

When, for any reason, he is unable to find a human being sufficiently similar to his ideal, to love and be loved by, he seeks a substitute in whatever other creature appeals to him most.

Rather than being indicative of a less high evolution this often indicates a higher-than-average nature on the part of the pet-loving person.

It is well known that cruel, selfish people seldom care for animals. It is equally well known that those who are kind to animals are gentle, refined, sensitive, idealistic—in short, highly evolved men and women.

These two facts are so universally known that when a motion picture introduces a character by letting you see him kick a dog or mistreating any animal you know he is the villain.

But when sweetness of nature, kindness of heart and goodness in general are to be pictured, the camera tells it all to you in a flash by showing the character petting or playing with some birds, lambs, dogs, kittens or horses.

One of the most beautiful, brilliant and famous young women in America is the cartoonist, Fay King, of whose hands we have spoken in "Realizing On Your Personality." Spirituality and gentleness of heart distinguish all her work.

In her room at the Hotel Pennsylvania, New York City, is her pet canary "Mike," whom she has had for ten years and whose imaginary sayings are familiar to the millions who see Miss King's stories and cartoons every day in the leading newspapers of the country.

Bill Hart's devotion to his beloved horse "Pinto" and Mary Pickford's to her big Danes are stronger proofs than even press agents can produce, of the natural goodness and inner refinement of these famous figures.

The Freudian theory that all our activities have a sexual significance is not only disproved by the ordinary facts of our own everyday lives, but
further disproved by the study of the human instincts.

Sex is a fundamental instinct and as such wields the great influence over our lives which any basic instinct wields.

But that it pervades our personal universe to the extent ascribed to it by the Viennese school seems scarcely possible, even when we allow the wide latitude and admit the great self-ignorance which the first psychoanalysts suggested.

In fact, measured by their effect upon our lives, a large group of instincts takes precedence of the sex instinct in the life of the average human being.

That there is a period, during adolescence, when the instinct of sex dominates our thoughts, feelings and actions, is undeniable.

But that that period of intense preoccupation with sex is of short duration is also undeniable. In the normal individual it is ordinarily not more than five years.

Even in the less-than-average lifetime there are, before it arrives and after it passes, some forty years when the instincts of assimilation, pugnacity, egoism and self-expression singly or combined—far overshadow the influence of the sex instinct.

With due respect to Freud, who has done so much to awaken mankind to its great subconscious forces, and whose contributions to the human sciences are immeasurable, he gives (or so it seems to some of us) undue weight to the ancient sex symbols of ancient peoples.

It is not unlikely that instead of these symbols running inward toward sex as the spokes of a wheel run into the hub, these sexual symbols were primitive attempts to picture, in the only language they knew, higher and non-sexual cravings.

Not only do we know that we have manifold and mighty impulses which are not related even remotely to sex, but we know that love itself is by no means wholly sexual—even the love between the sexes.

The lure of love goes far beyond and far higher than sex lure, as we see in that greatest example of human devotion—mother-love.

Every creature desires to be loved—and often to love and be loved by those with whom he cares to associate nothing sexual, even remotely.

Alienists, physicians and psychologists are all aware of the healing power of love and the harming power of hate. We have seen many a patient cured of a disease which medical science could not touch, by the patient's falling suddenly in love. And we have seen stalwart ones succumb to all manner of maladies when thwarted in a much-desired affection.

So all-powerful and so all-pervading is the demand for love and the desire to give love that every child, so scientists say, is in love with someone by the time he is three years old. From that time to the moment of death he is in love with some real or ideal person upon whom he showers, in imagination if not in real life, the flowers of his spirit.

Being instinctive, intense and impulsive, this love-urge, like every other, demands expression and, like every other, is forced to express itself in its environment.

The only environment the child knows is the home. The only people from whom it can demand love and draw love unto itself are the people in its environment.

To the average child this means his parents. They are the objects upon which he showers his own instinctive love-energy, and he tries, with all the subconscious powers he possesses, to induce them to love him in return.

None of this is reasoned nor "thought out" in any conscious sense, but is done inevitably and unerringly just as the new-born babe, consciously knowing nothing whatever, yet subconsciously knows how to satisfy hunger at its mother's breast.

Under normal home conditions, the child finds, ready-made, the ideal situation for the growth and expression of his instinctive love-urge.

His parents, craving always more love themselves and craving always to give more love, respond not only unreservedly to the child's demand for love, but encourage its further development by doing all the things which lure love from any one anywhere at any time since the world began.

Love begets love. It is practically impossible to resist people who truly, deeply love us and who self-sacrificingly continue to shower it upon us.

Thousands of marriages are consummated every year as a result of one of the pair having loved the other into loving him.

Between the child and the parent there are no barriers. Everything conduces to the encouragement, enhancement and full expression of love—to the child from the parent, from the child to the parents, and back again in an accentuating circle.

It is small wonder then that BY THE TIME HE IS THREE, EVERY CHILD IS DEEPLY, INTENSELY IN LOVE WITH HIS PARENTS.

In many instances, this first great love is never excelled in adult life.

Thousands of men and women fail to find, when grown up, any love situation to compare with this original one, and remain single, without ever realizing the underlying reason.

With every condition ideal and ripe for love on the part of the parent and the child, and with every tradition backing up the parents' love for their children, it is inevitable that parents and children should develop a devotion for each other that is all the more intense because all the rest of the world blocks love. For this very reason it is inevitable that this concentrated love should sometimes subconsciously exceed the bounds of cold reason.

It is always a surprise to outsiders to see the blindness of parental devotion. It is equally surprising, looked at from the standpoint of actual facts, to see the blind faith of the child in his weak or unworthy parents.

But all this is inevitable. We love those who love us. We believe in those who love us, even after we are old enough to know better. So it is hardly to be expected that the young child should refrain from pouring out its instinctive affection upon the parents who comfort, feed and shelter it and who shower upon it the affections it demands.

It is true in most cases (for reasons entirely apart from sexual ones) that the daughter loves the father more than she loves the mother, and that the boy loves his mother more than he loves his father.

But that the sexual element predominates even unconsciously in this relationship is as false as it is unfair. And it is proven in this fact: that at least one-third of all girls love their mothers more, while more than a third of all boys love their fathers best. "Oedipus" and "Electra" are indeed myths.

Which parent will the child love more? If we need any further proof of the fact that the ego-urge is more powerful than the sex-urge we find it in the answer to this question.

For, THE CHILD WILL LOVE MOST THAT PARENT WHO MOST APPEALS TO HIS EGO, REGARDLESS OF SEX.

The child will center its greatest love exactly where the rest of us do—on those who are most devoted to him.

If the father is more strict, more unyielding than the mother the daughter will love her mother best, and the greater warmth of her devotion to her mother will be in proportion to the differences in their treatment of her.

For instance, if a father is extremely severe with his children and the mother almost as much so, all the children, regardless of sex, will love their mother more, though not much more than their father.

If she is the opposite extreme from the father—if she gives them their way, pets, loves, fondles and forgives them where he punishes and tyrannizes—all the children will adore their mother and (whether or not they ever admit it even to themselves) subconsciously dislike their father. Regardless of how right he was or how wrong and weak the mother was, this will invariably be true.

On the other hand, if the mother is austere, undemonstrative and a hard taskmaster, her children may have great respect for her and consciously admire her more than a worthless father. But if that father indulges them, and shows more affection—though he be a drunkard, thief or murderer—still will all the children love him best.

Love, Courtship and Marriage

And they will continue to do so just so long as he is the more indulgent parent.

This love is from the subconscious and the subconscious, as has been stated before, knows nothing of these modern standards of conduct. It deals with the expression of the individual. It is for whatever and whoever serves his instinctive cravings.

The accuracy of all this can be proved at any moment by any person from his own experience.

Regardless of whether he is willing to confess it or not, he knows that the parent he truly feels the greatest affection for is that one who was the more kind, more loving and more indulgent with him.

If, as often happens, the severe parent selects one of his children for special favors—if he shows partiality to that child to a greater extent than does the other parent—that particular child will begin to prefer him to the other parent, whereas the recognition of this partiality by the other children will make all the others withdraw farther and farther from the father and nearer to the mother.

Here we come to the secret back of all the father-daughter and mother-son complexes. And like most secrets it proves upon investigation to be a perfectly simple thing after all!

It is true that most daughters love their fathers best simply and solely BECAUSE MOST FATHERS INDULGE THEIR DAUGHTERS MORE THAN THEY INDULGE THEIR SONS.

In other words then, because they are conscious of the difference in sex and have been trained to protect women, fathers more often do for their daughters than for their sons the things that inevitably win love from anyone at any time under any conditions.

Let a father who has thus won his daughter's love suddenly begin to favor his son while the mother, who has been partial to the son, suddenly commences to show extreme favoritism to the daughter—and both these children, after a few days or weeks of suffering and uncertainty, will interchange their affections and go on just as before with their new loves.

It is true that most sons love their mothers more than they love their fathers and for the same reason as that stated above. IN ALL SUCH INSTANCES THE MOTHER HAS SHOWN MORE LOVE AND INDULGENCE TO THE SON THAN DID THE FATHER.

Here, again, we come to the effect of tradition. Just as the father indulged the daughter because of the traditional protection of women by men, he is inclined to be strict with his son because tradition says sons must be made to stand alone.

But the old subconscious knows naught of these things which have come recently into the world. All the boy's subconscious knows is that he loves his mother best.

His affection for her is enhanced by her devotion to him—a devotion in which she too is the creature of tradition.

Women are expected to minister to males. Her son is a young male, a wee man. To him she naturally and habitually tends to give the best of things, and he inevitably and automatically to love her best.

All this is delightful to the child. He loves to love and be loved. His childhood is more wonderful by far than that of the children who, for any reason, do not receive this unstinted affection. But he often pays a tremendous price for it in later years.

To the boy who loves his mother, that mother becomes the epitome, the symbol of all that is desirable in love.

As a man he can love only those women who bear a real or imaginary resemblance to her.

If he can find no woman who seems to him at all like his beloved mother he will never fall in love.

The more superior the mother and the more deeply and exclusively he loved her, the less likelihood will there be of his finding any one resembling her.

Proof of how deeply submerged are some of our strongest impulses is seen in the fact that all this is unknown to the individual in whom it is operating so strongly.

He has never been consciously in love with his mother and may even imagine he would prefer women who are very different from her, but the fact remains that those who are different from her never appeal to him, while he will fall in love at first sight with one who recapitulates the mother-symbol.

The daughter who loved her father may never know why she cannot find it in her heart to marry any man. The real reason—that she is unconsciously still in love with her father, or rather with the image of him which she carries in her subconscious—is usually inconceivable to her.

She may care little or nothing for him now. He may be the kind of man her mature judgment and lifelong training tell her is beneath her affection; she may know he has always been beneath it; but it will not alter that subconscious symbol.

The man she loves is not her father as he is today, as he looks today, nor is it her father himself WHOM she loves.

What she loves is the IMAGE OF HIM—face, features, ungrayed hair, smiles, gentleness and all—that he was IN HER BABYHOOD DAYS.

She loves in men only those things which her father SEEMED to be in that far-off time. She admires only those men who have the traits her father SEEMED to have.

She will never truly love any man who does not, in some or several particulars, remind that subconscious mind of hers of this Father-image.

As in the man's case, this woman seldom dreams what it is that determines her attitude toward men. She was not consciously in love with her father, any more than he was consciously in love with his mother.

"What in the world did he see in her?" and "How did she ever happen to fall in love with him?" are questions the world often asks.

The real answer is never forthcoming because nobody knows it, least of all the person whose taste is being discussed.

Such a man may explain to you for hours at a time the many delightful traits he "saw in her," but the fact of the matter is that what he saw in her was his original love-image.

If as a child he was tenderly cared for and loved by some other woman because of his mother's death or absence, it will be her image as he loved it then which he will seek.

In all this it must be borne in mind that the person need not necessarily LOOK like the loved parent, for the reason (as has been stated in earlier lessons) that the subconscious tends to take, not the whole, but a part or section of a thing and let it stand for the total.

There is no knowing what element it will take as the symbol of the whole (much depending, as we saw in the "Emotions" lesson, on the emotional intensity accompanying isolated incidents).

So there is no way of determining, without a mental analysis, either by one's self or an analyst, what characteristic was chosen by the subconscious as the symbol of the loved parent.

The nearest one can come to knowing what symbolizes this parent in his mind, if he does not already know, or if he cannot be fully analyzed by an expert, is to ask himself this question:

WHAT IS THE FIRST THING THAT COMES INTO MY MIND WHEN I SPEAK THE NAME OF MY FAVORITE PARENT?

The difficulty with this question is that, having read this question before putting it to yourself, your conscious mind tends to short circuit the real answer.

It therefore tends to throw the switch on it, as it were, and deliver the answer in accordance with your conscious preferences, rather than the facts.

But if the question were put to you by an analyst without your knowing its significance, your answer would, under proper conditions, come direct from your subconscious mind.

If by any chance you are still in doubt as to which of your parents you loved more you can test yourself by the following:

WHICH ONE DO I THINK OF FIRST WHEN RECALLING MY PARENTS?

Under an analyst your spontaneous answer to this would be the name of the parent you had loved best.

There are several reasons why it is not easy for us to analyze ourselves, especially in the matters referred to in this lesson.

The first one is that when we know the significance and meaning of the question the surface mind almost invariably intercepts the true answer before it comes to the threshold of consciousness, and substitutes one in keeping with its own standards.

An illustration of this was seen a short time ago in a woman of middle age who had had a most lonely life. She had been in love but once, and then with a man who was already married.

She criticised herself for years for having cared for another woman's husband, though she had no overt acts to be ashamed of, and in fact had never indicated to the man nor to anyone else that she cared for him.

She left the city where he lived, but worked in uncongenial positions, with uncongenial people and, instead of caring less for him, felt that she was caring more as the years went on.

At last it so happened that this man not only moved to the city where she was but was employed in the same establishment as herself.

She was determined to rid herself of what she had all these years termed her "unholy affection."

She had no real respect for this man, who was mentally and morally her inferior. But his dark brown eyes made her forget everything save her love for him.

Analysis showed that she had really loved her shiftless father because he had been most indulgent to her in her childhood.

As she grew older and realized his mental and moral weaknesses she ceased to respect him and was not really sorry when he passed on.

She lived with and supported her mother who had suffered much at the father's hands.

So fully did she respect her mother's superior qualities that she supposed she cared more for her than she had ever cared for the father.

Two tests brought out the fact that her father had dark brown eyes and that dark brown eyes of a particular expression were to her the symbol not only of her father but of all love.

The similarity of expression in the married man's brown eyes, his shiftlessness, and moral and mental weaknesses, all combined to revive the old symbol.

When fully convinced that it was not the married man she loved but the symbols of which he reminded her, she ceased instantly to care for him.

A physician who had struggled for many years with a growing dislike for his wife was analyzed.

He had consciously refused to display this aversion or encourage it. It had assumed such proportions, however, and was arousing such dangerous emotions that he feared not only for his health but for the future of their family.

It was found that when he was seventy-eight he had had an accident which it was feared would make him permanently blind.

He spent nine weeks in a hospital with his eyes bandaged.

Long before they were unbandaged he had fallen in love with the waitress who brought the meals to his bedside, though he could not explain why.

When he saw her for the first time he found she did not look at all as he expected her to. But that did not prevent his marrying her two weeks afterward—as soon as they were sure his eyes would be normal again.

Analysis showed that what he had really fallen in love with was the girl's voice. It was low and sweet like that of his mother whom he had subconsciously loved but who had been dead many years. He pictured her face, before he saw it, as that of his mother.

By the time they removed the bandages from his eyes he was so deeply in love with the symbol-voice he forgave the difference in the face.

If the mother's face instead of her voice had been the love-symbol in his mind he would not have loved this girl.

But her face was secondary and thus relinquished, when necessary, from the ensemble.

The mother's voice was the real symbol of love to him and any woman with this voice would have appealed to him.

Before he had been married a week he realized that this woman's voice was the only thing she possessed in common with his beloved mother. The wife was, in fact, the almost exact opposite of the mother, most of whose traits he unconsciously loved.

Their marriage had been to him one disillusionment after another. His wife was unlearned where his mother had been highly educated. She was uncouth and crude where his mother had been refined; rough, outspoken and quarrelsome, where the mother had been amiability and gentility itself.

He tried to accustom himself to her, to overlook, to convince himself that this woman who loved him and bore his children was not to blame. He had been brought up to believe that a husband and father had no right, under any circumstances, to think of himself; that his family deserved his time, strength and love, regardless of everything.

To escape from the hated reality he drank much coffee, then other stimulants, and when we met him had been taking drugs some time.

It was very difficult for this man who had treated others for so long in his practice to relax sufficiently and confide sufficiently to the analyst to give her the story of the real (though hitherto unrealized reason) for falling in love with this woman so far beneath him.

It was not easy for him to admit that things medicine could not touch could be brought out into the sunlight and cured by mental analysis. But such was the case.

He was shown the exact facts—that he had not turned away from his wife for the reason that he had never loved her.

He had married what he supposed was a woman like his mother and she was utterly different.

His years of brave struggle to keep from hurting her—a large husky woman—had resulted in almost wrecking his own much more refined organism.

A recognition of the facts and the restoration of his self-respect enabled him within a few months to resume his practice and give up his drug habit.

This love between mothers and sons and fathers and daughters, with its far-flung influence upon human lives, is seen in almost every great love of history.

But nowhere is it more strikingly illustrated than in that most illustrious love-union of modern times—between Elizabeth Barrett and Robert Browning.

We will quote direct from its sympathetic and poetic raconteur, Elbert .Hubbard in his "Little Journeys":

"Robert Browning's mother was a woman of fine feeling and much poetic insight. She knew good books. The mother and son moused in books together and, according to Mrs. Sutherland Orr, his biographer, this love of mother and son took upon itself the nature of a passion.

"She was an infirm individual, a Shut-In, reclining always on a couch.

"The love of Robert Browning for Elizabeth Barrett was a revival and a renewal of the condition of tenderness and sympathy that existed between Browning and his mother.

"There certainly was a strange and marked resemblance in the characters of Elizabeth Barrett and the mother of Robert Browning; and to many this fully accounts for the instant affection that Browning felt toward the occupant of the 'darkened room,' when first they met.

"It also accounts for the answering love Elizabeth Barrett gave him that first moment. Robert Browning was, on first sight, much more the father type than the poet. His frame was compact and strong—like HER FATHER'S. His poise, his protective power symbolized the things her father had meant to her in her childhood days when he was all love for her.

"Edward Barrett had a sort of fierce, passionate, jealous affection for his daughter Elizabeth. He set himself the task of educating her from her very babyhood. He was her constant companion, her tutor, adviser, friend.

"The child's health broke. From her thirteenth year she appears to us like a beautiful spirit.

"But she did not much complain. She had a will as strong as her father's, and felt a Spartan pride in doing all the studying he asked and a little more. She read, translated, thought.

"To spur her on and to stimulate her, he published several volumes of her poems.

"Came a time when Mr. Barrett was jealous of his daughter—of the fame that was taking her away from him. The passion of father for daughter, of mother for son—there is often something loverlike in it—a deal of whimsy!

"'Edward Barrett's daughter—she of the raven curls and gentle ways—was reaching a point where her father's love was not her life.

"A good way to drive love away is to be jealous. He had seen it coming years before; he had brooded over it; the calamity was upon him. Her fame was growing; someone called her the Shakespeare of women.

"Edward Barrett scowled. He accused her foolishly and falsely of perverseness. He attempted to dictate to her—she must use this ink or that. Why? Because he said so. He quarreled with her to ease the love-hurt that was smarting in his heart.

"Mr. Browning, who had heard of Miss Barrett and admired her work, wrote asking permission to call upon her.

"Miss Barrett replied that her father would not allow it, neither would the doctor or nurse; that she lived in a darkened room. She added, 'There is nothing to see in me.'

"But this repulse only made Mr. Browning want to see her the more. He appealed to her cousin, an elderly gentleman who was the only person allowed to call.

"The cousin arranged it. He timed the hour when Mr. Barrett was downtown, and the nurse and doctor safely out of the way, and they called on the infirm prisoner in the darkened room.

"They did not stay long, but when they went away Robert Browning trod on air. The beautiful girl-like face, in its frame of dark curls, lying back among the pillows, haunted him like a shadow. She was slipping away. He would love her back to life and light!

"And so Robert Browning told her all this shortly afterward. . .

"She grew better.

"And soon we find her getting up and throwing wide the shutters. It was no longer a darkened room. The sunlight came dancing through the windows.

"The doctor was indignant; the nurse resigned. Of course Mr. Barrett was not taken into confidence, and no one asked his consent. Why should they? She was thirty-five—and her father a man who could never understand.

"So one fine day when the coast was clear, the couple went over to Saint Marylebone Church and were married. The bride went home alone—could walk all right now—and it was a week before her husband saw her, because he would not be a hypocrite and go ring the doorbell and ask if Miss Barrett was home; and of course if he had asked for Mrs. Robert Browning, no one would have known whom he wanted to see.

"But at the end of a week the bride stole down the stairs while the family was at dinner and met her lover-husband there on the street corner where the mailbox is. No one missed the runaways until the next day, and then the bride and groom were safely in France, writing letters back asking forgiveness and blessings...

"Health came back, and joy and peace and perfect love were theirs. But it was joy bought with a price— Elizabeth Barrett Browning had forfeited the love of her father. Her letters written to him came back unopened... He declared she was dead...

"We regret that this man, so strong and manly in many ways, could not be reconciled to this exalted love.

"Why could he not have followed the example of John Kenyon who had always loved her and who, it is said, did not smile for two years after her elopement?"...

The answer is to be found in human psychology which today shows us that many who THINK they love someone are really only loving themselves!

When you truly love, you want the adored one to have not YOU necessarily but WHATEVER he or she desires.

That John Kenyon truly loved Elizabeth Barrett was proven when in his will he left all he had—fifty thousand dollars—to the Brownings, to add the last touch to their happiness.

They were poor but his kindness placed them forever beyond financial fear and gave them perfect peace.

In this ideal mating of the Brownings, as in all great loves, it was again proved that it is LOVE rather than sex which most human beings seek in marriage.

People seek marriage IN PROPORTION AS THEY LACK LOVE AND FRIENDSHIP IN THEIR LIVES.

Many a handsome bachelor remains unmarried not because women do not care for him but precisely because they DO.

This satisfies his demand for love without the entanglements resultant from wedlock.

Psychology also explains why, at fifty or so, these men finally marry. They are beginning to lose their attractiveness, the love and friendships of women which have substituted for marriage became fewer in number and fainter in feeling.

Such a man awakens to the fact that if he is to be supplied with personal affection he must find a mate and "settle down."

While it is true that many supposedly celibate men and women live far different lives from what we imagine, it is equally true that the attractive, popular type of bachelor described usually lives a far more celibate life than the sophisticated would believe.

We base this statement not only upon observation and knowledge of psychology, but upon our experience with thousands of students throughout the United States.

Many of these men have stated in private analyses (where they can be even more frank than with their physician, and where there is the fullest understanding and consequent tolerance of every human weakness) that though they bore the reputation of being exceedingly gay, as a matter of fact they lived lives of chastity OUT OF PREFERENCE.

Many of these men desired an analysis largely to find why they preferred to live this life instead of the one popularly ascribed to them— the kind they also supposed other such men lived.

In many instances such a man has labored under the delusion that he was "eccentric," "freakish" or abnormal, and was relieved but not surprised when he learned that his was not only a perfectly normal but much more prevalent attitude than the world realizes.

It is not the popular man but the unpopular one (who gets little or no love from anyone) who seeks sexual expression and who, instead of the celibate life credited to him, lives on containing sexual experiences that would amaze his unsuspecting friends.

The same is true of the flirtatious attractive woman—and especially of the supposedly dangerous young widow.

It cannot be repeated too often that what the human being desires most is NOT sex but LOVE. If love of a personal nature can be obtained without sex, many there are, in both sexes, who prefer single blessedness to mating, and celibacy to sexual expression.

The attractive woman who can win and hold the devotion, attention, affection and love of men—to whom they send flowers, candy, books and other gifts—is never the sexual creature she is painted.

This also we know from private analyses of thousands of such women. The adulation which the ego is always subconsciously craving in love is satisfied by these attentions. The love-demand is met by the affections of a large number of men. Often they feel no further need of expression.

It is the quiet, self-effacing, timid, plain and outwardly puritanical woman who dwells on the matters of sex, searches the libraries for sex literature and finds sexual expression in the least suspected paths.

She it is also who is most easily induced to give herself out of wedlock because her heart is so starved for love.

Such a woman, if no longer young or if of the extremely repressed type, often refuses, but it is in the face of terrific struggle.

She desires NOT to refuse, more than the self-expressive woman can ever know. Her willpower deserves our utmost respect.

All these and myriads of corroborative situations, facts and conditions throughout all human experience prove conclusively that even LOVE IS FAR LESS CRASSLY SEXUAL THAN WE HAVE EVER SUPPOSED.

Every human being craves understanding, communion and the certainty of intimate personal interest.

We believe the time will come when all thinking men and women will recognize that THE THINGS OF SEX ARE RESORTED TO NOT SO MUCH FOR THEIR OWN SAKE AS BECAUSE THEY GIVE THE SUREST AND COMPLETEST SENSE OF THIS DEEP PERSONAL INTIMACY.

Look in any direction you will under any condition, observe any person or persons of any race, nationality, education, belief or training, and you will find what historians have always seen but never understood—that THE INSTANT THIS PERSONAL INTIMACY

IS FULLY ESTABLISHED THE SEXUAL ELEMENT ASSUMES A LESS IMPORTANT ROLE.

Once the sexual act has taken place the utmost intimacy known to humans is established. The sex urge is, to a far greater degree than we have ever dreamed, MERELY A MEANS TO THIS END.

Having fulfilled its mission it immediately takes a secondary place. This again proves to us how much more of the ego element exists in even the wildest love than we have ever recognized.

Hundreds of women and men wonder why no subsequent sexual experience with the same mate ever rises to the heights of the first. Many whose mates love them more than they did at first, imagine that because passion has died, love has flown.

The exact opposite is more often true.

Passion is always and invariably self-centered, egoistic and wholly SELF-EXPRESSIVE. It can not, by its very nature, awaken or exist minus these qualities—any more than you can become hungry because another has been without food, nor halt your own starvation by watching him eat.

To yield one's self without desire as the instrument of another's desire, is unselfish (though a most dangerous and reprehensible kind of unselfishness!)—but to satisfy one's own desire is the essence and epitome of self-seeking.

Many a wife and many a husband who recognizes this subconsciously withdraws from contact with his mate for no other reason than his aversion to being made merely an avenue of self-expression for another. This again illustrates the all-pervading urge of the ego.

The greater the ego of such a one the more certain is he to retreat from his mate when his subconscious finally becomes aware of the facts.

He may never suspect the reason for the cooling of his ardor. On the other hand it may be a fully conscious reaction.

If he has reached the age or stage of life when the sexual urge is less dominant this withdrawal and relinquishment of sexual expression may have no appreciable effect.

But if such a one still loves his or her mate and is still very much alive sexually, there may arise a conflict between the ego instinct on one hand (which refuses to adapt itself to utilization by another) and the sex instinct (which demands expression and knows nothing save its own desires).

In these cases — and there are tens of thousands of them — conflicts and complexes of various kinds arise — always in accordance with the type of the individual.

As time goes on and one finds that his mate bears little or no resemblance to his ideal-image, he will try to forget, or fight his aversion; seek new relationships or separate — depending again upon his type and temperament.

If you were one of a large family of children the probabilities are you did not have enough parent-love lavished on you exclusively to establish a too vivid love-image.

If you were brought up by someone other than your parents it is not likely that you were harmed by a too intense affection.

If you grew up in an institution you doubtless received too little love and were permitted to show too little.

But in any case, this lesson cannot fail to help you.

Read it carefully, be frank with yourself. Through it you will come ultimately to a deeper understanding of your own personal problems.

Though it is a startling, and to many a shocking fact, it IS nevertheless true that the people we love are desired, not for themselves but for OURselves, and loved to the EXTENT THAT THEY, DIRECTLY OR INDIRECTLY, AID IN OUR OWN SELF-EXPRESSION.

All of which proves again how the beloved ego in each of us makes or mars our world.

The child loves best the parent who most aids it in expressing itself. The man loves best those women who aid most in his self-expression. Women love best those men who aid them most in their self-expression.

Every unmated person is seeking, as we have seen, a lover who recapitulates the symbol of his first great love.

But such a one, even if found, will never bring him continued happiness unless he be, in addition to this symbol, of a biological type which automatically aids in the self-expression of his mate.

When a man finds a woman who recreates his love-symbol he can love her instantaneously, but if her biological type is such that she cannot aid in his CONTINUED self-expression he will eventually tire of her. The more she obstructs his self-expression, the sooner will he tire.

If she not only refuses to yield herself as an aid to the expression of his type and subconscious wish, but insists upon CHANGES in him which enable her to express HER OWN, he will gradually grow to dislike her. If she keeps it up he will ultimately subconsciously hate her, though she be the mother of his children!

The matter of biological types is too extensive to go into here and has been fully explained in our course, "The Five Human Types."

The present course deals with man's subconscious mind, but if you are interested to further understand human types and their effect upon our love-life, see "Types that Should and Should Not Marry Each Other," Lesson VI of the above mentioned course.

Whenever an individual goes through life without marrying it is not because he does not desire a mate, but because marriage with any of the people he has seen would, in his opinion, INTERFERE WITH HIS SUPREME SUBCONSCIOUS WISH.

Every unmated person desires a mate, but if he desires SOMETHING ELSE MORE—that is, if the desire for a mate is not his SUPREMEST desire—he will not marry until he finds someone who he is convinced will NOT INTERFERE with his supreme subconscious wish.

Many men and women mate with one who does not remind them of their subconscious love-symbol, and they marry knowing this.

Whenever this happens it is because the finding of a mate who shall repeat this love-symbol is NOT this person's supremest wish. He feels that the one he has chosen will aid in that supreme wish, whatever it may be, and strikes a compromise.

Since that supreme wish is for something which to him is more desirable than the possession of an ideal mate he sacrifices the lesser to the greater. You do the same thing in every decision of your life.

This supreme subconscious wish in each of us is a primal, instinctive thing. It may be founded in high, recent and civilized instincts, and often is; but much more often the deepest desire of the average organism is for the gratification of a primitive instinct, urge or tendency.

If this primitive thing is what he really wants more than anything else in the world, the law brings it to pass in his life. If it is too far removed from modern instincts his family, his friends and the world will call him a coward, a ne'er-do-well, a beast or a criminal—depending upon the particular instinct which, out of the primitive group, is most over-developed in him.

All the while he will be wishing to live up to his higher instincts. He has many others of high order. One of these—and it exists in every human being—is the instinct of approbation.

He wishes the approval of his fellows; he wishes to do and be and have the things that make them like, admire, respect and follow him; but his supreme want must and WILL express itself. All its enemies must go by the board. He makes excuses, he equivocates, he apologizes, he tries to justify his failures to the world, whose opinion he so much values.

Most of all, he suffers.

But he feels that he suffers less than he would were he to give up his supremest want—so he pays the price.

LESSON XII

Success and Your Supreme Wish

SUCCESS is, next to love, the most vital matter in one's life, for only through successful accomplishment of some nature can civilized men and women be thoroughly happy.

Not only does success fulfill a great personal need by aiding in the self-expression of the individual but through it he contributes to the progress of the world.

These two elements are necessary to the happiness of any normal man or woman.

First, the normal individual desires self-expression. But a close second is his sincere desire to help humanity. The latter is not a mere margin which he wishes to dispose of but a natural demand of his "success instinct."

Civilized man has two rôles and is taught early in life what they are. He is himself—and himself is ever his primary consideration. But he is also a part of society—a tiny section in a great mosaic.

The average individual thinks chiefly of that little self-section—not so much because he is selfish or narrow but because his own troubles, problems and difficulties are so great he has little time, energy or thought left over to give to the general pattern.

The greatest result of Mental Analysis is that it is helping the individual to untangle his own troubles.

The moment this is done the rest follows. He awakens to the needs of his fellows—his family's first, then his friends', next his acquaintances', and in time, the world's.

Every normal human being, to be happy, must know that he is the big world. One need not be "out in the world"—like the father who meets the public in his work—in order to have this gratifying realization.

The loving mother, the understanding wife in her little apartment, knows that in doing her work she is directly connecting with the work of the world through her husband—that she is the quartermaster, the Red Cross and munition plant behind the lines.

Subconsciously, every such woman demands that her man make a success of his work out there in the front trenches, for her sake as well as his own. She does not like to feel that all her efforts are being expended for losing army.

Many more lives than we realize are ruined from a lack of definite connection with the world of real work.

The individual himself (and especially if it be a herself) often wonders what is wrong and goes through years or a lifetime without realizing that it is the thwarting of this natural success instinct which is causing the difficulty.

The woman who has a home, a husband or children will find in them full satisfaction of this urge IF SHE HAPPENS TO BELONG PREDOMINANTLY TO ONE TYPE.

But if she belongs predominantly to either of the other four human types she will never find complete self-expression in the care of home, husband or even children.

She, like the men of these types, demands direct self-expression. To her some interest outside the four walls is essential to happiness.

Each type always selects the general kind of outside interests most appealing to it.

Until recent years home and church work were the only activities in which women could engage and keep the full admiration of the world.

Then the woman's club was born. Various charitable organizations inaugurated and backed almost entirely by women came into being.

The prohibition crusade gave thousands of women an opportunity to emerge and connect with a world cause. Later the woman suffrage movement, for fifty years, gave the same opportunity to thousands more.

It will be interesting to you to note how each of these crusades—churches, charitable organizations, prohibition and woman suffrage—was headed by different biological types of women and that the rank and file in each consisted chiefly of women of that same type.

The Franees E. Willard type still predominates in the W. C. T. U. The Susan B. Anthony type still predominates in the National League of Women Voters.

Whenever a woman of one of these crusades joined another it was for the furtherance of her real interest, as, for instance, when the W. C. T. U. joined the woman suffrage movement. It did so, not so much for woman suffrage per se as because it was convinced that woman suffrage would help prohibition.

When the Susan B. Anthony type joined the W. C. T. U. it was largely for the purpose of gaining co-operation in the suffrage cause.

These facts of type-preference were obtained by four years' first-hand observation of thousands of women in both these organizations throughout the United States.

Many other surveys show that women, like men, must have self-expression and that each invariably chooses, out of the possibilities in his or her environment, the particular kind of activity always preferred by his type.

He chooses more or less automatically because his choice is predetermined by his subconscious. But his subconscious is largely determined by his type. This is because the subconscious mind is the hereditary mind—the mind of instinct with which man is born. What he does after he gets here will affect its content but not its predominant trends.

Every individual of every type, temperament and combination, desires self-expression through some kind of outgoing activity.

He will be content, congenial and constructive only in those endeavors which aid in the attainment of his supreme subconscious wish.

If his supreme wish is to spend his life in some particular kind of activity, regardless of its tasks or drudgeries, and if he concentrates on this activity, he will become a genius. But if his choice of a vocation is secondary to his wish—that is, if it is selected only as an adjunct to the wish—an aid and abetter of something he desires more—and he gets into such a vocation, he will be in it only one of the many big successes.

If he spends his life in a kind of work which calls for traits which he has only in a small degree, he will be mediocre.

If his work demands activities that are the opposite of his natural ones he will be a failure.

In each case the subconscious mind registers feelings for or against certain vocations and for or against specific lines of work contemplated by the individual.

Your preference for or prejudice against any line of work is not an accident nor a mystery. It is an emotion based in the subconscious unreasoning feeling that this vocation would help or hinder the materialization of your supreme wish.

It automatically votes against everything which would interfere with your life's desires and for everything of any nature (including vocation) that aids and abets them.

The child destined to become a genius has, like every other, a supreme subconscious wish. But this wish differs from that of the average child in two things—INTENSITY and CONTENT.

The supreme subconscious wish of the vast majority of men, women and children is TO POSSESS THINGS.

The supreme wish of the genius child is TO DO A CERTAIN KIND OF THING.

The average supreme wish, though it may be fired with the deepest emotion of which that individual is capable, is much less intense and furious than that of the genius-child.

These two lead to the third element—opportunity—as inevitably as the desire and ability to sing point the song bird instinctively to an opportunity to unburden his silvery throat.

So we find that the requisites for the making of a genius are:

A desire to DO A CERTAIN KIND OF THING, regardless of good or bad consequences.

That this desire shall constitute the ONE SUPREME, SUBCONSCIOUS WISH of his life, in comparison with which all else is insignificant.

That this SUPREME WISH TO DO A CERTAIN KIND OF THING shall be so INTENSE as to allow no room for feelings of doubt.

These things and these only have invariably differentiated the genius from other men and women.

These intense inner urges COMPEL the genius to find opportunity for doing the thing he wants to do. He has no peace until he does it. Once started at it, satisfaction permeates his spirit, saturates his soul. He is at the business for which he was created; he has found himself.

In this supremest of human achievements—meeting and working with one's self face to face—the genius forgets all else.

Is it to be wondered at that such enthusiasm produces great things?

Other men give but a fraction of themselves to their work and none of their subconscious selves to work they dislike. The subconscious of the genius is in tune with the world.

Any man who WANTS to do a thing with the same intensity, the same selfless, concentrated determination can make of himself a genius.

But the average man does not want to DO; he only wants to HAVE WITHOUT DOING.

He is always expecting to "put one over" on Fate.

It can't be done.

"A genius is one who can not be kept away from his work." If nothing can keep you away from yours, if you love its toil and drudgery so much it is play, this means that to do this thing is your supreme subconscious wish. Whatever you supremely, subconsciously wish can and does come true, as you will see in the last lesson of this course.

Those who are not geniuses but the next highest—the big successes in any line—are those whose supreme wish is TO ACHIEVE A CERTAIN GOAL and WHO ARE WILLING TO DO ANYTHING HONORABLE

TO REACH IT, no matter how hard, how humiliating or how difficult the necessary sacrifices.

Such a man or woman will become ultimately a supreme success. For him, as for the genius, there is no question of opportunity. The world is full of opportunity and he knows it.

The trouble with the unsuccessful is not that they lack ability or opportunity. They lack none of the success requisites save one, and that one they can get any moment they want it—willingness to PAY THE PRICE.

The rest of the world wonders and complains at the success of certain well-known people, but it might better be learning a lesson from them.

We need not concentrate on the same goal but we can apply the one big secret of their success to higher ones. That secret is the one stated above—a willingness to make any sacrifice necessary to success in a chosen undertaking.

To other people self-complacency, inertia, pugnacity, and a hundred other things, take precedence of the success-desire, but to this one there is nothing but the goal.

You may kick this man down your front steps, but by the time you have closed the door you will find him smilingly entering at the back.

And the chances are he will leave with your name on the dotted line!

This type of person—regardless of race, color, nationality, training, education or environment—is bound to win. He can bear any humiliation and make any sacrifice for success.

A woman who has attained fame and fortune by her own efforts, despite poverty, ill health, ugliness and other handicaps, was talking not long ago to a small group of old friends whom she had not seen since she was a ragged little girl in the ragged little Western town where she grew up.

"Let me see, Helen, didn't you wait table once at the Smith Central? I seem to remember seeing you there when you were about fifteen," asked one of the friends.

"Yes," she replied, "and the Summer before I washed dishes at the Belvedere, and the Summer before that I had a strenuous position as cook, scrub woman and maid-of-all work on a big ranch where forty men were employed. The rancher's wife had a nap every afternoon and retired at nine. I was up at five and did not sit down from that time until midnight.

"But I had a wonderful time. I needed that $3 a week to buy books and clothes for high school that Fall. When Fall came I got another job—working for my board in a family of seven children—but I HAD to have an education and thought I was a lucky girl to even GET a job!"

After more mutual reminiscences one of the women turned to the now successful one and said, "Did you ever select anything and say you would NOT do that—didn't you have powerful aversions to doing some things?"

"There was one," the woman replied—"just one thing I always said even as a child that I would not do. I said it over and over, and it was, 'I will NOT fail!'"

If you care enough about being a success to stop flirting with failure you will find the work and the opportunities necessary to make you one.

People miss success because they want to eat their cake and have it too. They won't do this and they are too good to do that; they are above this and superior to that—in their youth. At middle age they are making excuses, and at sixty many are brought to a choice between those very same menial things and the poorhouse.

False pride has cheated more people out of success than any other thing in this world.

Pride that is REAL is too proud to drag you a frazzled failure through this world of opportunity!

The content of your own subconsciousness determines your success or failure.

To know whether you are going to be a real success you have but to ask yourself the following questions:

Which of these two attitudes predominate in my mind: the determination AGAINST doing certain things or a determination to DO certain things?

Do I keep my mental eyes fastened on the FEARS OF FAILURE or the CERTAINTIES OF SUCCESS?

Do I think more about the obstructions in my pathway—my troubles, my enemies, my handicap, my disadvantages, my weaknesses—than the GOAL I hope to reach?

The answer to these questions reveals the content of your subconscious as regards success-qualities. If you are wasting your strength AGAINST things, people, problems and life in general instead of expending it FOR the things you desire, you are running your car in reverse and backing yourself down hill.

If your mind has more fear than faith in it you are going to lose! Nothing on earth can make any man a winner who doesn't believe in himself.

Nothing can make you a failure save yourself.

If your subconscious is centered more on thoughts about your troubles; if your talk is full of them, you will have lots more of them, for you are putting into operation a great law and the law, being immutable, will bring them to you.

If you burn the candles of memory at the shrine of your enemies you are going to make more enemies and further embitter the ones you already have.

If you think and talk and act out your handicaps, your disadvantages, your weaknesses, you are planting tares and will reap bigger and bigger harvests of these very things as life goes on.

For YOUR SUBCONSCIOUS CONTENT MAKES OR MARS YOUR LIFE. IF IT IS DESTRUCTIVE YOUR LIFE WILL BE DESTRUCTIVE. There is no way on earth to avoid it, though millions have tricked themselves into thinking they could.

WHAT IS IN YOUR MIND COMES OUT IN YOUR LIFE. You can't fool the Force that rules the universe. That Force decrees that certain causes bring certain results and they always do.

The world calls the successful man an egoist and he is. But he is seldom a vain egotist. He believes in his own strength and proves he has it.

The mediocre and the failures BECOME mediocre and fail because they so overrate themselves as to imagine they can outwit divinity. This is not true of every failure but of most.

You can apply another little test that will tell you whether any man is this type or not. If he is forever expressing envy, jealousy, suspicion and criticism of the successful it has but one cause—the resentment of his own disappointed ego.

Those who have failed through little fault of their own are never embittered by the success of others.

If you are constantly deriding, pulling down, carping at the good fortune of others; if you call every successful person vain, selfish or a money grabber, wake up to yourself.

Realize that this attitude betrays you to every person who knows anything at all about human psychology. It tells him you are only judging others by yourself and that you are assuming they must be all these because your wounded vanity demands consolation.

Furthermore, it is a well-known fact that the motives you are in the habit of ascribing to others are what you know your own would be IN THEIR PLACE. If you can not see a man successful without calling him vain, it is because you would be vain in his place.

If you can not see a rich man without calling him mercenary, it is because you are mercenary. If you can not see another on the pinnacle of fame or fortune without thinking he is insincere it is because YOU lack sincerity.

All these are indications of your subconscious content.

Since your subconscious content determines your success, do you not see why some people have failed? People who worked and slaved and skimped—yes, and went to church!

You have got to have the pure air of right attitudes blowing through your mental windows if you want to be successful. Andre Tridon says, "The genius is always unselfish. In the neurotic, egotism is a mask for a sense of inferiority."

He and scores of other mental scientists declare that the successful are less vain, less selfish, less deceitful, less mercenary than the failures.

But that is not by any manner of means the most important thing upon which they agree.

They have found that it is chiefly BECAUSE OF THEIR MORE CONSTRUCTIVE MENTAL ATTITUDES THAT THESE PEOPLE HAVE SUCCEEDED.

Does this not contain a great lesson for every human being? And does it not prove, after all, that regardless of our particular belief or unbelief, the truth was spoken when it was said, "The letter of the law killeth but the spirit maketh alive?"

Your subconscious is a great standing army you personally own and control.

Through your conscious mind you are giving it orders every waking moment.

If you keep your mind full of destructive thoughts of any nature whatever you are giving destructive orders to your army and it will bring to pass in your life the destructive things you order.

If you have been getting what you did not want it was because, unknowingly, you have been giving your subconscious powers the wrong kind of orders.

Your subconscious is wrapped and woven around and over and under and through just one thing—your supreme life wish.

It has no function save to see that wish gratified; it never tires, never sleeps, never forgets.

It never accepts excuses; never takes No for an answer; never for so much as an instant lessens its concentration on the attainment of your one supreme aim.

It gathers from every source within your reach all manner of materials for your use in the furthering of this wish, much of which you never suspect until you start to do the thing you want to do.

A man has a deep desire for many years to write a certain book. He is so busy with his everyday affairs it is years before he sits down to start the manuscript. He thinks he has only enough material for a beginning.

But he soon finds that through his intense and genuine interest in this subject, his subconscious has gathered data for a dozen books—and hands it out to him.

He is amazed to discover how deeply he has thought on this subject and how many illustrations he has at his tongue's end. He can not write fast enough to keep up with his mind, which is bursting with material for the tangible products.

But if this man, instead of DEEPLY DESIRING for years to write a book only thinks for years that it would be a good idea to write a book, he will find when he sits down that he has almost no material.

He will awaken to the realization that he knows very little about the subject and that what he does know is unorganized, chaotic and distasteful.

When one truly DESIRES to write on a certain subject he has so much material in his mind he scarcely uses his notes. But when he attempts to write anything against his desires he gets little from even the most voluminous notes, memoranda or previous manuscript.

These facts and similar ones are known to every person who tries to do anything he has long desired to do.

The condition of your subconscious tells, with unmistakable certainty, whether you are achieving about what you are capable of, whether you are lagging behind or falling far short of what you have the ability to accomplish.

You can go far toward determining for yourself which you are doing by the following tests:

First of all, IN WHAT ARE YOU DISSATISFIED WITH YOURSELF?

And, IN WHAT WAY ARE YOU CONSTANTLY CONSCIOUS OF NOT COMING UP TO YOUR STANDARDS?

That standard comes from your subconscious and comes because you are capable of doing the very thing you desire to do.

Subconscious discontent is the method taken by your subconscious to register its disapproval. It never disapproves of you for not doing what you CAN NOT do. The fact that you regret not living up to a certain ideal is the proof that you are fully able to do so.

The man who can do wrong, weak things without regret is always a far lower-grade man than the one who suffers remorse. The one who knows the keenest suffering and self-discontent is the man who is possessed of the highest powers.

What is the amount of your ambition?

If you have little it is because you have little ability.

Ambition to do a thing comes from THE CAPACITY TO DO IT AND THE DEMAND OF THAT CAPACITY TO BE BROUGHT OUT AND UTILIZED.

A thing you have no ambition to do you have no ability to do. The man who, at thirty, has no ambition to be an architect will never be an architect.

The woman who, at thirty, has no ambition whatever to sing has no singing ability.

In this connection do not confuse the kind of work you REALLY WISH TO DO with the kind of work you imagine would bring you THE THINGS YOU WANT.

For instance, If you really WANT to sing, for the sheer love of singing and not for its rewards or the things it would bring, you have singing ability.

But if the real desire in the bottom of your subconscious mind is not to DO THE SINGING FOR THE SHEER JOY OF DOING IT but to HAVE THE EMOLUMENTS, HONORS, GLORY, FAME OR MONEY you think produce for you, you have little and perhaps no singing ability.

You will never succeed supremely in any line of work or endeavor which you do not truly, deeply, subconsciously, intensely WANT to do.

What you WANT to do you have immeasurable power to do—and the power is in proportion to the DESIRE.

Science has made one other amazing and illuminating discovery. It is that WE CRAVE SLEEP IN PROPORTION AS WE ARE UNHAPPY, UNHEALTHY OR SUCCESSFUL.

When we are happy, well, and successful we can stay in perfect health on much less sleep than we require at other times.

When we are disappointed, discouraged, depressed, ill or humiliated we want to escape from reality, and the subconscious furnishes the sleepiness necessary to bring temporary peace.

Napoleon required sleep wholly according to whether he was winning or losing battles. Three hours were sufficient when things were going well with him.

His biographers and all historians of the period degree that immediately following his most successful battles he often went several days and nights without any sleep whatever.

After his exile—when the light had gone out for him forever, and he knew it—he slept from ten to fourteen hours out of every twenty-four.

It is no mystery either to himself or to the psychologists why Thomas A. Edison requires less than four hours' sleep out of each twenty-four.

He is doing what he WANTS to do. He is achieving in real life, the things his subconscious self, his real self, desires. He is living life to the full.

His conscious and subconscious minds are working in harmony, aiding and abetting each other as they were created to do. There are almost none of the conflicts, interferences, oppositions, misunderstandings, or warfare which split and disintegrate the conscious and subconscious minds of the average individual.

THIS FACT ACCOUNTS NOT ONLY FOR THE SUCCESS OF EDISON BUT FOR THAT OF EVERY SUCCESSFUL PERSON WHO EVER LIVED.

No man can succeed through his conscious mind alone, for this conscious mind is so recent an acquisition in human evolution that it is not yet in good running order. The slightest thing sidetracks it.

Though far more powerful than we have ever suspected, the conscious mind is incapable of the deep concentrated activity of the subconscious. It is flighty, erratic, whimsical, superficial compared to the subconscious mind.

The man who puts only his conscious mind on a thing gets only surface results.

The saving fact here, however, is that the man who constantly turns his conscious mind on anything secures the co-operation of his subconscious also—and secures it to whatever degree this thing on which he centers his mind PROMISES TO FULFILL THE SUPREME SUBCONSCIOUS WISH.

For instance, you may consciously dislike to be a traveling salesman. You don't like the traveling, the constant absence from home and friends which it necessitates. But you can do them all provided your supreme subconscious wish is to be the star salesman in your district.

If your supreme wish is not for anything of this kind; especially if your deepest wish is to succeed at something entirely different, you will never get the co-operation of your subconscious mind in your salesmanship, no matter how long you keep it nor how hard you try.

And all the years you keep at salesmanship you will find relief whenever possible in some form of forgetfulness.

The safest and sanest of these forms of forgetfulness is our friend Sleep—who "knits up the raveled sleave of care" and tries, by giving the stage of the mind over to the subconscious manager, to further our supreme ambitions.

It takes the teamwork of conscious and subconscious minds, working in harmony both in sleep and in waking hours, to achieve anything great in life. If we sleep too much we hold back the other very necessary part of the team—the conscious mind.

As explained in the lesson on "Mental Miracles," whenever you are in trouble of any kind you tend to relieve the conscious mind of the strain—to "lose consciousness." Some types find this relief in long nights of sleep or frequent "naps."

Others seek it in various kinds of drink—the same types invariably choosing drinks furnishing the same kind of reaction.

Others seek forgetfulness in excitement, entertainment, society, travel and the hundreds of other modern attainments.

Any person's craving for the various "aids to forgetfulness" is proportion to the degree that reality, actuality—the facts of life—are disappointing or disillusioning him.

Thus the man who is discharged, jilted, financially ruined or worried, takes to drink if he is of a certain type.

If he is of another type this same disappointment turns him toward the deep oblivion brought by drugs—in which case he will again choose the particular kind of drug that appeals to his particular temperament. Every suicide is committed in the effort to escape reality. The fact that the rich, beautiful and apparently happy destroy themselves shows how little we know of the inner facts of any other human being's life.

That "dope" and drug "fiends" are often sensitive, keenly intellectual and idealistic individuals is not accidental. Such organisms, for a combination of reasons, find the harshness of reality too awful to bear.

For these reasons we are short sighted and narrow when we blame or despise the person who resorts to any of these things. He is in trouble. What he needs and deserves is our sympathy and understanding.

Success, as each individual sees it, comes from the materialization of his supreme subconscious wish. The man who makes a million but who has missed the one big thing he wanted does not consider himself successful;

but the one who wanted only to make money says when he does it, "I have succeeded."

Success is, after all, a matter of personal viewpoint. You may not know what any given individual's standard of success or happiness is, but there is one way in which you can tell with absolute certainty whether he is coming up to the standard he has set for himself, and that is by noting HOW MUCH OR HOW LITTLE OF HIS TIME HE GIVES TO THINGS THAT BRING MENTAL OBLIVION.

The man who is achieving his supreme subconscious wish is so happy in the realization of life that he feels little need of any kind of mental oblivion.

Facts gathered over large areas and through long periods of time concerning the life of men and women in all countries in all ages show that sleep is an instinct, just as is eating or sex, and that it is resorted to, as are other instincts, in the degree as other instincts are undeveloped or unexpressed.

Because sleep makes us harmless instead of harmful as some of the other instincts do, society has smiled upon it and encouraged it—unless it is carried to excess—in which case society (feeling itself endangered by it) will criticize it, and apply the much-feared appellation "lazy" to whoever over-indulges in it.

Carried to excess, sleep is as reprehensible as the excessive expression of any other instinct, but deserves more consideration at our hands even in its excess than we have been inclined to give, for no individual anesthetizes his senses save when those senses are suffering.

As man learns more and more how to coordinate his two minds he will be more and more successful and happy.

As more and more men and women emulate in their lives the perfect coordination of powers seen in Edison they will more and more emulate his four hours of sleep.

And, ages hence, when we have learned how to live, the instinct of withdrawal from reality (which came down to us from the ages when reality was almost unbearable) will fade away.

When that time comes there will be no beds, no skyscrapers honey-combed with "bedrooms" in which living men retire for hours from reality—and we will use constructively the THIRD OF OUR LIFETIME which we now spend in sleep.

Will you make a success of your job?

Success and Your Supreme Wish

The answer to this big question must have dawned on you while you have been reading this lesson. At least it has given you such insights into the real reasons for your own successes and failures as you never had before.

It must be clear to you now that the things at which you failed were things which, for some reason, lacked the complete co-operation of your subterranean, subconscious forces. It is these things and not just hard work that make any undertaking a success.

It must be equally clear to you why your own triumphs and those of other people often came from less work than you had devoted to the thing that failed.

You now know why, in the moment of winning, you could scarcely realize that the winner was really you.

You also know why you often felt you really didn't deserve such a lot of credit as people gave you; that the person who did this successful thing was not you but someone working through you—someone bigger stronger than yourself.

But to get back to the big question—will YOU succeed?

YOU WILL SUCCEED PROVIDED YOUR SUPREME SUBCONSCIOUS WISH IS FOR SUCCESS. If your deepest, most absorbing desire is success, nothing under Heaven can keep it from you.

If your supreme wish is for something else than success you will that something else. If it is for mediocre success you will achieve mediocre success. If it is for supreme, sublime success you will get it.

You will get it because it would then be your supreme, subconscious wish.

How that wish is to be attained will be made clear in the next lesson—a lesson containing hitherto unpublished and until very recently unknown laws of the most vital import to every human being.

What, more than anything else in the world, do YOU want out of life?

The answer you make, in your secret soul, to this question determines with utter, inexorable certainty WHAT YOU ARE GOING TO GET. Not the details—they don't count—but ultimately, eventually in YOUR LIFE AS A WHOLE.

In this lesson is published, for the first time, the most recent and by far the most startling psychological discovery concerning the real secret of human happiness that has been made in the history of scientific research.

It will show you to your complete satisfaction what has been holding you back and how to take your foot off the brake if you really desire to do so.

It is going to take the props from under some of your pet alibis, but if you are the honest seeker after truth which your study of mental analysis implies, you will be glad to part with them in return for the great self-revelation and self-realization this lesson gives you.

This lesson will show you, with intense clarity, why you have lost many things you tried to get. It will show you where the fault lay and where it came from. It will show you who was to blame and WHY. It will show you HOW that person was to blame for your not accomplishing the thing you attempted. It will show you exactly what stood in your path and who put it there. It will show you how to take obstructions away from your path in future if you really desire to be free of them. It will also show you why and how others have failed.

This lesson will show you why you succeeded when you did succeed.

It will show you why you seemed to do the biggest things most easily; why you had, through it all, a sense of not really doing it yourself but of being instrument, as it were, of a person bigger and stronger than yourself.

It will show you why you lived through some of your greatest tragedies in spite of the conviction that you never would.

It shows you the real, inner secret of all your own accomplishments and those of other people.

It shows you the great law which has brought every personal success, every personal achievement and every personal triumph that has ever been accomplished in this world.

It shows you why you always find time, strength and opportunity to do certain things and none for certain others; why you "give up" certain ambitions and reconcile yourself to going without all kinds of things you had supposed paramount in your life while clinging tenaciously to others which your common sense tells you are inconsequential.

It shows you why the people of the supposedly greatest gifts fail while others, who started with few, go to the top of Life's Ladder.

It shows you why you have permitted some of your own greatest talents to lie undeveloped while working hard to succeed at something for which you seem to have no ability.

You have sometimes wondered why you simply could NOT go on with a thing which you knew was for your own best good. You have marveled at your capacity for making the SAME KIND of mistake over and over.

You have become disgusted and often discouraged with yourself for the inexplicable reactions certain things and especially certain work cause in you.

You have thought of all these and a thousand other self-mysteries, and either arrived at some theory that appeals to your particular

Success and Your Supreme Wish

type and temperament, or you have given it up, thinking—and perhaps saying—"There is no accounting for us; a human being is a conglomeration of enigmas!"

The average individual is like a child seeing a moving picture for the first time. He sees an amazing, mystifying, myriad-sectioned drama unwind before his eyes. To him it is the realest of reality. All is as it seems on the screen—and all arises from and returns to the unseen, the mysterious.

The average unthinking individual lives in a maze of moving mysteries which he calls his life. The unexpected is always happening to him. The expected and longed-for happens but seldom and when it does he can not see how nor why, so is unable, in any way, to repeat it.

He no more attempts to understand the laws back of his life-dream than the three-year-old child at the movies attempts to figure out how pictures are made. He swallows it, enjoys what he can, registers verbal disapproval when things go wrong—but SITS AND TAKES IT, like the babe in the theater.

He feels helpless, often hopeless. But it is too big a tangle to understand or straighten out; so there he waits watching his life-story play itself out as it will.

This lesson is to prove to you that your life-movie doesn't "just happen"; that you are not at the mercy of Fate; that YOU and YOU ALONE make your own life drama.

It is going to show you that the play in which you are acting the life picture you see unwinding before your eyes each day, is based on laws as sane, simple and scientific as those back of the making of a motion picture. It is going to do for you, in explanation, what we would be doing for the child if we took him out of the theater—whose pictures he had always supposed to be magic-made–and showed him the camera, the studio, the actors and actresses, the stages and directors, scenarios, lighting effects—the mass of NATURAL forces through whose application every picture is made.

We hope this lesson will do for you much more than that. We shall show you how certain everyday, ever operative NATURAL LAWS are behind every individual drama; how everything in your life is made, directly or indirectly, consciously or unconsciously, BY YOU, through your use or misuse of these same natural laws.

We are going to show you how YOUR pictures are made—the machinery back of every movie you have ever put on in your own life; why you played the rôle you did and why you are playing, at this moment, the very part you are.

It is our sincere hope that you who read these pages will, from this day onward, apply these laws in your own life, for by so doing you shall attain your deepest and dearest desires.

We, like the babe at the movies, live in the delusion that things are only what they seem—a maelstrom in which we are caught, a moving mirage that whirls and swirls and carries us on against our will.

Science shows us that everything in the universe has a cause and that the same cause always and invariably brings the same results. Nothing "just happens." There are NO ACCIDENTS. All occurs in accordance with divine, unchanging law.

The world we live in today is exactly the same world the cave man dwelt in. But civilized man, THROUGH A WORKING KNOWLEDGE OF LAW, has brought out of these unseen and hitherto undreamed-of forces the things that make life livable, beautiful, uplifting.

The cave man called the lightning a god of wrath and fell down in fear when his flashes illuminated the sky. Civilized man, through a study and understanding of law, brings that same force to bear on his problems and with it lights the world, heats his home, travels around the globe and talks, without wires, from one end of the earth to the other.

In the last twenty years science has been discovering that human health and disease, human success and failure, human happiness and unhappiness—all the problems of human life—are equally controlled by law; that man is a part OF, not a part FROM natural and divine law; that the laws of the mind, body and spirit of every individual are ever operating and are ever bringing to him, in exact accordance with these laws, the things that come out in his life.

Every man and woman has many conscious wishes. They are in the surface mind, the busy brain that handles the affairs of the moment and the events of the day.

You have a conscious wish to arrive at the office in time to look through your mail before the opening hour. You have another conscious wish to remember a fact, statement, the amount of that check you must write.

You have thousands of these conscious wishes during the course of a busy day. They pass into and out of your mind without much ado.

As a result of your training, education, environment, experience, type, personality and several other things, you have acquired certain CONSCIOUS STANDARDS—of what you OUGHT to do and be and

Success and Your Supreme Wish

accomplish; of what you owe the world, society and your fellow-man; of the right and squareway to treat people; of honesty, justice, fair play; of how much and how well a man ought to work to get on in life; of how you ought to act under all conditions; of what you ought to acquire, achieve, accomplish; of the heights to which you ought to rise; the influence you ought to wield; the prestige you ought to have; the good name, fame or glory you ought to win.

In short, you have builded into that conscious mind of yours whole sets of ironclad ideals which you aspire to live up to.

Whether you have lived up to them in the past has depended on just one thing which you had in those past years; whether you are living up to them now, and in what proportion, all depends on how much of that same thing you have today.

Whether you will in the coming years live up to these standards achieve these things you consciously strive for, will depend upon how much you understand, amend and utilize that same something. That thing which determines it all—which has actuated directly or indirectly every act of your life—is your supreme, subconscious wish.

One of the most recent and revolutionizing discoveries of science is that every human being has, in addition to these temporary conscious wishes and conscious standards, ONE WISH WHICH OVERTOPS ALL OTHERS, A WISH WHICH IS OFTEN SECRET AND SOMETIMES SUBMERGED, BUT WHICH SATURATES HIS SUBCONSCIOUS MIND.

This wish is never for one specific thing nor does it deal with details. It is not for certain THINGS, nor even for specific PEOPLE in our lives, but for a CONDITION IN LIFE—an environment, a kind of expression—the untrammeled satisfaction of a basic instinct! The achieving of a great ambition in some general direction—the attainment of a beautiful character, the acquirement of riches or the winning of an immortal name. And sometimes—in fact all too often—the secret supreme wish is for none of these uplifting things but for others of a far different nature.

The second great discovery which is revolutionizing the science of psychology is that EVERY HUMAN BEING BUILDS HIS LIFE AROUND HIS SUPREME SUBCONSCIOUS WISH.

Some build their lives around the supreme wish consciously; others unconsciously or subconsciously; but each is building every year, every day, every hour, directly or indirectly toward the gratification of his deepest desire.

The average individual has never heard of this urge at whose behest he lays practically every plan of his life. He is often unaware of this intense yearning which dictates the direction of his energies, predetermines the trend of activities characterizing every week of his life; which actuates the manifold expressions of himself and which prejudices, pulls and pushes him in directions serving its purpose.

But this does not alter the fact that it is there and that it wields an influence upon our lives which, in the end, makes or mars them.

We often wonder why a promising man with brains, education, advantages, good looks and every possible chance makes such a mess of his life.

Especially do we wonder why this intelligent individual should make the SAME KIND of mistakes over and over, permitting this one species of weakness to ruin his existence.

"He is so unusual in so many ways," we say. "Why can't he see that it is only this one thing that is wrecking his chances? Isn't it too bad that a fine young man like that, with such splendid qualities should permit one little thing to destroy him!"

In every such case—and there are many of them—the individual's supreme subconscious wish is for something which the giving in to this weakness brings him.

A woman who was well known as a writer of superior magazine articles was an outspoken radical.

She lived in a suffrage state so had a vote and cast it consistently for a radical ticket. She believed in birth control and declared that if she ever married she would not feel entitled to bring children into the world—not only because it was, as she was fully convinced, too cruel to give them a chance, but because her mother had died in an insane asylum and her father in a tuberculosis hospital.

She lived in Arizona herself as a result of a prolonged siege of the disease which had taken away one lung, but which seemed now to be under control.

This woman had a most unusual mind. Her conversation was as interesting as a play, her writing was scintillating and extraordinarily clever. She was widely read, a deep student and a most convincing speaker on these very subjects upon which she held such radical views.

She finally married. Her husband did not care for children. But once every year for twelve years now she has presented him with a son or daughter, and once with both!

All her friends say, "What in the world has come over Agnes? What became of her convictions?"

The answer is not far to seek. Agnes, under all her conscious attitudes, had a deep, devouring, desperate desire.

Far back of and behind and beyond these surface things there was a supreme subconscious wish. That wish was to be the mother of a large family.

Reason, common sense, horse sense and her sense of justice told her that she—in whose veins ran two taints—had little right to jeopardize innocent lives.

Intelligence and human sympathy told her that life—never easy for the strongest—would be cruelly savage to the handicapped. Study and thought convinced her conscious mind that one hampered as she was might better be educating the world toward social and political betterment than adding to its population.

But the moment opportunity offered away went every conscious conviction, every standard of the years—and in came the subconscious urge! It took possession. Or rather, it KEPT possession. For it was the working out of that old subconscious longing which caused her to marry at all.

And this brings us to the third great new discovery:

This newest, hitherto unpublished and most far-reaching of all the discoveries concerning the laws of human life is that EVERY HUMAN BEING GETS HIS SUPREME SUBCONSCIOUS WISH.

At first glance he may question this; but five minutes of honest self inventory serves to convince every person that it is literally, UTTERLY TRUE.

You, for instance, may say, "That can't be true. Why, I wanted a college education more than I wanted anything else in the world. I have wanted it for years and I have failed to get it!"

You are sincere in saying this—just as you have been sincere all the time in telling the same thing to yourself and your friends.

But if you will look deep into your own heart you will find that at least one other desire—perhaps a dozen of them—takes precedence, in your secret list, of this desire for a college education.

You may never have stopped to think of it before (and the probabilities are you have said it so often you fully believe it) but when you come right down to it, there are several things you want more than you want that college education. Yes, I know, something was always happening to prevent you from going to college. There always IS something happening to prevent things, and it prevents them too—all but your REAL WISH!

When things happen to that, you go right over them. You find a way out. You do SOMETHING to counteract it. You invariably ride over the difficulty—and DO IT!

During the past ten years at least a hundred men and women have told us "the only thing on earth they had wanted most was to go to college but it had been impossible."

What were the psychological facts?

One young man who vehemently denied at first that he had ever desired anything as much as a college education, finally said that he believed he wanted to get married more than he wanted an education. This was the reason for his marrying instead of going to college.

Another who was certain that nothing had ever superseded his desire to go to college realized that what he had really wanted most was to travel. He hoped to go abroad and had decided a college education would help to give him a keener appreciation of the things he expected to see in his travels.

When he was given a position which took him several times a year to London and Paris, he subconsciously gave up the college idea, though continuing consciously to think and to declare that it was a great disappointment.

These are not deliberate deceptions we practice upon ourselves and our friends. We know very little about our real selves until we study the human sciences. The result is that only an occasional individual ever meets the stranger that lives in his skin!

A man once said to us, "I can not believe that every person GETS his supreme, subconscious wish. I have loved a woman for eight years. My subconscious wish was to have her. I haven't gotten her, and what is more, it doesn't look as though I ever would. Yet I have tried with all my might to win her."

We explained to him this other great law:

OUR SUPREME SUBCONSCIOUS WISH IS NEVER FOR ANY SPECIFIC THING OR PERSON BUT FOR A CONDITION, A CERTAIN AVENUE OF SELF-EXPRESSION.

The supreme wish saturates the subconscious mind but the subconscious mind never knows nor cares anything about details nor the fine points concerned with methods. All it knows is overwhelming DESIRE for a certain kind of SATISFACTION FOR YOUR PERSONALITY AS A WHOLE.

The conscious mind supplies methods, means, the vehicles for realizing these subconscious desires.

These two great minds of ours may be likened to the equipment of a freight train. The subconscious mind supplies the steam, the GOING POWER, the FORCES necessary to your arriving at a certain destination.

It is unlike steam in this, however: it knows the GENERAL DIRECTION in which you want to go and is concentrated on your getting there. But it allows the engineer (your conscious mind) to select the crew, the paraphernalia for the journey and to take whichever one of the tracks it prefers.

BUT IT GIVES YOU NO PEACE SAVE WHEN YOU ARE TRAVELING IN THE GENERAL DIRECTION OF ITS (AND YOUR) SUBCONSCIOUS AIM!

It stays out of sight, but goads, drives and lashes you whenever you start down a side-track—and gives you its full help only when you get back on the main line.

What this man really wanted was not this, nor any ONE SPECIFIC woman, but some general kind of SELF-EXPRESSION for his personality which he considered the possession of her would make possible for him. In other words, she was what every individual is to the subconscious mind of his lover—the MEANS TO AN END.

No adult man or woman lives who subconsciously loves another man or woman. The subconscious knows no individuals AS SUCH. It is not concerned with the personnel of anything—only with RESULTS.

YOUR subconscious knows no one but YOU. It has no desire, no religion, no aim, no interest save the accomplishment of YOUR WANTS. YOU are its world, its master, its adored. The result of the universe is, to your subconscious mind, only a place in which YOU function, a stage on which YOU act, the world in which YOU live and move and have your being.

"Where do I come in?" is the first question your mind puts to everything you ever hear, everything that is broached to you, everything that comes within the range of your consciousness.

If you can not see wherein YOU are going to get self-expression of some sort you stay away from it. Even our most generous acts are performed more for our own self-expression than for the persons for whom we do them.

The man who gives his money to the poor and dies penniless has not really sacrificed himself. His supreme subconscious desire was for THAT KIND of self-expression. He was happiest that way and did it because he could find more happiness in that than in keeping it for himself.

In other words, he BOUGHT with his money, the thing that appealed most to him, and though in so doing he proved himself a higher, finer nature than the average, and deserves our admiration and respect as a superman, he is NOT to be credited with self-sacrifice.

What we call self-sacrifice is always the sacrifice of something the individual wants for SOMETHING HE WANTS MORE—therefore is not self-sacrifice at all.

The big thing we must not overlook in this new understanding is that THE INDIVIDUAL WHO PREFERS TO USE HIS MONEY this way, who gets his GREATEST HAPPINESS OUT OF HELPING OTHERS IS A HIGHLY EVOLVED INDIVIDUAL, FAR AHEAD OF HIS TIME—SPIRITUAL IN THE HIGHEST, FINEST SENSE, SYMPATHETIC, SUPERHUMAN.

You need not regret that you can no longer credit him with self-sacrifice. This kind of human being is far more admirable than one who would reverse God's first law of self-preservation. We know it IS God's law because He puts it into every living organism.

Your first DUTY is to YOURSELF—to make yourself the highest, best, biggest and broadest being you can be; and the proof of this lies in every living thing in the universe.

You can never help humanity very much till you can walk alone. Your first duty therefore, to the world and to yourself, is to LEARN TO STAND ALONE! Don't lop and lean and loll on other people.

First, develop your own backbone. Then, as you go along, help everybody, inspire everybody, uplift everybody—and don't forget to START!

Don't make the mistake that thousands of well-meaning people have—of waiting till your own life is perfect before beginning to give others a lift.

"You will pass this way but once," so scatter real help as you travel, but keep your life-belt on! Keep your head up, your eyes open, your heart gentle—but KEEP CLIMBING.

If you would like to see what a great thinker says about these real human motives read the book Mark Twain wrote and which he directed should not be published till five years after his death, "What Is Man?"

In it he shows you, in better words than we can, how every act of every human being is for "the contentment of his own spirit."

LESSON XIII
Healing Ourselves and Helping Others

John D. Barry says, "At this moment I am thinking of a man who is going through a severe ordeal in the way of nervous illness. Escape lies in himself. But he isn't making the effort. He could tell anyone else what to do. But he isn't doing it. This weakness is one of his symptoms. It's the worst part of his illness. It's practically the whole thing.

"As all doctors know there are kinds of illnesses that, it would seem, could be cured if the victim would only reach out and take the cure."

This man is suffering intensely from what seems like neurasthenia. For hours at a time he will lie in bed or on a couch, wide awake but seemingly helpless. And yet he's one of the strongest looking men I've ever known.

"One of his friends says, 'His case is really mental. Though the problem seems to be in his body, isn't it really in his mind?'"

Vehicles travel on the right side of the road in obedience to a law of the land and a natural law as well.

To obey law is to avoid accident or punishment. To disregard law is to invite, court and cause suffering. It is not possible to travel on both sides of the road without accident, so laws were enacted requiring pedestrians and vehicles to keep to the right. The right side of the road belongs to YOU. It is yours by law. You have your own place on it just as everyone else has. The right side of the road of health also belongs to you, according to natural law. It is yours by divine right. Health is an inheritance in which you have a vested interest. Don't lose your place in the forward march toward harmonious well being. The highway of Health is beautiful and easy to travel if you follow the rules of the road.

Don't hurry and don't worry. If you do you may run into a health accident. A few ways to keep on the right side of the road will be given in this lesson.

William F. Warren, former president of Boston University, said, "No command or entreaty occurs so many times in the Bible as the emphatic one, 'Fear not!'" There are millions of people in this and other parts of the world whose minds are forever filled with the fear of something. Where there is fear there cannot be perfect health. Fear throws its black pall over mankind from the cradle to the grave, thus hastening the individual's march to the latter by every feeling it engenders. It mars and stunts multitudes of lives, makes people ill, wretched, insane, poverty stricken and inferior.

The National Public Health Service recently sent out from Washington a bulletin explaining the evil effects of wrong moods on health, and especially in breeding nervous diseases, mental disorders and old age. Though only a few years ago the doctors derided the psychologists for teaching that the mind had a powerful influence in creating health or disease in the individual. The complete conversion of these material scientists was shown in the theme of this bulletin which was, "Don't worry. Worry is health's worst enemy."

The law of thought can be used to create malformation just as a weapon that has been given to you for your defense can be turned by you against yourself. This is what has happened in most diseases. The sufferer has turned an impersonal psychological law against himself and CREATED disease, without realizing it.

The first steps in getting rid of pain are the exact reversal of the first steps one takes to GET pain. Millions have manufactured pain for themselves by THINKING ABOUT PAIN, LOOKING FOR PAIN, CONCENTRATING ON ADVERSE SYMPTOMS and PREPARING FOR DISEASE.

These are the four steps which set the gage. By means of these four stages you can bring ANYTHING ON EARTH to yourself, good or bad. By thinking of the bad, looking for the bad, concentrating on the bad and preparing for the bad it will arrive, and by reversing the process you can bring the good. It depends on the DIRECTION in which you are thinking, looking, working, preparing whether what comes to you shall be from the good or the bad side of life.

If you permit yourself to dwell on the notion that you are weighted down with a tendency toward this or that disease, that you "inherited" a weakness you are going to set the gage in the very direction you do not desire, for our thoughts produce actions and actions produce RESULTS.

I presume most of us have had to face some such possibility or even probability during our lives. It is certain, since our ancestors are all dead, that we could easily convince ourselves that there was in us a strain of whatever caused their deaths if we were so disposed. But we know that Mother Nature, who sends perfectly formed children to the deformed parent, will stand between us here as everywhere, and that our health or disease depends largely on our own ways of living, and especially our ways of THINKING.

Without the slightest hereditary taint in their direction one can bring upon himself certain diseases BY THIS THINKING, or he can, by the same process, ward off the fruition of a tendency that is really there.

Some try to bluff or bully themselves into health. They are braver or more deserving of success than those who will not try, but they use a wrong method. Being faced with the idea that they have hereditary tendencies toward some malady they say to themselves, "I am going to look at this matter bravely now. I am going to be just as careful as I can. I will give myself the best of care. I will not expose myself and I will be temperate and hope for the best."

Without admitting it to himself such a one is harboring a SECRET dread, a suspense, a ghost that casts its shadow over almost every thought and action thereafter.

To remove all this and revel in the genuine freedom whose counterfeit he has been simulating one need only to recognize the fact that THE UNIVERSAL SOURCE OF ENERGY, whatever, wherever or whoever it be, CREATED US and is forever CURING us of every malignant or destructive thing just so far as we permit it to do so.

This source of life is the eternal enemy of its rival Death, and fights far harder for you and me than we can ever do. No physician and no medicine cures. Nature, in the working out of law, heals. It is only when we obstruct its work by setting in operation against it our own thoughts and actions that it ever halts, and then it does so not a second longer than we compel it to. Whenever we encourage a happy thought or even relax the fear thought, healing sets in. You can FEEL its effects after every pleasant emotion.

There is no incurable disease. There are PEOPLE who perhaps cannot be cured, because they WILL NOT be. There are men and women so egotistic as to find it difficult believe even in the power they created their own marvelous selves. "Except as ye become as little children" there is no certainty that you can be free of disease. From the moment you become as a little child in your reliance upon the infinite you will note improvement.

The oft remarked characteristic of most of the patients who were cured at Coué's famous French clinic was childlikeness. "According to your faith shall it be done unto you" is not a mere phrase. It has stepped out of the Bible and walks, a living law, up and down the land. With your religious or non-religious beliefs this law has nothing to do, nor is it affected in the slightest by them. It is a scientific FACT and applies to every human being. The tragedy is that so few human beings can believe it.

You may not be able to believe that the food you have eaten will digest, because you cannot SEE HOW it could. But if you DO YOUR PART the laws of assimilation will do the rest. The same power that set these laws in motion, to build up and keep your body strong, is operating every instant to eliminate everything that interferes with health. What we must learn is not how to rend the veil and SEE HOW we can be cured, but to LET GO, to substitute for the thwarting, benumbing fear-thought the REALIZATION that the same divine force that made us will begin to heal us the instant we let it have full sway.

"Every church, like every medical organization, will soon be teaching people how to heal themselves by releasing this brake in the mind," said Rev. John Murray, pastor of the Divine Science Church, in a large meeting recently at the Waldorf Astoria.

"The age of miracles did not end with Jesus. He revealed a power possessed by every person. He healed by means of this universal power.

"Christ, Coué, Christian Scientists, New Thoughtists and psychologists, though they call it by different names, are all talking about the same law, and any and all cures performed are performed BY that law—the law that THOUGHTS OF HEALTH BUILD HEALTH and THOUGHTS OF DISEASE BUILD DISEASE."

ANY individual, ANYWHERE, at ANY TIME under ANY conditions can operate this law and get its corresponding results. Change your thoughts ABOUT YOURSELF and you will change yourself. You will change your feelings, your environment, your success, your health, your future, your destiny.

Thousands of people are making themselves ill at this very moment by means of thought, yet if you should ask them if they believe in the power of thought over health they would disgustedly say, "I certainly do NOT!" These very people have, at some time or another experienced mind-cure. Everybody has, though few have realized at the time what it was. The ailment from which they were suffering may have been a headache, indigestion or cold. The unexpected arrival of a friend, the receipt of good news, a good book or some other incident cured them.

Or the trouble may have been more deep seated or of longer duration—nervous disorder with all the accompanying physical disturbances, a big disappointment, mental shock, fear, unhappiness, sorrow or chronic worry—with the cure effected by the descent upon him of some such thing as a great responsibility, the stimulation of a new love, a new job, a raise in salary, getting religion or going on a trip around the world.

Everyone who refuses to harbor resentment, jealousy, anger or fear is giving himself mental treatment of the most effective sort whether he realizes it or not. The results are always more far-reaching and immediate when he DOES realize it, however. Everyone who looks on the bright side of things, everyone who says to himself when things look dark, "I shall not let this spoil my outlook" is successfully applying a law that keeps him in physical as well as mental health.

The cultivation of sunny, happy, confident mental attitudes has delivered thousands of men and women not only from mental depression but from various physical ailments.

"How much is there in this mental stuff anyhow?" a man asked a famous New York physician.

"Enough," said the physician, "that you can tone up your physical condition tremendously and cure yourself of all manner of minor ailments, by mental means. By this I mean THINKING GOOD THOUGHTS AND REALIZING THAT HEALTH, NOT DISEASE, IS THE NATURAL AND DIVINE PLAN TOWARD WHICH ALL THE FORCES OF THE UNIVERSE ARE AT ALL TIMES MOVING.

"Enough so that you can learn to master the emotions that cause many of your illnesses. Enough so that anyone can entirely eliminate depression, irritability, discouragement, sensitiveness—the cause of so many of man's maladies. Enough so that you can entirely remodel your disposition. Enough so that you can make yourself into a happy man, a much more successful man. Enough that you can be able to meet life with a poise and power you never dreamed of exercising."

The human mind is well-nigh supreme over the human body. That is why ill-thinking makes us ill and well-thinking makes us well. The healing powers of the mind appear to be limitless. It is apparently a dynamic power-plant of physical energies. Whenever the masterful command is sent deep into the energy-chambers of the subconscious mind the miracle of restored health is performed. This can happen as soon as the command ACTUALLY REACHES the depths of the subconscious, whether that takes years or months.

The greatest factor of power in the subconscious mind is THIS REALIZATION ON YOUR PART. Such realization of the law removes all obstacles for it compels the arrogant conscious mind to step aside and give the stage to the great subconscious. Springs of vitality are everywhere within us but we do not reach down and drink from them. Instead, we live on the surface of ourselves, operating only the conscious, surface powers. We depend too much upon outside influences. We look for help from without, like the man who set a pail under the eaves to catch the rain water when all the while there was a deep well of cold water in his own back yard!

Remember HEALTH IS THE LAW OF LIFE. It is the PURPOSE of life, of the all-powerful force that has created every living thing, including YOU and me.

Place yourself in harmony with it and it will do the rest. Disharmony in mind and heart—fear of yourself or hatred of others—closes the gates and shuts you away from your rightful inheritance.

No person can be well who dislikes others for hatred is a poison and will eventually kill the hater years in advance of his allotted time.

The most pronounced skeptic will agree that the conscious and subconscious minds control a great proportion of the body's activities. Every physician and physiologist knows it to be true. Every medical school teaches the young doctor what we have seen manifested by every physician for fifty years—never to express a destructive thought in a sick room. If we would cease our destructive thoughts we would have little use for him at all.

A mind full of discontent, selfishness, impatience, anger, jealousy, envy or revenge is a hotbed of disease. Give yourself the purifying experience of relaxing for a few moments each day while you give yourself and all that hurts you into communion with WHATEVER IT IS THAT MADE YOU.

You will find yourself amazingly restored, refreshed and renewed. One thing we know: THE POWER THAT CREATED US IS STILL WITH US. It renews every organ in the body at least every eighteen months. It did not make us as a toymaker builds a doll, and set us down here to live or die. It gave life to us and it continues to supply us with life every moment as long as we live. This power, wherever and whatever it is, cures everything from the little cut on your finger to our broken hearts and diseased bodies. The NAME it has doesn't matter. I would not trouble too much about WHAT it is, WHERE it is, WHY it does the things it does, or anything else. I would just realize that the force BIG ENOUGH and POWERFUL ENOUGH to create this marvelous universe and kind enough to put me into it and look after me in so many wonderful ways was, WHETHER I COULD SEE IT OR NOT, MY FRIEND AND PROTECTOR. And I would just stop trying to run the universe and let that power do it—even to my poor little part of it—once in a while.

After a sickly childhood, a frail girlhood and semi-invalid adulthood, I so completely cured myself of illness that for many years now I have lectured almost every night the year around without missing a single engagement, without having a cold, a touch of weariness, a headache or ANY AILMENT WHATEVER.

I did it by following two sets of laws: those of physical health and those of mental health. I do not eat or drink harmful things. I do not abuse or neglect any organ or system in my physical mechanism. I treat each one with respect—respect for IT, for MYSELF and for the POWER that created it.

I keep in mental health by saying, thinking and KNOWING the following concerning myself: "My body shall obey my mind. Though ten thousand fall at my side, no disease shall come near me. I am immune to each and every germ in the air, the water and food I come in contact with. The power that created me wants me to be well and strong and I shall do my mental and physical part to help that power, not merely ask it to help ME. I go forth in strength, I walk in health, happiness, joy and peace. I will not only BE health, I will TALK health, LIVE health, RADIATE health and HELP OTHERS to health. I will be the living embodiment of physical and mental vitality."

The idea of any bodily action tends to PRODUCE THE ACTION. Emotion always causes numerous and intense bodily effects, inwardly, whether we recognize it or not, just as furious anger causes the outward physical reactions of grinding teeth, frowning brows, clenched fists, contracted jaws, growling cries, panting breath, purpleness or paleness of the face, without our being conscious of any of them.

Fright often produces wild beating of the heart, a gasping motion of the lips, deathlike pallor, protruding eyeballs and the bodily rigidity known as "rooted to the spot."

Grief produces various physical reactions with which we are all familiar.

If mental states can thus affect those parts of the body which we see we may be sure it affects many other parts which we do not see and that all of those destructive reactions separately and collectively affect the health. They create and throw into the blood stream toxins which go to every part of the physical organism. Likewise, all constructive emotions—happiness, joy, contentment, love, generosity, etc.—create and inject into the blood certain sustaining elements. It is the effect of these that causes us, a few moments afterward, to feel so strong and stimulated.

There is such a thing as "exposing yourself to health" as well as to disease. Therefore, mingle with, associate with, live with, go to hear and see and come in contact with people who are well and who know HOW they got and kept health—those who understand and practice the laws mentioned here. Do not, save as a helper or healer, cast your lines with the sick, the ailing, the chronically ill people who "enjoy" their poor health.

If they desire your help or will avail themselves of it, go to them by all means. Stating to them the laws of health will keep yourself reminded. But if they refuse your help or, for any other reason, cling to their illness do not persist in spending time in their company.

It will become evident to anyone who thinks about it that the threefold aspects of life in the individual are mental, physical and spiritual.

Physical health is largely dependent on mental health. Anyone who will enter enthusiastically into the expression of healthy mental attitudes can improve his actual physical condition in an hour's time. He who will adhere to these thoughts habitually and express them aggressively can cure himself of a hundred minor ailments, ward off more serious ones and lengthen his life immeasurably.

Fear, discord, anxiety, inharmony breed disease as surely and truly as microbes do, for they lower the threshold of our resistance, our one protection against the millions of germs, bacilli and other enemies that surround us.

We must not deny, overlook or neglect the physical body. IT too is an expression of the life-principle and its laws are as sacred as those of the mind. The body should receive proper care, attention and rest, but if we are to get and keep health we must also observe the laws that govern the conscious and subconscious elements within ourselves. The cleanliness of the outside of the cup will avail little if the inside remains unclean. Food, however wholesome, will poison the body if eaten to the accompaniment of furious anger, intense worry, jealousy or revengefulness. On the other hand, men and women, deficient in one or several vital organs have lived healthily to a great age by cultivating calmness, temperance, serenity, love and a sense of humor.

Health is our inheritance. It is the normal, natural condition of all living things. We lose it only by withdrawing from it, by violating the laws of mind, body and spirit.

That the condition, not only of the mind and body but of the SPIRIT, exercises a tremendous influence over our physical well-being and will eventually make for health or disease, can be seen in two kinds of illustrations, one remote and one immediate.

Do something you know to be very wrong and note how this act affects your appetite, your bodily vigor, your ability to sleep, to breathe, to do your work well, to concentrate your mind, to walk erect, to laugh, to look people in the eye. The voice of conscience speaks to both body and mind. Contrariwise, note the mental and physical uplift that follows a good deed,

Healing Ourselves and Helping Others

especially one performed at a sacrifice to self without hope of reward, and more especially one which the recipient is unaware of the source of our gift.

In such instances as this where no one but God and ourselves—or ourselves and the Ruler of the Universe, if you prefer—knows of our good deed, where all selfishness is eliminated, where spirit alone shares our secret, there will be felt an unbelievable PHYSICAL as well as mental improvement.

I saw this law illustrated many years ago when a young woman who had been ill for years and had exhausted every means known to materia medica, regained her health as a result quite certainly, of a generous, self-sacrificing act.

For several years she had been very deeply in love with a young man who, while he liked her, did not share her ardor. He was a clerk on a salary. She still had a few hundred dollars of the inheritance left her by her mother. On the day when he was to start East he came to tell her the crushing news that he had lost the savings he had painfully gathered—every cent of the money that was to have taken him to New York to look for an opening in his work. He had withdrawn it from the bank in greenbacks and it had been stolen from his room the night before.

He returned to his old position to start over again, heartbroken from the fact that it would require at least two years to rehabilitate his bank account.

His disappointment so absorbed her that she forgot herself and her illness for over a week, at the end of which time she evolved a plan. It looked as though it might cost her her chance for recovery or even her life, but she decided to carry it through.

A few days later the young man called to announce, in wildest joy, news as good and unbelievable as the other had been bad and unbearable—that the thief had repented and returned the money! His excitement proved her ally for it kept him from noting any lack of spontaneity in her when he read to her the supposed thief's note wherein he declared "his conscience forced him to give it back."

The young man left the next day for New York. In his happiness she found full compensation for her loneliness and for the realization that now, since she was penniless, she must, sick or well, earn a living.

Within six months her baffling illness had completely disappeared. She had gained in weight, youthfulness and beauty to such a degree that when the young man returned, after a lonely winter in New York, he fell in love with her and they were married. They have been very happy. But to this day she has never told him where the "returned" money really came from.

Examples of the more remote effects which wrongdoing and wrong thinking have upon the physical health are to be seen in the chronic illnesses of the selfish, moody, stingy, unkind person. Heads of many of the penal institutions of this country have told me that convicts are seldom well and that those whose criminal doings or thoughts extended over a long period before they were incarcerated, are afflicted, almost without exception, with deep-seated diseases of long standing.

The admonition, given by that most successful living minister, Aimee Semple McPherson, and every great healing evangelist, that you must obey your conscience and live purely if you wish to be sure of a cure, is founded on an eternal, natural law.

That people who live in good health to a great age have, invariably, been of clean moral character, serene spirit, and possessed of gentle tolerance is a fact too well known to need repetition. It is equally well known that the selfish, the hoarder, the grasping, the cruel, the unprincipled, the vicious and the ill-tempered die earlier than others. The rich man who refuses to be open-handed will find Death loosening the grip of his fingers many years earlier than necessary.

To heal one's self or others, one should familiarize himself with the LIMITATIONS (or what up to now appears to be the limitations) as well as the POSSIBILITIES of healing the body by mental and spiritual means.

It is conceivable that there are in reality NO LIMITATIONS WHATEVER. I am convinced that limitation exists only in the individual, NOT IN THE LAW, and that as individuals rise above their own personal, limiting consciousness, disease will for the most part be prevented, cured at all stages when it does arise, and that as the race develops disease will completely disappear from the earth.

Today man possesses a very definite, tangible physical body which reacts to his mind. He possesses a mind that acts upon his body, and he possesses a spirit that acts upon and REACTS TO BOTH. All three are and must be recognized as interdependent at this stage in human evolution. The road to health is a triple-track with the spirit acting as the living "third rail."

That the body, as well as the mind and spirit, is divine is proved in the fact that it renews itself from year to year. It should not be despised but respected and treated as the thing it really is—a vessel for holding the living flame, for guarding and keeping it operative on this earth just as long as possible.

Because the body IS sacred the discovery of every law which preserves it and prolongs its life is a step nearer to divinity. Material science should be recognized as one of the many steps by which, from various directions and in varying degrees, man is reaching toward perfection and rising upward toward the power that made him.

By obeying the laws of physical health, by turning destructive thoughts away from the door of his mind and by recognizing his oneness with the Life-Power that created him, whatever that may be, anyone can vastly improve his physical condition. When he can do the latter WITH FAITH he can cure himself of disease.

"Ah," you say, "There's the rub! How CAN I have faith when I've had no evidence?" I do not mean PERFECT faith. What I do mean need not trouble you. Said the centurion, "Lord, I believe; help thou my unbelief." That is the spirit. Believe as much as you can, meanwhile SEEKING for more belief. It will come. It will come quickly because you will get results immediately. Then your faith will be sensible and sane and SOLID because founded on EXPERIENCE, FACTS which you've demonstrated. And it will grow greater all the while because you will use it. It will plant and replant, seed and reseed itself. Only be receptive and refrain from active opposition in your own mind and RESULTS WILL COME, bringing a living, vibrant, fruitful, unshakable faith with them, to stay forever.

Coué, the great little Frenchman, taught the most effective modern method for treating disease when he told his patients to rub the affected place lightly with the hand while repeating over and over in an assured, matter-of-fact, monotonous tone, "It is going, it is going, it-is-going, it is going, it is going." The object of the rapidity of the repetitions is to exclude other contrary ideas, to prevent their slipping in between phrases, as it were. In a few moments the pain either disappears or greatly decreases.

If this phrase does not appeal to you personally make up one that expresses just what you WOULD LIKE TO HAVE HAPPEN, and say it in the same way. The results will amaze you.

Many of those for whom I have prepared formulas or who have prepared their own in accordance with the directions given just above, have told me they got results within five minutes. Some had to use their formulas a day or even two days, before it seemed effective, but not one has failed to attain results.

You can cure yourself of disease WITHOUT A SHRED OF REAL BELIEF, if you will put this formula into practice. Unbelief resides in the conscious mind and if it steps aside only sufficiently to let the law GET AT the subconscious remarkable results can ensue.

Going only so far as to TRY the formula constitutes a sufficient abdication of the conscious, doubting mind to let the law become operative. We do not know how or why this is so and we do not need to. We only know it DOES IT.

This much we do know: that the subconscious mind controls the automatic functions of the body. It is the central power station from which come impulses that determine bodily health and strength, disease or weakness. The subconscious mind, so long as we refuse even to TRY to apply it, is held in subjection to the conscious mind which is skeptical because it has never dealt with any but material things.

But once let this bigoted conscious mind step aside long enough to let us implant in the vast subconscious the conviction of health and it is CERTAIN that our health will improve. From the complexities of the science of psycho-analysis we give you these fundamental truths. If you will simply try them THEY will perform miracles for you. YOU need not do it. In fact, you cannot. THE LAW working in and through you, does it all.

The earth's millions go through life little dreaming that they have, stored up in the subconscious, more power than is necessary for them to get all the things which they crave.

These lessons will give to you the key to this strange inner storehouse of treasures. Thousands have profited by these simple truths. You can do the same.

When mankind learns how to put the subconscious to work there will be no more failure, poverty, unhappiness or pain.

"Miracle men" will no longer be necessary when we learn to perform our own miracles. The miracle man can help us only when he is near us, but when we learn how to use our own instrument of healing we cure ourselves wherever we are, whenever we need to.

One of the most vivid illustrations of the power of the mind once a healing formula is implanted in the subconscious, can be seen in these four different types of men, each of whom is SUFFERING FROM THE IDENTICAL MALADY, but cured by four different methods. The man who BELIEVES IN DOCTORS is cured by HIS DOCTOR; the man who BELIEVES IN A CERTAIN MEDICINE is cured BY THE MEDICINE; the man who BELIEVES IN CHRISTIANITY is cured BY AN EVANGELIST; and the fourth man, BELIEVING IN CHRISTIAN SCIENCE is cured by reading "Science and Health."

Each of them, without knowing it, was supplying the VERY SAME SCIENTIFIC PRINCIPLE—THE LAW OF THE SUBCONSCIOUS

Healing Ourselves and Helping Others

MIND. He applied it in the way and FOR THE REASONS which most appealed to his subconscious and was cured when he communicated with his own God-given powers in the language that his brain would let pass. The self-same power cured each one as soon as the suggestion got past the arrogant old censor, Mr. Conscious Mind.

We can kill or cure with thought. Thought kills some slowly and others instantly. It cures some instantly and others slowly though none the less surely. Habitual thought stretched out over the years, or intense, burning thought concentrated in an instant—the results are the same.

In thinking for health it is better not to think always directly about a cure, but rather to go about it indirectly by thinking constructive thoughts of high aspiration and achievement. Concentrating his mind on success, especially when unforeseen developments in his business or profession kept his mind focused for days or weeks at a time on practical problems, has cured many a sick man.

A heartful of goodwill, of kindly tolerance, of forgiveness to those who have wronged us and of generosity to those who misunderstand us will help us to get and keep health, while their opposites will eventually bring upon us various physical discomforts.

Abnormal methods of thinking and living are health destroyers. From all such you can easily free yourself if you will.

Live normally, think constructively, "love thy neighbor as thyself" and hate no man, "even those who despitefully use you"; forget every unhappy experience of your past and recall every happy one; get busy and keep busy in the present and trouble not too much about the future; look at tomorrow hopefully, confidently, knowing that today is a glorious adventure and eternity the greatest of all.

Helping Others

Every really successful physician has recognized the effect of his own moods, words and actions upon his patient.

A good doctor first equips himself with the knowledge of the facts of man's physical body, then recognizes the suggestibility of mankind. He recognizes that his first address must be TO THE PATIENT, not to the disease. Separate diseases are cured by obeying laws, but the PATIENT must be helped by an individual doctor. Such is the power of personality and the law of suggestion.

No pains should be spared to gain a sympathetic understanding of the one we hope to help or heal. We must realize that there is no ailment from which a man suffers in which some of his malady does not depend somewhat upon his STATE OF MIND.

This applies not only to the vast field of psycho-neurosis but to infections, organic diseases, heart troubles and all other disorders.

Thus all good healers, like all good doctors, will take into account not only the interplay between the body and mind of the patient but the interplay between the physician's actions and those of the person he is trying to help.

Many persons of great power, who could help and heal others with unbelievable effectiveness never try to do so because they imagine that capacities for healing are confined to a few individuals of peculiar endowments or qualifications. On the contrary, EVERY PERSON HAS SOME CAPACITY TO HEAL OTHERS and this capacity will manifest itself whenever the laws governing it are complied with and the right methods followed.

As soon as he learns how, every person can heal himself and help others to overcome various indispositions, disorders, ailments and disease. Once we know this, each of us is under obligation to develop these powers for the sake of those with whom we live or come in contact, and to exercise them for the good of anyone and everyone when the request, opportunity or demand arises. "No one liveth unto himself alone."

In varying degrees different talents inhere in different individuals, and this one is possessed to a greater extent by some than others. Each is responsible for it to the degree he possesses it—a degree which will surprise him if he ever puts it to the test.

Certain men and women have forceful dynamic personalities, and to this kind some illnesses and some individuals respond most quickly. Other persons react more readily to quiet, simple, modest, soothing personalities, and still others to people whose natures lie somewhere between these extremes.

Other things being equal, the very aggressive individual can be helped more quickly and completely by his opposite, and vice versa—a fact which accounts for marriages and friendships between individuals of widely differing personalities. Opposites do not so much "attract" as complement each other. Competition is eliminated. Their traits supplement each other. Their strengths and weaknesses "dovetail."

To be most successful in healing and helping others, whether toward health, happiness or other achievement, you should bear the above facts in mind and be guided by them. In the treatment of different types of people, first of all, BE SINCERE. That is, be yourself—genuinely, straightforwardly unpretending, but "temper the storm of your nature to the shorn lamb" so to speak. If you are by nature loud voiced, positive, masterful, all these will be welcomed and will inspire strength in the very timid who by your example will feel greater confidence in themselves. But when dealing with one who is a replica of yourself in these traits, whether in the capacity of healer, friend, teacher or acquaintance, you should "tone down" considerably if either of you is to secure the utmost from the association.

I wish to call the special attention of parents to the differentiation just mentioned. Children whose natures are distinctly unlike should not be treated (at any point in any problem, in sickness or health) in exactly the same way. Many other kinds of differentness will be apparent in children and adults but the ones referred to are the most significant in all our treatment of others.

You or any other person of average intelligence can be instrumental in helping and healing others. The only persons who cannot heal others are the feeble minded, and these, as we all know, are astoundingly successful in the treatment of animals, especially the pets they love.

Accept the fact that YOU POSSESS this power. If you cannot realize it now—and I can well believe that to many of you it is a surprise—simply try it some time. You will never doubt it again. Study the rules presented in this lesson, read and reread them until you know them so well that you feel friendly toward them. Apply them whenever, wherever and for whomsoever you chose. Confidence will come with your first attempt. It will increase every time you apply your power. As confidence increases you will find expertness in the use of your power increasing, and as both confidence and expertness increase the power to help those in your own household or who appeal to you from outside it, will express itself more and more. I do not say the power itself will increase. IT is already there, in far greater measure than you can realize. What you need is to learn how to use it, apply it, harness it and put it to work for you.

The principles cited in this lesson have been applied to the needs of people within the intimate circles of my family, friends and private students and to thousands of members of my classes. Having a horror of unscientific methods, especially of undependable healing methods, and having set the standard that I would confine myself, in all my lessons, to RULES THAT NEVER FAIL, rules which would work anywhere, for anybody under any conditions when faithfully followed, I preferred to keep silent on the matter of healing until I had thoroughly tested every rule, method and law. I therefore include herewith only those that have withstood every test over a long period of time with many different kinds of people. I shall cite comparatively few rules but those few can be relied on to help any person to whom they are properly applied.

Rule 1. Live as pure, noble and kindly a life as you can. Think of yourself for what you really are: a channel through which the powers of help, healing and inspiration are meant to flow. They WILL flow onward and outward to everyone with whom you come in contact just to the extent and in the measure that you OPEN YOUR HEART AND MIND TO THE GOOD IN THE WHOLE WORLD.

Whenever you close your heart and mind to the power that created the world, to the good in yourself, the good in your fellowman, just to that extent you close this channel and restrict your own ability for helping or healing others.

It is not the most brilliant, learned, beautiful, powerful or even masterful people who help you and me and EVERYBODY ELSE most. Who is it? The PURE, the GENTLE, the TOLERANT, the ones who have most of JUST PLAIN OLD-FASHIONED GOODNESS, KINDLINESS, SYMPATHY AND LOVE. When you and I are on the top wave, when things are sailing along, when we are well and happy and successful we may find a certain thrill or excitement in the other kind, but when sickness, sadness or failure comes—when we really NEED somebody—these harsh, selfish, brilliant folks are the last ones we want to see, aren't they? Someone who loves us, just for our own little selves, faults and all, and who WANTS to help us—how wonderful they are in that hour!

Part of it is due to our love for them, but a great big wonderful part—a part we've never understood—is due to one of the simplest facts in the world: that this person is good and kind and gentle TO US. We naturally prefer our nearest relatives or oldest friends at such a time and for a reason few have ever analyzed: that we feel THESE people DO care more for us than outsiders do.

But anyone who truly FEELS, LIVES and EXPRESSES this love for us and especially if he is acquainted with scientific laws of healing, can often do the impossible for us.

Rule 2. Whether healing yourself or others have in mind two sets or lines of thoughts: first, the improvement of GENERAL HEALTH throughout the body; second, the EXACT SPOT you desire to be healed or from which you wish pain to be removed.

Concentrate definitely, positively vividly upon the thing desired, keeping it in the foreground of the mind while entertaining in the background the command for perfect health in every other part of the organism.

Rule 3. Do not waste time, energy or power trying to FORCE yourself to believe that healing will come to you. Some healers teach that this is necessary but, confidence in these laws is NOT essential to healing. The laws I shall herewith present are scientific, unchanging, eternal. Nothing and nobody can nullify them, for they concern the forces given you by your creator.

Rule 4. There are certain principles of healing and helping which can ALWAYS be applied BY anybody, for himself or for others. Every parent, teacher, minister, physician—every leader in every walk of life—should know and apply these principles in his contacts with others, for his own unfoldment, for the good he may do, the lives he may save, the hearts he may soothe, the pain he may relieve. Every person who comes in contact with others owes it to himself, to his fellowman and to the Power that made him, not to wrap his talent in a napkin, but to develop and use it.

Be assured that you are not required to grow ten talents from one, but you ARE expected to use that one, if one is all you possess. Many of you will be surprised, however, to discover, as soon as you put it to the test, that you have many healing talents.

The happiness and uplift that will come into your life and spirit, from this knowledge, rightly used, is beyond computation.

Remember this, YOU HAVE SOME KIND OF INFLUENCE ON THE MIND AND SPIRIT (and therefore indirectly on the HEALTH) of EVERY PERSON YOU COME IN CONTACT WITH. As a matter of fact and because of this, each of us is hurting or helping, weakening or strengthening EVERY PERSON WE ASSOCIATE WITH—and because both of these powerfully affect the health, we are MAKING PEOPLE MORE WELL OR MORE ILL, PHYSICALLY, DURING EVERY MOMENT WE SPEND WITH THEM.

Many times in the life of each of us we have felt acutely ill after a few moments in the presence of certain people. At other times we have found ourselves miraculously relieved or even cured of pain after some particularly pleasing, loving or sincere person had called upon us, or talked to us for five minutes on the street. One hurt us, sickened us; another helped us and one day we lost a perfectly good headache while talking to a dear friend.

Each of us has been pleasurably or painfully aware of the effect of OTHERS UPON US, in this connection, but few persons have ever realized that THEY TOO exert this influence on everybody to a greater or less extent.

So, whether we have ever given it thought before or not, we cannot, when we look at this fact, refuse to recognize our responsibility. It behooves us, then since, as long as we are alive, we are influencing others, to learn how we may always be a good and uplifting influence, mentally, spiritually and physically; how to prevent our being even indirectly responsible for the unhappiness, illness or depression of another human being; and how we may, through service to others, find that peace and joy which passeth understanding—the peace to which no one ever attains till he becomes a HELPFUL FORCE IN THE WORLD.

You will find that certain people amongst your circle of acquaintances go up and down the land helping and healing their friends by their very presence, and others, by the same token leave mental, spiritual and physical wounds in their wake. That sensible, decent, conservative, hard--headed business friend of yours—how he would laugh at the idea of one person's power to heal another! Yet he, with the best motive imaginable, makes everybody in his concern half sick with fear by his severe, cold, critical manner! And that jolly young salesman, wouldn't he smile at the idea too—and all the while he is helping everybody he meets, to actual physical improvement, just by his manner. "A cheerful heart doeth good like a medicine."

Rule 5. There is a peculiar and definite magnetism in sincerity, goodness, truth and honesty that can be felt but not described. Other things being equal, therefore, the purest, noblest, most consecrated persons will be the most efficient in helping and healing others.

The obedience of such people to the highest laws gives them an authority that seems to speak directly to the subconscious minds of those they meet. It is equally true that, though they may help many, the false, the insincere, the pretender cannot rise to great success in this field and are doomed to ultimate downfall.

As explained before, a faith in the LAW, the formula, or the methods which we use upon OURSELVES OR OTHERS is not necessary to healing either ourselves or them, but when we are to be healed BY or THROUGH someone else, faith IN THAT PERSON, in his honor, sincerity and goodness, is absolutely essential to the best results.

Therefore, if you would become a great healer or helper of others you must be first of all sincere in your desire to help THEM, not merely to help YOURSELF. The desire to help yourself, in every way from personal unfoldment to financial returns, is justified, fair, businesslike. "The laborer is worthy of his hire" and no man or institution can accomplish anything in this day and age without funds. But if you are doing this MORE for money than for the joy of service, or if you are thinking A GREAT DEAL MORE about yourself than of your patient or subject, your results will be meager. If, by any chance one heals ONLY FOR THE FINANCIAL RETURNS he will invariably fail in the long run. Because, in such case he would be concentrating not on the idea of healing, as the law requires, but actually UPON THESE FINANCIAL RETURNS, and the law of healing not being operated, could not bring the desired results.

Do not misunderstand me. I am not saying that one should heal without remuneration. As a matter of fact Americans dislike charity and many persons are so humiliated by it that this consciousness restricts the subconscious through embarrassment until the best results are not obtainable. Americans like to PAY for what they get, and to GET what they pay for. Furthermore, the greater one's natural healing power the more does he owe it to the world not to hide it under a bushel. Without funds he cannot go far; without funds he cannot reach many; and it is sad but true that in this country unless he make a fair financial success of his calling thousands who need his help will not have sufficient confidence in his ability to approach him or ask for his help.

It is a matter of putting first things first. He who puts a sincere desire to help others ahead of his own selfish interests will heal far greater numbers and this will lead, without his giving it much thought, to greater financial success than anyone can ever have who thinks more of himself than of the needy who come to him.

The first step, therefore, is to GET RIGHT WITH ONE'S OWN SPIRIT. No man has ever yet succeeded in downing, silencing or outwitting his conscience. No power under Heaven will enable a selfish man or woman to heal or even to convince great numbers of their fellowmen for very long. The ring of the voice, the glance of the eye, the manifold movements of the human body all tell their story, a true story which he who runs may read.

Since we cannot make our inner selves over in a moment, since instinct is strong and selfishness a thing that is not to be overruled in a day, it will be well not to demand perfection of ourselves at first, but we should demand decided improvement in our own motives and KEEP AT IT till we have weeded out the dank growths that enjungle our minds.

Do not wait, before beginning your healing, till you have made yourself perfect. Do not wait at all, in fact. Begin at once to help someone you do deeply love, someone concerning whom you are NOT selfish and extend your ministrations, as your love spreads, to others. Some day you will be able to love utter strangers because of their need of you and just because they, like yourself, are among God's creatures.

Rule 6. To be of the greatest service to others and to achieve the highest success in healing, self-control is essential. Next to faith in the SINCERITY of the one who tries to heal us, we must have confidence in his STRENGTH and this is impossible if he is lacking in self-control.

A nervous manner, jerky movements, a harsh voice, impatience or "fussiness" will nullify almost anything the healer says.

Dignity, discipline, courtesy and considerateness should never be forgotten when treating others or for that matter when contacting others in any capacity, for we know not what moment we may wish to help them.

Rule 7. Faith in the healer's sincerity, Faith in his strength, and next, WILLINGNESS TO LEAN UPON HIM, to give one's self over to his care, are the other essentials.

Skeptics are seldom cured, not because belief is necessary to the cure, but because this turning one's self singly and sincerely toward the healer IS essential, and the skeptic will not do this inwardly. He may do so outwardly but usually his conscious mind has really refused to let the message by, and his mental reservations create an impassable barrier.

Everything, from personal habits to one's inner spirit should receive earnest attention, since the former may, if neglected, make it impossible for one to help sensitive, fastidious patients or friends.

Rule 8. Never contradict, criticise, or above all, ridicule a sick person, no matter what he says or does. Even well persons cannot stand this, and to permit yourself this luxury with ill ones will offset everything, make you powerless to help them and ADD to their illness by adding to their stock of resentments.

Sick people, whether their ailments are physical, mental or both, are supersensitive, and most "touchy" on the very point or weakness that the healer, doctor or well person feels impelled to criticise. Both know that this wrong attitude in a certain direction is doubtless the very thing that is causing the patient's trouble, but this is the ONE THING he cannot bear to be told. He cannot bear to think you suspect it. The cure must be achieved, in these cases, indirectly.

People who are causing their own illnesses through certain complexes are always afraid you are going to suspect this, and will oftentimes go to extreme lengths in their attempts to conceal this from you, just as one who is concealing something in a closet will often stand in front of the door and try to direct your attention elsewhere.

Let them think they have accomplished this. Do not, under any provocation, allow your own egotism to defend itself or you at the cost of an opportunity to help someone else. What if he does insult your intelligence? You insult something within yourself far finer than intelligence when you retaliate to a sick man or woman.

Rule 9. Never approach a patient or anyone you wish to help in an unkind, disinterested mood. The greatest scientist in the world, if he came to our bedside impersonally or coldly, cannot help us as much as one of far less knowledge who comes with warm friendship shining in his eyes. Better to die in the presence of those who love us than be manhandled by "experts" who look upon us as just another "case."

Rule 10. Direct the patient NOT to talk of his troubles to others and tell him why. Doing so will only impress the wrong order on his subconscious besides putting into the minds of others the thoughts and visualizations of his illness, which will be sent back to him in their conversations to re-impress his own mind with disease instead of health.

LESSON XIV

How to Let Your Subconscious Help You in Your Work

WE all work better and easier under certain conditions than others. For reasons known or unknown to us our thoughts flow more freely in the presence of certain things and are inhibited by others. Sometimes these things seem silly to everyone else, but that should make no difference to you. Tell nobody about these little idiosyncrasies or peculiarities of yours. Waste no time trying to dispose of these powerful aids or in combating your aversion to others.

Also do not try to teach yourself to adopt those of other people just because they help someone else. The other fellow's and yours are purely personal matters, these preferences or prejudices being lodged in the sub-conscious of each as a result of his own past experiences. These experiences though forgotten themselves, are associated thereafter with this peculiar condition in such a way as to leave pleasing, constructive feelings; or unhappy ones.

For my own part, I can never write at my best save before an open fire in a room with many windows. A fireless room—however bright, handsomely furnished and stocked with every other convenience—never enables me to do my best, whereas I can forego many of the other things I enjoy if only these two elements are in my environment.

The cause of this peculiarity is known to me and the time and place of its origin distinctly remembered.

I had written in many cities, under many different conditions, but it was not until we spent a winter at Elbert Hubbard's Roycroft Inn at East Aurora, N. Y., that I was able to write with ease. There I occupied the Ruskin room on the top floor of the tower. It had windows on all four sides and a beautiful fireplace in which a log was kept always burning. My own study when built was designed first of all to include these two things.

I hope you will pardon my personal references in these lessons. I make them only because my own experience has taught me much of what I am trying to explain, and also to make clear that you will do better to yield to these deeply imbedded, innocent preferences than to oppose them. I do not relate these to everybody, and advise you not to air your own promiscuously. Everybody appears more or less "strange" to everybody else, even under the best conditions, so it is just as well to refrain from publishing your own unnecessarily.

For similar reasons almost every person finds that he works more easily and happily at certain kinds of work in certain kinds of weather than at any other time. One man whom I know and who never cares to touch his tools ordinarily, likes to "carpenter" around his home on cloudy days. A woman friend who sometimes comes to visit me brings in her trunk a certain kind of sewing which she never touches except on rainy evenings and another never enjoys reading except when it snows. Then she likes nothing so much as to curl up in a window seat and devote the whole day to it. No one can drag her away. She will cancel any engagement she may have in order to keep this particular one with her own subconscious self.

Poe, as we know, was unnaturally despondent, but what many do not know is that he was always happier and more productive in dreary weather.

The fact that almost everybody is depressed by dark, drab days and stimulated by bright ones (due to the biological memories of millions of years when our ancestors were exposed to weather) makes all the more significant these personal preferences.

In order for a "dark-days" preference to gain a foothold in the individual's subconsciousness, this kind of weather must needs have been intimately connected in his past with some very pleasurable emotion or experience. That this emotion or experience was so pleasing as to overcome a prejudice indicates its power, and this power should be utilized to help the owner. Efforts to oppose it mean the wastage not only of time but of a valuable opportunity.

One of the colleges I attended was a university in the windiest city I have ever visited. Though I had never given the matter any thought up to that time, it became evident to me that there was a decided difference between the morale, quality of recitations and general feeling of the students on calm days and on very windy ones. Faculty members when interviewed said they had noted it for years, and always dreaded the general "scatteration" caused in the average young person's mind by extremely blowy weather.

Though one cannot lay aside his regular work just because the weather fails to aid it, he CAN learn to know what it is that brings on these heretofore unaccountable feelings, and instead of laying it to other and more serious causes, take whatever steps he prefers to counteract it, when it is necessary to work in spite of it.

One student who came to me several years ago had begun to fear he was in danger of insanity, for no reason except that on brilliant days he always had an uncontrollable desire to give up his regular position (on which depended the living of his wife and three babies) and to go forth in search of the one kind of work he had always preferred.

He has been brought up by a Southern mother who couldn't bear to see him in anything but a "white collar" job, but he had always been interested in mechanics and liked nothing better than to don a pair of overalls and dirty his face and hands puttering over his car or any other available machine.

By doing his work at the bank in daytime and attending an automobile school at night he was able to transfer from the one to the other about a year later, and ultimately invented an oil-regulator that has made him rich.

The whole world is familiar with the enthusiasm for work and for all creative effort which comes with the Springtime; also with the workless feeling accompanying Autumn's "melancholy days." Spring housecleaning and the general campaign for refurbishment which takes place at that time are only two of the customs bred and born of psychological work-tendencies.

The thorough cleansing of the home is, as a matter of common sense, more necessary in the Fall, when everyone is to be housed in it for months, than in the Spring when fresh winds romp through it and when everyone spends much of his time away from it. But we are creatures not of common sense so much as of "our senses," and so far as possible should reserve for each season the kinds of work we most enjoy doing in that season.

Rule 1. It will behoove you to study yourself for, and take advantage of, all these "high tides" that come within yourself.

The average person works best in the early hours of the morning, more effectively in the forenoon than afternoon, and more enthusiastically in the afternoon than the evening. This is due to three factors, the physical, mental and spiritual. The body is more alive just after its rest, the mind more keen after sleep, and the spirit, in addition to being affected by both of these, is more uplifted than after the day's experiences or disappointments.

But there are exceptions to this, as to all the other general habits mentioned above, and each individual should study his own reactions with a view to availing himself of the constructive and of rising above the destructive.

Herbert Spencer and many another writer, scientist and inventor worked best and easiest from 2 to 6 a. m. Many advantages do inhere in this period. First of all, the organism has been found to reach its high-water mark in the average individual between these hours. Greater stimulation is felt then, mentally, spiritually and physically, than at any others during the twenty-four, as anyone knows who has ever made a practice of arising at that time. Everyone who has sat up with the sick or who for any reason has remained up all night remembers the wide-awakeness he experienced at about this time in the morning. The sleepiness, the weight of heaviness which enveloped him earlier in the night entirely disappears, and he feels as much or more refreshed than he usually does after a full night of rest.

A second great advantage to be seriously considered, especially by those who are sensitive to noise, interruptions or activity, is that in these hours the world is more quiet and there is far less danger of interruption than at any other hours of the twenty-four. The sense of security which this consciousness brings is not the least of the advantages to be gained from this period. Many persons can accomplish in one hour at this time what requires two or three later in the day.

Almost all writers arise early, do much before breakfast, the remainder before lunch and give the afternoons to rest, recreation and sociability. Most of them feel also that their minds gather as much of value from this recreation period, which though outwardly inactive is inwardly alert, as from the hours of concentrated thought and work.

There can be no question that "fallow" periods are as essential to the growth of the mind, work and personality as work periods, the only great danger being that we shall let this resting period extend too long, or that we shall not enter into it with the attitude which creates while we are not working.

All of us have experienced this growth and been happily surprised to find that after we had dropped a problem from the conscious mind for a time we could solve it easily upon returning to it.

The most familiar of these illustrations came into the lives of most of us I fancy during school days. I remember with much gratitude a teacher of my own childhood who understood the laws of the subconscious mind better than even she realized.

After watching for an entire term my vain struggles with arithmetic she passed me to the next grade under condition that I "make it up" during the Summer. When I told her I couldn't let one study hold me back for a year and that I was going to start in the day after school closed and work at it till I could understand it she said, "No, you mustn't do that. You have worked hard enough. Rest a while. You have fought with yourself so long your mind is all tired out. I want you to drop your arithmetic completely for two months. Don't try to work it out, don't try to think about it, just forget it completely. Turn your back on it and LET IT ALONE. Then, one month before school opens in the Fall, come back to me and I think you will find it much easier."

It worked for me in that instance as it has in thousands since. The veil seemed to be lifted from my mental eyes. From the first moment of returning to it it seemed amazingly clear and simple. I had, as she explained it, "tied my mind up in a knot" and while I was doing something else my subconscious untangled it for me. I had done what we always do when we wrestle too long and too hurriedly and worriedly with anything: drawn the string so taut there was no play. The best simple illustration of this is seen when we try, by main force, to remember a name or anything we intensely desire to recall.

"Why CAN'T I remember that?" we exclaim. "Oh, WHAT is it? I know it as well as ANYTHING! What can be the matter? I must think of it!" It doesn't come. We are demanding that the conscious mind produce it for us when as we now know, memory is lodged in the subconscious. The more we pull and haul and scold at the conscious the less opportunity has the subconscious to bring it up to us. We can never hear what the subconscious is trying to tell us if we are quarreling with the conscious mind. This fact accounts for many of our blunders.

Call it what you will, do with it as you will, and think of it as you may—religiously or scientifically—there IS a "still small voice" within each of us. It is spiritual but also very practical, and will help us in the most common, everyday affairs as well as with larger ones if we only let it.

One of the first ways to let it, is to recognize its existence and then listen for it instead of wrangling with the large loud voice of the conscious mind. You will get a clear idea of just what I mean if you will think of yourself as possessing two workmen. One is Mr. Conscious and one is Mr. Subconscious.

Conscious is a large, brawny chap, mighty valuable and powerful in his way, but lacking understanding. His great muscles are the ones you must depend on to do the actual labor of accomplishing things, but Subconscious, who is a frail little fellow as far as muscles go, has a better head on him. He is much older, more experienced in the world and understands you and your needs far better than Conscious does. But Conscious doesn't give you much chance to find out how capable Subconscious is. The schools and our parents and preachers and the world in general have praised Conscious and made so much of him he is a little arrogant.

Until recently nobody paid any attention to Subconscious. He has such a retiring nature, and is so above all these things anyhow, that he never thrusts himself upon us, while Conscious was always such a handsome young creature we rather enjoyed thinking he was the whole staff.

Conscious is always stepping in front of Subconscious and diverting our attention, especially in waking hours and when we are trying to get something done in a hurry. In headlong fashion he pitches in and makes a great fuss trying to work out a solution, when all the time if we would only say, "Step aside please and let Subconscious decide what we had better do," we would save much time and failure. He won't put on any fuss or feathers, but as soon as you stop arguing with Conscious and he can get your ear he will tell you what it was you wanted to remember. After this, when you are trying to remember something simply say, "Never mind, it will come to me." Go about your business and pretty soon—just as soon as Conscious gets out of the way—Subconscious will tap you on the shoulder and say, "Here it is." This is precisely what has happened every time the thing "came to you" afterward.

Rule 2. These two things are necessary when turning over to the subconscious any piece of work, any problem or solution: you must previously have DONE YOUR BEST WITH IT CONSCIOUSLY and you must turn this work over to it in the RIGHT ATTITUDE. If either is missing it can not work it out for you as quickly or successfully.

The story of the arithmetic will serve to illustrate what I mean by "doing your best with it consciously before turning it over to the subconscious. I had battled with long division and fractions a whole term. I had done my part to understand them consciously. If I had not I should never have been able to reach so quickly and completely into the subconscious, because the conscious mind is the anteroom, the front hall that leads into the subconscious.

Through the conscious is the proper avenue for getting in to see the Subconscious and he does not respond as readily for you if you overlook this any more than the head of a big business would like it if you ignored his secretaries and forced yourself into his private office.

There are certain rules to follow, certain RIGHT ways of doing things; certain methods which bring the quickest and surest results and this is truer of our own peculiar organisms than of anything else in the world. Our forces simply do NOT react constructively under destructive treatment and they always DO under the constructive, confident kind. There are many wrong ways but only one best, RIGHT way to do anything and everything.

Rule 3. So, if you would reach your subconscious and set it to work at once on any piece of work, go through the formalities and proper steps beforehand. Learn as much about it as you can. Become "conscious" of as many phases, angles and facts as possible. Gather all the data you can. Then, if the secretary, Mr. Conscious Mind, cannot handle your business (and he can most of the time), you will be justified in insisting upon seeing the head of the concern.

Rule 4. When you have done your part and are ready to turn the whole matter over to the Subconscious there are right and wrong methods of doing it. The right one consists of four things: first, that you turn the work over to him in an attitude of TAKING HOLD OF THAT PIECE OF WORK IN A DEEPER WAY YOURSELF, instead of LETTING GO OR SHIFTING ALL THE RESPONSIBILITY; second, that you HOLD HIM RESPONSIBLE FOR DOING IT; third, that you EXPECT him to do it; and fourth, that you SET A TIME LIMIT at the end of which he should complete it.

We will use the story of the arithmetic again for it still serves as a good illustration of the RIGHT way. The teacher didn't let me think I was giving up arithmetic entirely just because I was not to think of it consciously for two months. She made me understand that I was really BUILDING UP, not GIVING UP the matter; in other words, I was taking on a new kind of responsibility concerning the arithmetic, not simply throwing responsibility aside. By telling me that I should take this way to DO IT she implanted the idea that my subconscious mind was being given a definite responsibility to do that very thing. By saying I should find that it would come out all right she impelled me to EXPECT my subconscious to do it and by SETTING A LIMIT she showed me how to demand results within a specified time.

Rule 5. In setting your time limit use your good common sense, so as not to ask the impossible. Also use your higher senses and KNOW it can and WILL be done whether your everyday conscious mind can see HOW it is to be accomplished or not.

Then give your subconscious every encouragement, every constructive pat on the back you can, pass on to it new ideas as they come to you, precisely as you would add to the data you had given to anyone else who was working for you. In brief, give it the work to do, then stand behind it in every way, especially with your confidence.

In other words, submit a PATTERN to the subconscious in order to simplify its work and to enable it to know exactly what we want with the minimum of effort on our part. It will work out ways and means of completing the product.

Robert Keable, noted writer and author of "Simon Called Peter," says, "I believe intensely that it is our subconscious mainly that writes—actually plots—a book. And I add my conviction that the more one can give rein to one's subconscious in writing a book—as with housekeeping, working at a machine or hoeing a potato patch—the better it is. For, in the genesis of a book, the theme has been driven down into the subconscious which has already worked it out in its own way. I am convinced that the subconscious will plan for and help execute anything we try to do, and that it can do much for us when we recognize this fact and give it the utmost to perform."

There is a way to do great things easily—so easily it looks like a miracle. That way is to GET READY TO DO IT. The ease with which any person does his work is made possible by the fact that in his subconscious mind he has stored away the knowledge and built the habit-tools he now brings into use.

Rule 6. In order to obtain the fullest co-operation of your subconscious for any achievement you must not shackle it with regrets. You cannot expect it to move forward consistently if you constantly turn it toward the past and compel it to give its attention and power to gazing backward. If you do it will make about the same progress as a man does who stumbles backward up a hill.

Extract the LESSON from your past experiences and then drop them. Use them just as you would food. Eat them, digest them while you go about your business; grow strong on them and face the future.

We CAN grow strong on our very defeats and failures if we will but look upon them as so many school books which we had to master before we could be ready for the next higher grade. But we are through with them when the lesson is learned, and they should be discarded when they have served their purpose just as your old school books are.

How to Train and Develop the Subconscious Mind

Have you ever stopped to think what perfect control your mind has over your hands? You have educated them until they are expert servants, performing their work almost automatically.

One of the most glorious facts of life is that YOU CAN TRAIN AND EDUCATE YOUR SUBCONSCIOUS MIND TO DO THE SAME. The power of your subconscious is UNLIMITED, IMMEASURABLE, INEXHAUSTIBLE. So great is it that no one has ever yet plumbed its depths. When the proper methods are used there is nothing, seemingly, that it cannot do for us. Certainly it has never failed to do anything demanded of it by every person who ever obeyed its laws, all of which will be clearly explained in this lesson.

The great general phases and possibilities of the subconscious—the steps by which it operates to bring us anything we want, have been referred to in previous lessons in this course, but in this one we shall recapitulate, sum them all up, remind you of the necessary steps and give the final instructions for setting into operation at any given moment for any given purpose the entire mechanism of this vast power house.

You need not take my word for this. When we put this great subconscious force to work in the right way its immediate results in health, confidence and tangible returns are so abundant that we can only wonder why we have never used this almost omnipotent power of ours before.

> "Only a thought, but the work is wrought,
> Could never by tongue or pen be taught;
> But it ran through a life like a thread of gold,
> And the life bore fruit a hundredfold."

We are building, by the thoughts we entertain and ENCOURAGE, an unseen but enormous web of the greatest magnetic power—a web that extends out from, beyond and about us as does the spider's and which catches in it the things that correspond to it, the things it ATTRACTS.

To build, therefore, a wonderful network that shall draw unto you the things you desire, realize every thought you DWELL UPON, BROOD OVER or CLING TO—good or bad—becomes thereby a tiny silken strand in this great unseen but powerful network.

Rule 7. To build a web that shall draw unto you the things you desire, the first thing you must do is WATCH YOUR THOUGHTS! Too many people think to themselves, "I will DO such and such a thing, but I'll THINK what I please about it," never realizing that this secret attitude has a drawing power in it. He never suspects that it brings to him in accordance with ITS nature sometimes more than any external, overt act could because an act is something that, important as it may be is often over and done with as soon as committed while a THOUGHT sets into some kind of motion every fiber of his body, and BUILDS INEVITABLY IN A THOUSAND DIRECTIONS in his remote and immediate environment.

Everything in the universe GROWS BY WHAT IT FEEDS ON. Feed your mind, moment by moment, with good thoughts, serene thoughts, kind thoughts, and you will grow like them. Some day the better things for which you have striven will come within the reach of your hand.

Every divine thought you take into your mind and dwell upon builds for divinity in you, in your life, in your character. Every foolish weak thought tears down. Every strong thought strengthens, every uplifting thought lifts us up.

Rule 8. "Great works," said Johnson, "are performed not by strength but by perseverance."

When you feel discouraged or impatient, just remember the Children of Israel, who spent FORTY YEARS IN THE WILDERNESS before reaching the Promised Land.

Rule 9. Go at things wholeheartedly.

> "If you gently grasp a nettle
> It will sting you for your pains;
> Grasp it like a land of mettle
> And it soft as silk remains."

When you have a disagreeable thing to do, a disagreeable person to meet, a disagreeable situation to face, WADE INTO IT. Otherwise it will wade into you.

Don't you remember as a child when you were called upon to take a dose of medicine, how much WORSE you made the whole thing for yourself by halting, dreading, whining and playing with the spoon? It took ever so much longer to work up sufficient courage to take the stuff than when we gulped it down and got it over with. In fact, whole chunks of courage seemed to ebb out of us for every instant we delayed, till at last when we HAD to swallow it we were so weak we trembled all over. Sometimes the message we'd sent into our stomachs over the solar plexus wires of the subconscious made it come right back again, and no wonder! "Look out down there!" you subconsciously called to your stomach. "Here comes something horrible. I hate it but I've got to send it to you!" Little Mr. Stomach, thinking only to help you, took you at your word and did the thing he supposed you wanted. If this happened many times he finally got into the habit which you boast of today—that you simply can't take medicine.

The subconscious mind is marvelously sensitive. It learns easily. Like a good and faithful servant, it is constantly on the alert to see what you want, to do things as you want them done and adapt itself IN EVERY WAY to your wishes and desires.

If you dally and dawdle whenever something unpleasant has to be done it soon comes to the conclusion that this is the way you want things handled and will always furnish you with excuses, justification and supposed "reasons" for the delay, precisely as a good servant would bring forth defenses in your behalf if outsiders insisted on compelling you to do something it knew you disliked to do.

But the moment you give it orders to go straight forward into things it will make it so easy for you that you will wonder why you haven't always done it that way. It will go ahead, pave the way, find out the easiest routes and do all the hardest work. And the glorious reward when it's DONE! Heaven can hold nothing sweeter than the gratification we have when a difficult task has been squarely faced and mastered!

We suffer a thousand times more in ANTICIPATING things than we do when we get into the things themselves. To put off the disagreeable, to postpone the unpleasant, is only to GIVE IT POWER OVER YOU for that period of time, to CONFESS its tyranny over you, all of which tears down your self-respect.

The temptation to take it easy, to get out of doing the hard thing, to postpone the difficult task just as long as we can and get out of it altogether if possible, is natural to the old weak side of human nature, but when we resist this temptation we rise above human nature and become superhuman. To the superman or superwoman all things are possible, and most of them easy.

Rule 10. Always start the day by tackling the toughest job first, by grappling with the next worst next, and so on, reserving the easy, pleasant things for the last. This doubles the fun of doing the pleasant one because your state of mind (which is always the important thing) is so much more peaceful and happy.

If you will do this the day will come when the habit of conquering the unpleasant things will become so fixed and firm that the going forth to meet them will be more pleasurable than painful to you—give you a thrill of victory and a sense of personal power, the equal of which is never found in any other way.

To think of every tough piece of work as an enemy we are to vanquish is to call forth all our self expression. Such a habit finally relieves us of all pain when doing the difficult thing, in fact puts pleasure in its place. But the longer we stand in fear and trembling of the hard things of life the longer will they rule us, the more tyrannical will they become and the less will we be aware of our vast unused resources.

Tackle the unpleasant thing vigorously, masterfully, determinedly if you would remove its sting. Do not hesitate or sidestep and you will always find it easy.

Rule 11. "If you are ambitious to expand your life to its utmost possibilities, never shrink from whatever will make you GROW, however distasteful it may be, never shirk responsibilities, however disagreeable they are at the time, however it may interrupt your regular routine of life or interfere with your ease and comfort. Only the shouldering of responsibility develops manhood and womanhood, enlarges life and makes it worth while."

WE MUST CALL OUT OUR RESERVES if we expect ever to realize what a strong standing army we have within us, ready to do anything and everything for us at our command.

It is so human to play with the spoon all through life when we have anything disagreeable to swallow! If we only knew how much easier it is to take the bitter medicine quickly we would save ourselves endless loss, pain and humiliation.

Marden tells this story:

"I remember a Harvard student, son of wealthy parents, who had been in the habit of living well and who went into training in the football team. But he was so unwilling to take his medicine, to eat the plain fare and submit to the discipline and the hardships of training that the captain, much to his regret, was compelled to drop him. The young man loved athletics, possessed godlike physique and would have been the star player. But he would not take the training and later had the mortification of being an outsider when his team was victorious in the season's games."

The most sublime moments of life often lie very close to the most painful situations.

All everyday men and women have much more power than they realize. But most of them continue to be "just average" because they have "fenced in" their talents, shut them off from themselves and the world, and even forget their existence.

To do your very best and be your very best it is just as necessary for you to get yourself in tune as for the musician in an orchestra to get in tune.

This lesson will show you how to "tune up" the greatest instrument you will ever have in this world—your subconscious. To get into harmony with what you are going to do, give your subconscious the order, just before falling asleep and many times during the day, to dissolve every inharmonious thought, feeling and mood.

The content of your subconscious mind is constantly changing; you are rebuilding your innerself every day; and the material you use for this rebuilding is composed of the thoughts you think hour by hour, moment by moment. It is the thoughts you are thinking today and tomorrow that will determine whether your subconscious will be more or less expert next week and a month from now.

Rule 12. Recognize every thought as a "brick in the wall" of our life structure and select your thoughts as you would the separate bricks to be used in the building of an actual wall around your home. Each of us IS surrounded by an invisible wall, inside which we live our personal lives. To dwell in peace, harmony and safety, to be secure from the inimical forces that would break through and steal, to be immune to disease, unhappiness or failure, we need only to make these thought-bricks strong and true. The storms will find no weak places then, the floods and winds of fate will have to pass us by.

When people "go under," "give up in despair," "lose their grip," or go "down and out" it is because they, unknowingly, built so many weak bricks into their wall that it crumbled when the pressure came.

If I were you I would decide today, right now, THIS MINUTE, on a certain course of action, and I would live up to it. I would decide to build me a BRAND NEW WALL and gradually move myself and my belongings COMPLETELY out of this old enclosure.

I'd build for myself a "City of Refuge" like those I saw in the Hawaiian Islands. In accordance with their ancient religion a high, thick wall of lava rock was built in an open space or clearing, and any persecuted person, innocent or guilty, was safe from his pursuers if he could outwit his enemies and get inside it.

Each of us has such a city of refuge, within himself where the stress and storms and persecutions of life cannot come, and we can move into it if we only will.

The chief reason that life for the average person is so full of hardship and unhappiness, is not that it HAD to be this way, but because the average person has never tried to censor, control or organize his thoughts and feelings.

Every child should be taught by its parents and during its school years HOW TO THINK RIGHT. This knowledge is a thousand times more valuable than everything else he is taught. Information and instruction we can gather any time, so long as the mind is open and teachable, but the right ATTITUDES of mind mean more to us than all the "learning" we can ever acquire.

The change that would result in this country in ten years, from teaching children how to USE their minds, would be beyond belief. WHAT to think as well as what to LEARN, what to FEEL as well as what to KNOW, these are vital things which, if trained into the child's subconscious, would enable him to build a life from ten to a thousand times more happy and successful than he is able to do under the present methods.

Rule 13. Iteration and reiteration, these are the two great steps in training and educating the subconscious mind. We are using them destructively or constructively all the time, according to what we are saying to ourselves, thinking to ourselves and then repeating to ourselves. As soon as any impression, good or bad, is firmly fixed in the subconscious it begins to externalize itself automatically.

Thus the impression you print upon your subconscious by constantly giving the constructive reaction to the events of life finally sets in motion vast inner machinery that DOES THE WORK for you almost without your being aware of it. The same is true if you give, for a long while, a destructive reaction.

It is this which makes us sometimes feel that the calamity which has befallen even our enemies is really worse than any recent act of theirs deserved. But it was the ADDED-UP REACTIONS of a long time previous that really brought it about. Do the right thing, say, think and feel the right thing when things go wrong and sooner or later the reward will come, with interest. Character can be modified and re-made to an unbelievable extent through the proper use of the subconscious mind. Direct it to accomplish certain things in your nature, BACK UP THIS ORDER WITH YOUR EFFORTS and, most of all, BELIEVE IN YOURSELF, and you can do practically—yes, everything—you desire.

Thoughts are seeds, each and every one of which drops into the soil of the subconscious and brings forth in accordance with its nature.

Anyone who persistently indulges in thoughts of despondency, depression or discouragement, will reap a harvest of like nature. Out in the bright daylight of his everyday life there will finally arrive the very surroundings visualized in the inner chambers of the mind.

Think of yourself as unsuccessful, abused, "down and out," and these undesirable conditions will materialize in your life.

What does all these prove? That before we can HAVE what we want we must THINK it, VISUALIZE it, DWELL on it, ACT, TALK and PLAN for it exactly as we have been doing for the things we didn't get. Reverse the process!

Any man's nature becomes discolored, bent, twisted by destructive thinking, and good, pure, uplifted, confident thinking will STRAIGHTEN OUT THE KINKS.

Many persons believe that their weak, undesirable characteristics are natural and inevitable, that they are a part of their temperament and cannot be changed. Temperamental weaknesses can be overcome. The life history of all the worthwhile men and women of the world is the story of a series of mistakes, errors and fallings-down, but followed by persistent gettings-up again.

What we must have is not freedom from the bumps and falls but the persistence to start over again. This habit will eventually prevent most of the things that now discourage us.

Rule 14. Incisive, vivid, graphic self-suggestions are best and secure the quickest, best results. Next to this in importance comes the FULL INTENTION to attain what is desired. Settle on what you want, SEE IT IN YOUR MIND'S EYE, decide to GET IT. Thereafter pay no more attention to the things that would prevent it than you would to the carpings of his rival after you have ordered a certain architect to build you a house.

Rule 15. Constant reiterations of your strength and poise will prepare the subconscious mind to withstand adverse conditions, unforeseen events and other emergencies, not to mention the great number of calamities this poise and confidence will prevent ever coming to you at all.

Constant reiterations that you are going to "LIKE AND ENJOY" a difficult piece of work "BECAUSE OF WHAT IT WILL BRING" WILL MAKE IT COMPARATIVELY EASY IF NOT ACTUALLY PLEASANT. One earnest, sincere application of this law will produce results that will forever after convince you of the truly miraculous power of your subconscious.

Proper application of the law of self-suggestion will bring harmony out of discord in one's life, cure ailments, turn enemies into friends, failure into success, inner darkness into brilliant day. For helping one's self it is a method that surpasses all others. It can make his ideals into realities, unfold his inner self, strengthen his soul, clear his brain and REMAKE HIS LIFE.

It will reveal and put to practical use in his everyday life innumerable factors, previously unguessed, which have been lying buried in his inner citadel. No one who has not made the acquaintance of and lived on intimate terms with his subconscious self knows the tenth of what he is, or a thousandth of the achievement he is capable of.

Freedom from everything that enslaves can be attained through the right use of this great power. There is literally nothing it cannot do for us in the way of attainment if we will but throw every vestige of our support behind it. No person secures the highest and best results in life without the co-operation of his subconscious, though most of the world's famous men and women, up to recent years, worked in harmony with this strange inner force without ever guessing its real nature. It has been called "the secret of genius," "the intuitive faculty," and many other things, each aiming to express the great unseen energies which rise in such men and women under certain conditions. We now know what the conditions are which bring these unlimited energies out to the surface and put them to work and can now create knowingly and deliberately the conditions they had to wait to stumble upon when "the mood" or the "muse" seemed willing. We know today that these moods make our lives, but we know something they never guessed—that WE make the moods!

Effects, good or bad, weak or strong, happy or unhappy, will arise in our lives which EXACTLY CORRESPOND to these long-continued moods. To make our lives what we want them to be we must remake our moods and to remake our moods we must invite into our mental house the good thoughts that come to the door of the mind and turn the bad ones away. After a while the evil ones will cease to trouble us.

Suggest illness to yourself over a long period (or over a short one if the suggestion is INTENSE) and illness will follow. Merely suggest—not even expect—harmony, discord, unhappiness, and these will walk in upon you sooner or later. If you BELIEVE in as well as suggest them they will arrive sooner, that is all.

The law of suggestion operates the subconscious mind and sets it to work in accordance with whatever you suggest to yourself, REGARDLESS OF WHAT YOU BELIEVE. It is a divine law and the belief or nonbelief of a mere human being affects it no more than it would the starting of your car once you step on the gas. Belief is helpful in that it makes you more quick and efficient in starting the inner mechanism.

Rule 16. Suggest to yourself only THOSE THINGS YOU WANT TO HAPPEN. Never think about, talk about or act out the ones you do NOT want. Suggest peace, quiet, harmony and achievement, and in a very short time you will begin to see opportunities for attaining them which have never been apparent to you before. Some of these opportunities will have been created by the new tendency and some will be old ones that have been there all the time but which, in your preoccupation with their opposites, you did not recognize.

An idea that is DWELT UPON, continually THOUGHT ABOUT or ENCOURAGED tends to monopolize a great proportion of the total manifestation of consciousness, to crowd out other and especially inimical thoughts, and to REACH OUT IN EVERY DIRECTION for the materials it requires for its fulfillment in the external world. It is this which enables the so-called genius to accomplish so much. He sticks to one thing. It is also just this which when carried to extremes in DESTRUCTIVE THOUGHT, FEAR THOUGHT or DREAD, brings that suffusion to the brain area handling this kind of thought, which causes insanity.

People who go insane are insane on only one subject at first. The genius concentrates CONSTRUCTIVELY on one or two great ideas and because his concentration is outgoing and creative, becomes stronger. All the elements are on his side. This is a constructive universe. But he who concentrates destructively wrecks himself and his life. He is opposed to the order of the universe, and the very universe opposes him whereas it literally comes more than half way to aid him who is doing anything CONSTRUCTIVE.

Many chronic invalids keep themselves in that condition from HABIT ALONE. Hundreds of people have remained bedridden for years from no earthly cause save self-suggestion. Most of the well, healthy people who do the world's work and carry its burdens could be sick next week and stay that way as easily as these others if they sat down and took the trouble to report every little ache to the subconscious as the chronically sick do.

I know many busy men and women who have now trained the forces within and around them until they are practically immune to undesirable things.

Most of the invalidism of the world could be overcome if there was real DESIRE on the part of the afflicted to be WELL. But in all too many cases there is not this desire. "Wherever the invalidism of any individual brings him attention, love, care, comfort or other things which he desires more than the things health could bring him and which HE COULD HAVE WERE HE WELL, he may insist on staying ill. Such a one is not curable because he refuses to pass the order for health on down to his subconscious mind. He may go through all the motions and pre-tenses but he takes the suggestion only as far as the door of the subconscious and is careful NOT to take it inside. Such a patient may really believe himself ill, and may have kept up the practice referred to until it is automatic with him.

The one who says, in reply to the true stories of miraculous healings, "Maybe so, but I'll bet he couldn't cure ME" is clinging, subconsciously to his illness. The supreme subconscious wish often operates not only to keep one ill himself but to suggest illness to another if the illness of that other promises to aid his own great wish.

I have in mind a case which aptly illustrated the above. A young man had been taught from babyhood by his mother (who wanted to keep him near her) that he was "frail," "not strong," "unable to enter into games like other boys," etc. He was a handsome, broad-shouldered lad, so thoroughly WELL physically, that two of the greatest diagnosticians in America pronounced him after complete examinations ABSOLUTELY NORMAL IN EVERY WAY.

He had been filled with the suggestion from childhood that he was not equal to the exigencies of life. This was his first difficulty and one for which he was in no way accountable. The mother, whose only child he was, and who desired above all else in life to keep him by her side, knowingly or unknowingly suggested to him the ideas of illness which would make him so dependent upon her that he could not go out into the world away from her. By this mother's supreme, secret wish he was MADE an invalid through the constantly reiterated suggestion of invalidism planted and replanted in his subconscious mind, and thus compelled to remain with her.

He, on the other hand, KEPT this invalidism (despite actual physical normality) because of a supreme, subconscious wish of his own—the wish to spend his life reading. Every time he attempted any work which interfered with this, he gave it up. After just about so much effort he would resign his position, take to his bed and spend weeks of apparent physical illness and all too apparent mental joy, reading, reading, reading. Though he was a perfect example of the power of mind over matter, he ridiculed its possibility. Between his own supreme wish (to spend his life reading) and his mother's wish (to keep him near her) he was the victim of suggestion from within and without, and of course remained an "invalid." Both were really innocent but that did not prevent the consequences of their acts being visited upon them.

Parents who suggest weakness, frailty, unfitness or inadequacy to their children are committing crimes.

Necessity, hardship or real desire on the part of the one afflicted will enable him to rise above this provided he will apply the law of suggestion to himself. SELF-SUGGESTION is far more powerful than any outside suggestion. He can often undo the evil work of years or a lifetime in a very little while. I have known of many people who are made ill or inefficient through the suggestions of others which they accepted and made into auto-suggestions, but not one is compelled to remain so when he knows what has been explained in these lessons.

Rule 17. Never use self-suggestion to your own disadvantage. DO NOT DWELL UPON the unpleasant things that happen to you, the unpleasant things people say to you, the unpleasant events of your past, etc. Just remember that these are INSIGNIFICANT except as YOU give them power over you, and that when you do so it is YOU, not these things, that harms you. All right, decide not to hurt yourself just because somebody else TRIES to. You are in armor. No man's arrow can penetrate that armor. But if you take to heart what he tries to do to hurt you, YOU are sending his arrow into your own bosom.

Rule 18. When working it is well to dwell on what you are trying to DO rather than on your own feelings, and it is always better not to look inward as much as outward. Look inward enough to give a definite order to your subconscious and then get busy to do your part to help it, out here in this external realm.

Whatever happens, don't watch yourself all the time. Give what you have planted a chance to grow. If you do not you are like the gardener who was always digging up by the roots the things he had planted to see what was happening to them.

When you give your subconscious an order in accordance with the laws referred to in these lessons you have complied with the requirements and you WILL GET RESULTS if you will but go on about your business and give them a chance to work. You do this for your vegetable garden. Don't do less for your own inner one.

Rule 19. After you have given the order to your subconscious, REALIZE IT IS BEING ATTENDED TO, precisely as you know this about your grocer once you have telephoned your order to him. How these things are to be gathered together by him, wrapped up and DELIVERED TO YOU are not matters that concern you. But there ARE matters that DO and these are the ones you should be giving your attention to.

For one thing, you should keep all thoughts that are in contradiction of what you want out of the parlor of your mind. Do not entertain them. That is your job. On the other hand make yourself a committee of one to invite in and entertain all thoughts that would aid or inspire the subconscious in carrying out your order.

I can best illustrate this by telling you what the mother of one of our well-known women novelists used to do for her. The daughter had certain hours for writing and while thus engaged no one was permitted to interrupt her. They lived in a friendly neighborhood where the young woman was very popular, and often people whom she could not herself have refused to see, came to call. But the mother resolutely refused to allow her to be disturbed and by giving her the attic room for a study was able to prevent even the noises of the rest of the household away from her. If her mother had failed to do this or if she herself had insisted on interrupting her we might not have had this woman's great books today.

Most persons devote a great many more thoughts to their failures than to their successes, regardless of the fact that they may TALK to you a great deal more about the successes.

Rule 20. Extract the LESSON which every unhappy thing brought you (and be sure it brought at least one), then let it PASS OUT OF YOUR MIND.

No effort you put forth for good is ever lost. They are always creating results. Though you cannot see yourself grow, if you are TRYING to be better and stronger and PERSISTING in repeating the order for it to your subconscious mind, nothing can keep you from developing. You are simply growing as the plant does—imperceptibly—and if you continue to comply with the laws of growth, some day the fruit will appear.

Sometimes you may seem to be standing still—to have been stationary for a long time, or to be backsliding—but when you least expect it you will discover that some of the things which were hardest to bear served the greatest purpose, that every discouraging thing furnished its quota of growth, despite the appearances at the time, and that you are a DIFFERENT AND STRONGER PERSON than you were only a little while before.

At this stage of evolution certain things are within the range of possibility, and apparently others are not, but here is a fact never to be lost sight of: THINGS WHICH WE THINK ARE BEYOND THE RANGE OF HUMAN POSSIBILITY ARE PROBABLY WELL WITHIN THAT RANGE AND THOUSANDS MORE WHICH WE IMAGINE BEYOND OUR OWN INDIVIDUAL POWERS ARE ALSO WITHIN IT.

I will illustrate how this applies in mental control of physical conditions. If a man's leg is cut off it would probably not grow again no matter how hard he believed it would. Man's subconscious mind is evidently not yet evolved to that degree, or at least he has not practiced this particular habit long enough to produce new limbs in us as, for instance, the subconscious of the lobster has done for him. The reason for this appears to be that legs compose so much more important part of the lobster than of man, and are so vital to him that much of his habit-mind has been concentrated in that direction for millions of years. Man has concentrated on the development of his MIND, which accounts for the superiority of his mental development over that of all other creatures.

One of the world's greatest naturalists declared that the eagle developed wings because of his intense subconscious desire to fly; that the giraffe grew his long neck in order to browse on higher and higher branches; while Dr. Paul Kammerer, a biologist of Vienna, has recently, after ten years of experimentation, produced in his laboratory a newt, WITH EYES, the first little creature of this variety ever to possess them!

I will quote from Dr. Charles Fleischer's article in the San Francisco Examiner, of December 17, 1923, the details of this remarkable experiment. He says:

"Living in submarine cages for thousands of years, this little amphibian did not have the power of sight. Its eyes were mere rudimentary organs under the skin.

"Dr. Kammerer exposed one of these blind newts to red light for several years. Generation after generation of this sightless little animal were thus created—and at last one group appeared IN WHICH THE EYES PUSHED THROUGH THE HEAD. All succeeding generations CONTINUE TO BE BORN WITH SEEING EYES!

"The newt theory promises to become as important as the Newtonian theory."

You Have The Book... Now It's Time To Put It Into Action!

This Is Your Exclusive Invite To
JOIN A SECRET GROUP OF HIGH PERFORMERS
Who Are Successfully Achieving Their Goals With Absolute Certainty!

Discover How To Put The Success Teachings Into Action For Real-World Results!

- ✓ Test-drive Secrets of Success Mastermind Community for 30 days for FREE

- ✓ BONUS! Claim your 3 FREE gifts today just for saying "maybe"

- ✓ And so much MORE – including real, actionable strategies first taught by some of the greatest thought leaders who've ever lived!

JUST SAY "MAYBE AND THE 3 GIFTS ARE YOURS FOR FREE

To claim your 3 free gifts, go to the URL below, or scan the QR code:

www.SecretsOfSuccess.com/roundpegs